P9-BYN-285

THE COMPLETE IDIOT'S GUIDE® TO

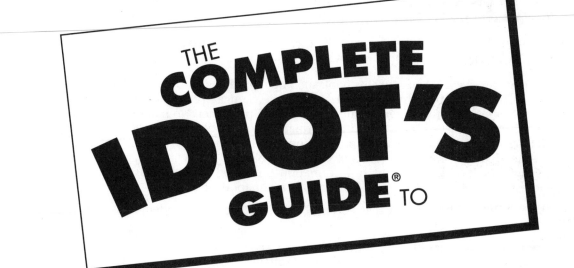

Meeting and Event Planning

*by Robin E. Craven and
Lynn Johnson Golabowski*

alpha
books

201 West 103rd Street
Indianapolis, IN 46290

A Pearson Education Company

This book is dedicated to our children, Clayton, Charley, Morgan, and Taylor, who make it all worth the effort.

Copyright © 2001 by Robin E. Craven and Lynn Johnson Golabowski

All rights reserved. No part of this book shall be reproduced, stored in a retrieval system, or transmitted by any means, electronic, mechanical, photocopying, recording, or otherwise, without written permission from the publisher. No patent liability is assumed with respect to the use of the information contained herein. Although every precaution has been taken in the preparation of this book, the publisher and authors assume no responsibility for errors or omissions. Neither is any liability assumed for damages resulting from the use of information contained herein. For information, address Alpha Books, 201 West 103rd Street, Indianapolis, IN 46290.

THE COMPLETE IDIOT'S GUIDE TO and Design are registered trademarks of Pearson Education.

International Standard Book Number: 0-02-864004-7
Library of Congress Catalog Card Number: Available upon request.

03 02 01   8 7 6 5 4 3 2 1

Interpretation of the printing code: The rightmost number of the first series of numbers is the year of the book's printing; the rightmost number of the second series of numbers is the number of the book's printing. For example, a printing code of 01-1 shows that the first printing occurred in 2001.

Printed in the United States of America

Note: This publication contains the opinions and ideas of its authors. It is intended to provide helpful and informative material on the subject matter covered. It is sold with the understanding that the authors and publisher are not engaged in rendering professional services in the book. If the reader requires personal assistance or advice, a competent professional should be consulted.

The authors and publisher specifically disclaim any responsibility for any liability, loss, or risk, personal or otherwise, which is incurred as a consequence, directly or indirectly, of the use and application of any of the contents of this book.

The Complete Idiot's Reference Card

Ten Tips for a Successful Meeting

1. Include all stakeholders to determine goals, objectives, and return-on-investment measuring tools.
2. Create a request for proposal (RFP) for your site-selection process. Make it specific and detailed and include all your needs.
3. Understand contracts before you sign them. Seriously consider asking a meetings industry attorney to review them.
4. Keep up with technology and use it to enhance your planning process. Use e-mail whenever possible!
5. Outsource parts of your meeting to save time and money.
6. Track your meeting history. Include rooms, food and beverage, audio-visual usage, and attendance figures.
7. Use your timeline and budget as meeting road maps.
8. Submit your meeting details in writing to the meeting facility. Read and update all banquet event orders (BEOs) and convention resumés before signing.
9. Don't have a meeting just to have a meeting. Know why you are having it.
10. Say thank you. Acknowledge *all* the people who made your meeting work. They deserve it!

Ten Common Pitfalls When Planning a Meeting

1. Failing to refer to your goals and objectives when making planning decisions.
2. Ignoring the return-on-investment (ROI) process as a tool for measuring the success of your meetings.
3. Making assumptions. Good planners learn to ask lots of questions and anticipate problems.
4. Picking the wrong site for your meeting. The best "deal" may not be the best match for your needs.
5. Hiring speakers without seeing them in person or seeing a tape.
6. Not keeping the meeting facility up to date on changes to your program or other issues regarding your meeting.
7. Underestimating your meeting costs or not adhering to your budget.
8. Packing too much into your agenda.
9. Failing to prepare contingency and crisis-management plans for every meeting.
10. Ordering too little or the wrong kind of food. Food makes a powerful impression.

alpha books

tear here

Goals and Objectives

A *goal* is the general purpose of the meeting and is strategic. A meeting goal answers this question: Why have the meeting? An *objective* is a measurable statement supporting the goal. Objectives answer the following SMART questions:

➤ Are they *Specific?*
➤ Are they written in such a way that they are *Measurable?*
➤ Can they be *Attained* within the time constraints of your meeting?
➤ Are they *Relevant* to the information presented?
➤ Can they be achieved in a realistic *Timeframe?*

Meeting Room Sets

Room Set	Definition
Classroom	Rows of tables with chairs facing the front of the room.
Theater	Like classroom but without the tables.
Chevron or herringbone	Rows are angled or curved; used with classroom and theater.
Conference, board, T-shape, U-shape, or hollow square	Eight-foot conference tables are placed in different configurations. Used for smaller meetings such as board, committee, and staff meetings.
Crescent (sometimes called one-half or three-quarter rounds)	Round banquet tables are set facing the front with chairs around half to three-quarters of each table.
Banquet rounds	Used for food functions. Standard tables are 60 or 72 inches in diameter and seat 8 to 12 people.
Reception	Rounds and smaller cocktail rounds with bars throughout a room.

Food and Beverage Guidelines

➤ There are 20 cups of coffee in a gallon. As a general rule, order 70 percent regular and 30 percent decaffeinated.
➤ Order 65 percent hot and 35 percent cold beverages in the morning.
➤ Order 35 percent hot and 65 percent cold beverages in the afternoon.
➤ There should be 1 server for every 20 to 25 people at a plated meal.
➤ There should be 1 bartender for every 75 to 100 people.
➤ Host bar: The meeting sponsor pays for the drinks.
➤ Cash bar: Attendees pay for the drinks.
➤ On consumption: You pay for only what was consumed.
➤ À la carte: Each menu item is priced and ordered separately.
➤ Guarantee: The final number of people that you tell the facility will attend a meal function. You pay either the guaranteed number or the number of people served, whichever is greater.
➤ Banquet event order (BEO): A hotel information sheet for staff members; it lists the details of a meal function including times, the number of people, the menu, special instructions, audio-visual equipment, and billing information.

Publisher
Marie Butler-Knight

Product Manager
Phil Kitchel

Managing Editor
Jennifer Chisholm

Senior Acquisitions Editor
Renee Wilmeth

Development Editor
Michael Koch

Senior Production Editor
Christy Wagner

Production Editor
Kathy Bidwell

Copy Editor
Amy Lepore

Illustrator
Chris Sabatino

Cover Designers
Mike Freeland
Kevin Spear

Book Designers
Scott Cook and Amy Adams of DesignLab

Indexer
Amy Lawrence

Layout/Proofreading
Svetlana Dominguez
Gloria Schurick

Contents at a Glance

Contents

Foreword

Dear Readers,

In my meeting-planning seminars I always start with a disclaimer that meeting planning is complex and requires careful attention to detail. In fact, I always say it's *more* than brain surgery: Brain surgeons are responsible for one life at a time; we who plan meetings often are responsible for tens of thousands of people at a time. I am excited to see a book that explains the meetings industry and communicates this message, which is so near and dear to my heart!

Individuals who are responsible for a few or a multitude of people at a meeting have to plan and manage carefully. We are responsible for the education, care, feeding, and safety of all those who attend our meetings and events. If one detail is forgotten, such as checking to see if the meeting dates conflict with a holiday, we might not attract the right audience. If the sessions are not designed to maximize interaction and education, people will walk out. If the entertainers or speakers we engage are not briefed about the audience (gender and age mix, ethnicity, level of experience, and so on), they may either fall flat or worse, insult the audience. If the implications of alcohol consumption are not considered, we are liable for the consequences. The list goes on and on.

Those who plan meetings and events often don't understand the breadth of the industry in which we work. This book will help you understand the complexity of meeting and event planning. It is a great resource for learning about the meetings industry and provides an instant grasp of meeting and event planning fundamentals. It also provides a multitude of resources including software, Web sites, associations, higher education, and much more.

This is also the perfect companion book to the texts and manuals already on the desks of seasoned meeting planners. It is the consummate resource for those who think that "anyone can plan a meeting"—this book explains why it is a specialized profession that requires knowledge beyond brain surgery!

Suppliers who provide facilities and services for meetings and events should read this book, too, because the best way to market and sell is to know your customers and help them do their jobs better. Planners are most loyal to those who have empathy for their work!

After you've read this book, read it again. All the best planners know that education is a lifelong process. Make lists of what you still need to learn and, with the resources in this book, determine where to turn for networking, assistance, and finding the right vendors.

Make a promise to me and others in our profession: Do what you do with the skills of a brain surgeon, with the compassion of the kindest person you've ever known, with the curiosity of the child who has yet to be told that asking "why?" is not okay, and with the knowledge that when you stop learning how to do this job better, you will get out.

—Joan L. Eisenstodt

Joan L. Eisenstodt, President of Eisenstodt Associates, LLC, a meeting planning and consulting company based in Washington, DC, has been in the meetings industry for 30 years. Recognized for her expertise and contributions to the industry by numerous organizations, she has been on every list of "Most Influential People in the Meetings Industry," published by *Meeting News Magazine*, since the first list in 1992, and honored as "One of the Power Players: 10 Women Changing the Industry" by *Successful Meetings Magazine* in 2000.

Introduction

Did you know there is an entire industry dedicated to planning meetings and events? People we talk to are surprised to find out that there are industry associations, suppliers, and other resources available to make their lives easier when it comes to planning meetings and events. Maybe you plan one or two meetings a year or are faced with planning a volunteer event in the near future. How do you know where to turn for help?

Some of the meeting-and-event-planning books available today are more like a textbook or manual than this book. We promise no in-depth mathematical equations and hard-to-follow formulas (well, maybe one). When it comes to finalizing your food and beverage, audio-visual equipment, sound, lighting, and stage production needs, we urge you to rely on professional vendors who make their living doing just that. This book will give you the basics so you can talk intelligently throughout the process.

This book offers insightful tips and information gained by working many years in the industry. As with any endeavor, there are many ways to accomplish the same thing. Since we have experience from both sides of the industry, the planner side and the supplier side, we are able to give you perspective from both sides of the fence. You need your suppliers as partners in your meeting, not just as a contractual entity. On the flip side, suppliers should know what it is like to plan a meeting.

We have tried to give you as many resources as possible in this book. The main challenge is keeping the information current as time elapses. We'll make you a deal. We promise to keep our Web site up to date and post changes to the book as they occur. As technology changes and you need to know about a fantastic new program, we'll post it on our site. As Web sites become available, we'll add them, too. So, bookmark www.meetingscoach.com and use it as an additional resource with this book. You won't be disappointed.

How to Use This Book

This book is divided into four parts that are all designed to lead you step-by-step through the planning process.

Part 1, "Bird's-Eye View," sets the stage for understanding the meetings industry. Things like setting your goals and objectives, determining the value of your meeting, and knowing who's who in the industry are all important in the planning process. We'll also take a look at technology and what it's like to book a meeting from the other side of the desk—the supplier side.

Part 2, "First Things First," explains what you need to do to get the planning process rolling. Creating your timeline (roadmap) and budget, writing and distributing a request for proposal (RFP), and negotiating with vendors are all things you need to do in the very beginning. Then we have a guest author, an attorney, to walk you through the hotel contracting stage. Finally, we discuss marketing and exhibits—both very important components.

Part 3, "Care and Feeding," is all about taking care of your attendees. How should you set the meeting rooms? Where do you buy all the things you need to produce a meeting? How do you find and hire speakers? What about travel arrangements? What about registration and housing? How do you determine your audio-visual equipment needs? This part is the heart of the planning process, so you'll want to pay close attention!

Part 4, "Center Stage and Beyond," addresses onsite meeting issues and all the other "stuff" that needs to be done. You'll learn about going onsite, preparing for unexpected crises, putting closure to a meeting (like paying the bills), preparing final meeting reports, and discussing ethical dilemmas. There is also a chapter for suppliers only that addresses what planners really want from suppliers. Also, you'll find a bit about certification and certificates/degrees in meeting and event management. Finally, there's a chapter on how to keep from becoming overwhelmed with all of your responsibilities.

Conventions Used in This Book

You will find helpful tips and hints for survival in the fast-paced world of meeting planning. Look for these fun and useful features throughout the book:

Don't Drop the Ball

Meeting planners juggle many, many tasks. Pay attention here so you don't "drop the ball" and lose precious time and money in the process.

Meeting Speak

Planning a meeting calls for a new set of vocabulary words. Here is where you will learn to speak the language. It's not really a foreign language, but it may seem like it on occasion.

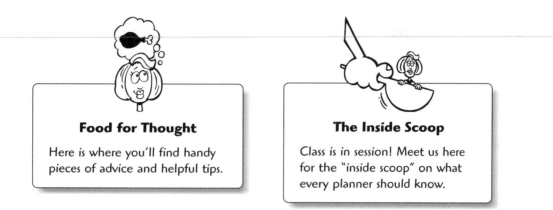

Food for Thought

Here is where you'll find handy pieces of advice and helpful tips.

The Inside Scoop

Class is in session! Meet us here for the "inside scoop" on what every planner should know.

Acknowledgments

Writing this book was a huge and fun endeavor for us. It's one we wanted to write for many years and finally got the chance, but it wasn't written alone. We have had many wonderful experiences in our combined 46 years in the business, and it is through those experiences that we are able to write about the meetings industry. Our careers have led us to many people and places, and all of these interactions play a part in what we know today. We are grateful for all of these experiences.

We have one special person who kept us on the right path in order to finish the book. Many thanks to Glenn Brill, who has an answer for just about any question and who is always there for us if we need something. We also extend warm thanks to all the editors we worked with at Pearson Education. We appreciate their assistance and the opportunity to write this book. There are also the people who contributed to the book. These people include John S. Foster, Esq., CHME, who wrote the legal chapter; Corbin Ball, CMP, for www.corbinball.com, the world's most comprehensive site about meeting planning and events technology; Joe Guertin, who helped us with information on generation learning styles; Chris McMasters and Gene-Michael Addis from MeetingMatrix, who provided the room diagrams; Nick Topitzes, CMP, of PC/Nametag, for the nametag photo; and finally, Robert M. Eilers from the Meeting Professionals International Foundation and Donald Dea and Hugh K. Lee from Fusion Productions for giving us permission to share their return on investment (ROI) model with you.

Last and most important are our families who supported us when we worked until the wee hours of the morning for months on end. For Robin, this includes her husband, Charles Bonham, and her two sons, Clayton and Charley. For Lynn, it includes her husband, Barry Golabowski, her two daughters, Morgan and Taylor, and her in-laws, Nancy and Ray Golabowski, who are always available to take care of the kids when work duties call.

Special Thanks to the Technical Reviewer

The Complete Idiot's Guide to Meeting and Event Planning was reviewed by a leading industry expert and one of the 25 most influential people in the meetings industry, as named by *MeetingNews* magazine. Special thanks to Joan Eisenstodt of Eisenstodt Associates, LLC, for her time, expertise, and brain cells. We couldn't have done it without her.

Trademarks

All terms mentioned in this book that are known to be or are suspected of being trademarks or service marks have been appropriately capitalized. Alpha Books and Pearson Education cannot attest to the accuracy of this information. Use of a term in this book should not be regarded as affecting the validity of any trademark or service mark.

Part 1

Bird's-Eye View

Before you start planning a meeting or event, you need to know a few things about the meetings industry in general, and meetings and events in particular. You also need to know who you can call to make your meeting-planning journey a bit easier.

We'll also look at the big picture to set up your meetings for success, including processes such as creating goals and objectives, determining a meeting's return on investment, and utilizing technology tools to get the job done. Finally, we'll take a look at what it is really like to sit on the other side of the desk when you call a facility to book your meetings. You'll learn how your business is evaluated and what you can do to make your meeting a better piece of business for the meeting facility.

Chapter 1

What Is a Meeting or Event Anyway?

In This Chapter

➤ Discover how big the meetings industry really is

➤ Learn about various types of meetings

➤ Learn what meetings and events have in common

➤ Distinguish between a meeting and an event

The time has come to recognize meeting, conference, and event planning as an official profession. This chapter gives a bird's-eye view of the profession and discusses the types of meetings and events held today.

Flying High

In 1995, the *Convention Industry Council,* or *CIC* (formally known as the Convention Liaison Council, or CLC), released an economic-impact study that discovered that the meetings industry is the twenty-second largest contributor to the gross domestic product (GDP). Who knew? In the United States alone, we estimate 250,000 to 450,000 individuals plan meetings and events. Although it is impossible to count everyone—even those who plan as part of their job or as volunteers—the number is huge, and the hotels, conference centers, and resorts know it. They have meetings in their facilities every day of the year. If you include the planners of festivals, parades, weddings, sports competitions, concerts, and fundraising events, the number is even higher.

Meeting Speak

The **Convention Industry Council (CIC)** is "composed of leading national and international organizations representing more than 81,000 individuals and 13,000 firms or properties involved in the meetings, conventions, expositions, and travel and tourism industries. It provides an important forum for member organizations to work together to enhance the industry." Contact them at www.conventionindustry.org.

Don't Drop the Ball

Meetings should support the organization's goals and mission. Don't get caught up in the logistics and lose sight of your meeting's purpose.

According to the CIC, the meetings and incentive travel industry accounted for more than $80 billion in annual spending in 1994. The industry supported more than 1.5 million American jobs and generated more than $12 billion in annual taxes. Hotels and other meeting venues reaped the greatest share of attendee expenditures, and the airline and restaurant industries were the next greatest benefactors of this spending.

Yet most people do not even know that the meeting-planning profession even exists. They say, "Oh, that sounds like fun, planning a party!" As most professional meeting planners will tell you, planning a meeting or event can be one of the most challenging things you will ever do. It involves a variety of skills covering oodles of details that are very time consuming and both logistical and strategic in nature.

United We Should Stand

Meetings management has just in the last 10 years become an "official" profession. Meetings-management/planning titles include Director of Meetings, Meetings Coordinator, Meeting Planner, Conference Manager, and Event Manager. Many meeting planners do not carry a job title with the words "meeting planner" in it. Many individuals do not even know they are meeting planners. Administrative assistants, executive secretaries, and managers at all levels frequently have a prominent role in planning meetings for their organizations, but they are not recognized as such.

Our industry is awesome! We get to create, organize, manage, implement, and improve upon an essential communications tool—meetings. We can use cutting-edge technology, we can be as creative as we want, and we can make a strong impact. What we do has value. The bottom line is that all of the players in our industry need to be champions of it.

The Purpose of a Meeting

When you begin to plan your next meeting, the first question you should ask is—why? What are you trying to accomplish? The primary reasons that meetings are held are to inform, teach, exchange ideas, discuss problems, make decisions, and communicate issues. Of course, there are other reasons to have a meeting, such as to raise money for a good cause or to make money for the organization. Getting acquainted, teambuilding, or just old-fashioned public relations are other valid motives. It is important to recognize why you are having a meeting and to set your agenda to accomplish your most important goals.

Why do people attend meetings? In most cases, the answer is to obtain information—to walk out of the room knowing more than when they came in. However, coming in a strong second is to network or develop professional relationships. Many people spend so much time focusing on work that they don't have a lot of time for, dare we say it, fun. Meeting new people and catching up with old friends or acquaintances is a key reason people want to go to a meeting or event.

What Are Meetings and Events?

Board meetings, staff meetings, technical and scientific conferences, product launches, annual conferences, training seminars, fundraisers, galas, conventions, tradeshows, and incentive programs are just some of meetings and events that make up the meetings industry. Since one of our biggest challenges is to categorize meetings and events, let's focus on some of the more widely held definitions.

➤ *Conferences* generally bring together people who have a shared discipline or industry, usually for educational reasons.

➤ *Conventions* are assemblies of delegates to formulate a platform, select candidates, and sometimes take legal action. They also focus on a common topic or issue.

➤ *Expositions* and *tradeshows* are designed to communicate services and products to consumers and members.

➤ *Special events* cover a wide variety of areas such as sporting events, fundraisers, tributes, community programs, festivals, parades, road shows, and more.

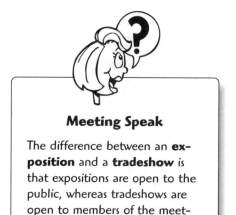

Meeting Speak

The difference between an **exposition** and a **tradeshow** is that expositions are open to the public, whereas tradeshows are open to members of the meetings' organization.

➤ *Company* or *institutional meetings* are for those from the same company or organization. They include board, staff, and sales meetings and focus on information exchange, problem solving, and decision making.

Before we go any further, you should know that meetings and events are two different birds. We have searched the world over to find a concise comparison between meetings and events. However, we've had no luck. As we go along, you'll learn more

The Inside Scoop

For-profit organizations budget and pay for meetings out of their own pocket. Nonprofit organizations ordinarily charge a fee for their meetings and break even or turn a profit depending on the meeting goals.

Don't Drop the Ball

Consider outsourcing some parts of your meeting to an independent planner or meetings-management company. They can save you time and money in the long run. (See Chapter 4, "Who Ya Gonna Call?" for more information.)

about the skills you need to plan both. It also is helpful to understand the role that for-profit and non-profit organizations play when developing meetings.

For-profit organizations have employees who attend mandatory training, sales, motivational, and other meetings. The key word here is "mandatory." Their boards of directors meet several times each year, and their marketing departments have product launches and strategic-planning meetings. These meetings are almost always paid for by the organization. Events may include a tradeshow, a fundraiser for a charitable cause, a company picnic, or a holiday party.

Nonprofit organizations and professional societies have meetings for their members that are not mandatory. Members have the option to attend an annual meeting, conference, convention, exposition, congress, tradeshow, or workshop. Each participant pays a registration fee. They are often responsible for their own expenses. Their company may reimburse them for the cost, but this is different than a company meeting. It is very important for these meetings to be of value to potential attendees; otherwise, attendance will be low. Events may include a fundraising dinner, a holiday gala, or a thank-you dinner for sponsors.

Who Are These Meeting Professionals?

The U.S. meetings industry puts planners into three distinct categories: *corporate planners, association planners,* and *independent planners.*

It is hard to pinpoint exactly how many corporate, association, and independent planners exist in the United States. However, if we look at the membership breakdown from the industry associations, we estimate that corporate planners make up the largest segment at just over 50 percent. Association planners probably make up about 30 percent, and independents come in at around 20 percent. Many corporations and associations are large enough or have enough meetings to warrant full-time, in-house planning personnel. However, many organizations do not have these resources and look to their secretarial or management staff. In other cases, they outsource some of their meeting needs to independent planners. Independent planners may work alone, partner with other planners, or be part of a meetings-management firm.

Here are three of the key professional organizations for the meetings industry:

➤ **Meeting Professionals International (MPI)** is "the premier educational, technological, and peer-interaction resource in the meetings industry." The organization is the largest association for meeting planners and suppliers. You can find them at www.mpiweb.org.

➤ **Professional Convention Management Association (PCMA)** "serves the association community by enhancing the effectiveness of meetings, conventions, and exhibitions through member and industry education and to promote the value of the meetings industry to the general public." Their Web site is www.pcma.org.

➤ **American Society of Association Executives (ASAE)** is another valuable resource for planners. Although their purpose is "to advance the value of voluntary associations to society and to support the professionalism of the individuals who lead them," their Web site is a valuable resource for everyone in the meetings industry. Check them out at www.asaenet.org.

The Inside Scoop

There are many professional organizations dedicated to the education and professionalism of the meetings industry. To find what you need quickly, go to www.corbinball.com. This site includes articles and spreadsheets for planners and has the most complete listing of meetings-industry Web sites bar none. It is a valuable resource for every planner.

But wait! There's more. Meetings and events don't just happen because meeting planners make it so. There is an entire flip side of the industry—the suppliers. Suppliers are all of the people, vendors, and organizations that supply products and services for meetings and events. They are very important, and their role will be addressed in Chapters 7, "Supplier Secrets No More," and 11, "Negotiating the Best Deal."

Least Common Denominator

Whether you are planning a meeting, an event, or something in between, there are several key factors they all have in common.

The Right Time

All meetings and events are held on a specific date and at a specific time. Deciding when to hold a meeting or event is a critical factor in its success.

Before selecting dates, research other industry- or company-related meeting and event dates. It is imperative to check the dates of other industry functions during your selected timeframe. A quick way to do this is to check the Web site of your industry's association or go to www.asaenet.org. Chances are, if there is an association Web site, you will find it here.

The Right Place

Location, location, location ... is everything. One of the most important decisions in the planning process is the venue. Although this may not seem like a big deal, it sets the tone for your entire experience. You are providing participants with an environment that reinforces why they are there in the first place.

There are a wide variety of site options to choose from. For example, a resort or conference center setting is used to foster a relaxed, laid-back atmosphere. A downtown hotel sets the tone for a serious business meeting. An airport facility is the perfect place for a board meeting for busy people who have to fly in and out quickly. An all-inclusive conference center may be the place for training workshops where the attendees need a professional atmosphere in a comfortable, quiet setting. This book mostly addresses what you need to know about planning meetings in hotels, but conference centers are wonderful places and should definitely be considered. To find one and to learn more about them, check out www.iacconline.org.

Alternative meeting sites are places such as museums, zoos, gardens, and other facilities with meeting rooms. Consider these venues for a change of pace. These venues do not always have food and beverage available and may have limited audio-visual equipment. However, all of these services can be brought in to an alternative facility.

Don't Drop the Ball

Make sure the dates you select do not conflict with any other industry or national event or company function. This will help increase attendance from the get-go. It will cost you money if you have low attendance or if you have to cancel and pay vendors a cancellation fee. Check out www.aglobalworld.com for holiday information.

Food for Thought

Create a master calendar to track meetings and events that might conflict or coincide with your event. Keep this document up to date so you avoid scheduling over another meeting.

The Right People

Remember who you are doing this for—your attendees. If you don't identify and reach the right people, then why have the event? Create a target attendee list and keep adding to it when appropriate. Take the time to consider where your attendees come from. Naturally, if you are working for an association, then the attendees will be your members, but what about potential members? If you work in a company, you have a defined attendee list. If you are raising money, you need to decide whose checkbooks to go after. Decisions, decisions.

The Right Leader

Having the right speaker or speakers to deliver your message is critical to your success. There are many speakers available, and you need to decide what message you want to get across to your audience. Larger meetings typically have a general session with at least one *keynote speaker* and numerous breakout sessions.

To find a keynote presenter, contact the National Speakers Association at www.nsaspeaker.org, research the numerous speakers' bureaus on the Web, or tap into your own network. Another organization to check out is the International Association of Speakers Bureaus at www.iasbweb.org.

Breakout sessions are back-to-back shorter sessions ranging from 45 minutes to 2 hours. The speakers for these are normally people from your industry who are experts on the topic. If your budget is tight—and whose isn't—you can probably find good speakers for free if you take care of their travel expenses.

Meeting Speak

A **keynote speaker** is a speaker with a wealth of expertise who is a respected authority on the subject at hand. He or she is sometimes a celebrity or a well-known personality from the industry.

The Inside Scoop

Some organizations spend upward of $50,000 to $125,000 for a sought-after keynote speaker. Ouch!

The Right Scoop

A well-thought-out agenda or schedule is critical to staying on track. Whether it is a meeting for 2 or 2,000, every meeting needs an agenda. Always start with an overview of the meeting and the key people. You should set the tone and direction of the meeting at the beginning.

The agenda is the road map for a successful meeting. Allowing time to interact with attendees at breaks, meals, and social events is very important. Remember the "fun" component. A good agenda not only will take care of business, it will also make a positive, lasting impression.

The Big Event

An event is somewhat different from a meeting because it can have a higher profile. A lot of events are stand-alone affairs; however, that does not exclude you from having an event associated with a meeting.

Don't Drop the Ball

Event planners: Consider joining the International Festivals and Events Association (IFEA) at www.ifea.com. Another organization to check out is the International Special Events Society (ISES) at www.ises.com.

Types of events include, but are never limited to, the following:

➤ Awards banquets

➤ Concerts

➤ Fairs

➤ Festivals

➤ Fundraisers

➤ Galas

➤ Parades

➤ Political rallies

➤ Public shows

➤ Road shows

➤ Sporting events

➤ Tradeshows

➤ Weddings

One big difference is that an event usually has entertainment, decorations, and music. That's not to say these can't be part of a meeting, but these characteristics tend to apply to an event. An event is something to be invited to or is open to the public—a special occasion.

Another difference can be size and number of attendees. Many events are open to the public and span several days. A festival can have a million attendees over a two-week period. A state fair is another good example of an event. You have different issues to deal with at events as opposed to meetings, such as security, animals, decorations, alcohol sales, and big-name entertainers, to name a few.

For some companies, both a meeting and an event occur during their big conference of the year. For instance, a sales meeting may take place for three days, and to end it with a bang, a gala awards dinner is scheduled. These are still categorized as meetings but have a final gala event.

No matter what you call it, meetings and events require careful planning in an organized, detailed, step-by-step fashion. This book will walk you through the myriad of details so that your next get-together, meeting, or event is a success.

The Least You Need to Know

➤ Meeting planning is a recognized profession.

➤ The meetings industry is a multibillion dollar business.

➤ Meeting professionals are growing in numbers.

➤ Meetings are focusing more on strategic goals.

➤ There is a lot to planning meetings and events, and it's fun!

Chapter 2

One, Two, Three ... Goal!

In This Chapter

➤ Understand the importance of goals and objectives

➤ Learn how to create goals and objectives

➤ Develop a goals and objectives worksheet

➤ Define what makes a meeting successful

Meetings should be held with purpose. Too many times, meetings are held because someone thinks a meeting is necessary. How often have you attended a meeting and walked away feeling like it was a big waste of your time? You are too busy, and going to another meeting just takes time away from your ever-growing to-do list.

In this chapter, we'll discover how to set goals and objectives and how to communicate them to the stakeholders, attendees, and others. Goals and objectives define your entire event.

Why Bother?

Imagine that you receive two brochures in the mail for different meetings. One is black and white, and one has splashes of color all over it. Immediately, you sense a difference. Upon reading the material, you find that the black-and-white brochure has a basic agenda, location, and registration form. The colorful brochure describes how you will learn several new techniques, network with your peers, and go home with helpful tips. Of course, this is Marketing 101, but the colorful, descriptive brochure illustrates the goals and objectives of the meeting. The basic brochure just gives you the logistical details. Which one are you more likely to attend?

Meeting Speak

A **goal** is the foundation of a meeting. It explains why the meeting is being held and provides a road map for the planning process. An **objective** is a measurable, attainable target that, when completed, contributes to the accomplishment of the goal. A meeting can have one or more goals. Usually, there are multiple objectives supporting the goal(s).

Goals and objectives mean different things to different people. These words are often used interchangeably, and the difference between them can be blurry. In this book, we define *goal* as the general purpose of the meeting, and *objective* as a measurable statement supporting the goal. You can call them what you want, but setting goals and objectives is a necessary part of meeting planning.

Creating your goals and objectives, in writing, is the essential first step in the meeting-planning process. Read on for guidelines to help make accomplishing this critical element quite a bit easier.

Big Picture

What do you do first? Think big picture. What goals do you want to achieve? They should be strategic in nature, setting the stage for creating objectives to support them. If the question is why have a meeting, then the answer is in your goal(s). Ponder the following questions to get your creative juices flowing:

1. What is your meeting's primary emphasis? Recognition, education, networking, training, reward, entertainment, to conduct business, teambuilding, or to display products?

2. Will this emphasis be more on the organization or the attendee? How much new information will be communicated? Or, will the meeting reemphasize current information and procedures?

3. Is the purpose to reinforce the company/organization's mission? Is the purpose to train attendees or employees?

4. How important is financial success?

Here are some sample goals:

➤ To provide futuristic, cutting-edge technology education for seasoned banking professionals

➤ To teach new hotel sales managers how to increase their sales and establish loyal customers

➤ To foster an atmosphere for networking within the meetings industry

➤ To provide hands-on instruction for establishing a strong Web site presence within the pet-food industry

➤ To celebrate a milestone like the twenty-fifth anniversary of the company

➤ To communicate the new company direction and business plan for the next year

Note that these goals are not task oriented. They do not tell you how they will be accomplished; they only tell you why the meeting is being held. In some cases, your goals will be the same from year to year. If you have past goals, start with them. If you are starting from scratch, brainstorm with key people, but in either case, make sure they are in line with your organization's mission.

The most difficult thing to do is to get started writing goals and objectives. It's far easier to start on the logistical planning—booking the hotel, hiring the speakers, and doing the other detail work. If you resist this temptation, you will be rewarded with a meeting that is worth the time, effort, and money.

Little Picture

After you have determined your goals, it's time to look at the little picture—the objectives. Does the thought of writing objectives send shivers up your spine? Well, help is on the way. Create objectives that mean something and that answer the following SMART questions:

➤ Are the objectives **Specific?**

➤ Are they written in such a way that they are **Measurable?**

➤ Can they be **Attained** within the time constraints of your meeting or event?

➤ Are they **Relevant** to the information presented?

➤ Can they be achieved in a realistic **Timeframe?**

SMART is an easy-to-remember set of rules that is frequently used to create objectives. By using the SMART criteria, you create solid objectives that support your overall goals.

The Inside Scoop

Remember that, when it's all over, you want your meeting to be a success. Clear objectives give you the measurement criteria you need.

Don't Drop the Ball

Make sure the final decision-makers have input on the meeting's goals and objectives. The last thing you need is a hidden agenda to come in from left field and create havoc!

There are many ways to get started setting goals and objectives. Take a look at the following scenarios:

Scenario 1: Happy Camper Company

You work for a Fortune 500 company that produces camping equipment, and the vice president of sales has asked you to help plan the annual sales meeting. It is scheduled for September, which is six months down the road. You begin by meeting with the vice president and the rest of the key management staff to discuss the meeting. The first question is, why are you having this meeting? A typical answer could be, because we always have it, and the sales managers get a chance to have fun. So, the goal is to have fun. Right?

Wrong! Asking the key people at Happy Camper what they want their salespeople to take away from the meeting is the question. Ahhh, now they get it. Well, an increase in sales would be great. Okay, now we are making progress.

Having fun could be an objective on everyone's list. But let's face it. Who wants to pay for fun with no other benefit? It isn't going to happen in corporate America. Finally, you and the other Happy Campers decide that the goal is to motivate and train the sales managers so they can return to the office and increase sales. When finalizing your goals and objectives, you also want to think about the following:

Food for Thought

You need to be strong when trying to establish goals and objectives. Resist the temptation to skip this step. This will be especially hard when your boss doesn't want anything to do with this process. Hang in there and do it anyway.

1. What is the most important message you need to convey to your sales team?

2. What works best to motivate your salespeople? Has something worked well in the past, or do you need to try new methods?

3. Are there new processes and techniques you could teach your salespeople? Do you need to train them on any new software?

4. How does this meeting fit into the overall company goals and objectives? How can this meeting support them?

To help you in your task, you may want to draft a worksheet that lists the meeting's name, goal, and objectives. For example:

Meeting Name: Happy Camper Company—Annual Sales Meeting

Goal: To motivate the Happy Camper sales team by providing fun, interactive education so that they meet and exceed all revenue projections for the company this year

Objectives:

➤ Increase sales by 25 percent over last year.

➤ Teach how to prospect for business in the new economy.

➤ Provide training on how to use the Internet as a sales tool.

➤ Motivate the sales team so they are excited about selling our products.

➤ Hire a motivational speaker to entertain at the final dinner.

➤ Emphasize the new strategic plan and how the sales department is an integral part of its success.

➤ Roll out the new company logo and branding initiative.

What do you think? Are they good objectives? Do they seem reasonable, logical? Do they help reach the company's goal(s)? Actually, there are two important things wrong with them. First, they do not meet the SMART criteria. Read each one and apply SMART. Some are not specific enough or measurable. How, for instance, will you know you have motivated the sales team?

The second thing is that they are written in the wrong perspective. They are written from the planner's perspective. It may be the aim of the organizers to roll out the new company logo or to hire a motivational speaker, but how does that benefit the attendee? The real issue is what will the sales team be able to "do" once they go back to work?

If we rewrite the objectives using SMART rules *and* keeping the attendee in mind, they might end up like this:

Don't Drop the Ball

All stakeholders have their own objectives. Just make sure they agree with the primary meeting objectives that are written from the attendees' perspective. Your meeting can't accomplish all things for all people.

17

By attending the annual sales meeting, the Happy Camper sales team will do the following:

> ➤ Increase all product sales by 25 percent in the next six months.
> ➤ Learn five ways to prospect for new business.
> ➤ Pass a 35-question test covering the five customer service links on the company Web site.
> ➤ Identify three ways they contribute to the company's new strategic plan.

Now these objectives are definitely specific, measurable, attainable, relevant, and time based. They will keep you on track for achieving the goal of the meeting.

The Inside Scoop

As companies and organizations move to measure meeting results, determining goals and objectives is *the* critical element in the planning process. If you skip this step, you do not have a basis to make key decisions. Senior management and association executives are under constant pressure to evaluate every dollar spent, and they need to understand why they are having their meeting.

Scenario 2: Big Association of Rare Cat Owners (BARCO)

You are an employee at a nonprofit association that provides resources for owners of rare cats. Since there is not a dedicated meeting planner on staff, everyone helps with the annual conference. There is a lot of competition for attendees in your industry (really!), so your meeting has got to be the best. You need to sit down and write a detailed plan.

The first thing you do is have a meeting to plan your meeting. (Huh?) You schedule a meeting one year in advance of the conference with the conference committee, association officers, and staff. The first meeting is to determine the goals and objectives and to explain everyone's role. When determining your goals and objectives, you want to take into consideration the following:

➤ Attendees comments from last year: What did they like? Dislike? What do they need?

➤ What are the hot topics in your industry?

➤ Do the attendees need networking time?

➤ Is there a recognition program to reward members? Does this need to be incorporated into the program?

➤ Does your board of directors need to meet?

➤ Do you need a formal business meeting?

➤ Are there any burning issues to resolve?

Let's take a look at a worksheet:

Meeting Name: BARCO Annual Education Conference and Tradeshow

Goal: To introduce new products and services and to provide industry education and networking opportunities to our members

Objectives:

By attending the BARCO conference and tradeshow, attendees will do the following:

➤ Meet at least 10 new members who share their interest.

➤ Learn three new ways to prolong a rare cat's life.

➤ Understand the latest technology in rare cat breeding procedures.

➤ Meet vendors who sell BARCO products and services on the Internet.

➤ Learn how to join the online discussion group and how it helps you take care of your rare cat.

The great thing about these objectives is that you can use them in your marketing collateral. Attendees will be interested to know that they will meet at least 10 new members who share their interests and see vendors who sell BARCO products and services. These objectives explain what they will get out of attending the meeting.

Roll Up Your Sleeves

Now it's time to roll up your sleeves and put it in writing. Make sure all the players, including the decision-makers, understand and embrace it. Begin by creating a worksheet with the goals and objectives, similar to the examples in Scenarios 1 and 2.

What? More Objectives?

The objectives we have focused on so far are based on outcomes for the attendee. They are primary. However, it is perfectly okay and maybe even necessary for you, the planner, to develop an additional set of objectives. These objectives are called *process objectives* and they will give you direction on how to accomplish your primary objectives.

You will make better decisions about the meeting location, speaker selection, program agenda, marketing strategies, and other important details if you always ask yourself what impact they have on your goals and objectives.

Meeting Speak

A **process objective** refers to the how-to approach for accomplishing something. An **outcome objective** is defined by the needs of your attendees and should identify what the attendees will learn at the meeting.

A Tisk, a Task

Now you need to create an agenda to support the objectives. This process will get you ready to create your timeline in Chapter 8, "Creating and Following a Timeline." Take a look at a sample agenda for the preceding BARCO scenario. Your meeting is for two days and two nights. This is a basic agenda just to get the ball rolling. It will be modified as you delve deeper into the planning process.

Wednesday/Date	Agenda
Evening	Check-in
8:00 P.M.–10:00 P.M.	Hospitality Suite Open

Thursday/Date	Agenda
7:30 A.M.–8:00 A.M.	Breakfast
8:00 A.M.–10:00 A.M.	Opening session
10:00 A.M.–10:30 A.M.	Refreshment break
10:30 A.M.–12:00 P.M.	Three breakouts
12:15 P.M.–1:00 P.M.	Lunch
1:15 P.M.–3:00 P.M.	Tradeshow floor open
3:15 P.M.–4:45 P.M.	Three breakouts
5:45 P.M.	Reception/dinner
	Theme: "Cats Are the Purrrfect Companion"

Friday/Date	Agenda
7:30 A.M.–8:00 A.M.	Breakfast
8:00 A.M.–9:45 A.M.	Tradeshow floor open
10:00 A.M.–10:30 A.M.	Refreshment break
10:30 A.M.–12:00 P.M.	General session
12:15 P.M.–1:00 P.M.	Lunch
1:15 P.M.–2:45 P.M.	Three breakouts
2:45 P.M.–3:15 P.M.	Refreshment break
3:15 P.M.–4:30 P.M.	Closing session

Food for Thought

Send a note to each member of the conference planning committee saying thank you for his or her assistance in creating the meeting goals and objectives and that you look forward to a successful meeting.

The first basic agenda incorporates the goals and objectives into a schedule. It only states the day, time, general schedule, and any special event associated with the meeting.

Thanks for Your Support

After your goals and objectives are agreed on, the first thing you need to do is distribute the goals and objectives worksheet and tentative agenda to the people who attended the brainstorming meeting(s). Ask them for updates or changes or any other input. Tell them that planning is underway and that every part of the meeting will be designed to support the goals and objectives.

Now it is time to address who is responsible for making decisions and getting all of this done.

Don't Drop the Ball

Although you may report to a person or group we call the decision-makers, *you* have a vested interest in the outcome of the meeting and need to take ownership of the meeting.

Who's the Boss?

The lead meeting planner is really the boss. In meeting planning, many things can go wrong or slip through the cracks. Sloppy decisions, or ones that stray from your objectives, will ultimately make more work and cost more money. Someone needs to manage the entire program. In most cases, it's the lead meeting planner because this person understands the objectives and is close to the details. This ensures that the goals and objectives are met during every step of the planning process.

In today's industry, more planners are taking on the responsibility of program planning as well as "just" logistics. This is a welcome trend and one that is frequently discussed in trade publications, educational programs, and networking forums. However, addressing the issues and challenges of this next step goes beyond the focus of this book. Stay tuned.

The Least You Need to Know

➤ Goals and objectives are the key first step of meeting planning.

➤ Create SMART (Specific, Measurable, Attainable, Relevant, Time-based) objectives.

➤ Decision-makers should be involved in setting the goals and objectives.

➤ Goals and objectives should support the organization's mission.

Chapter 3

Is It Worth It?

In This Chapter

➤ Discover who has a vested interest in your meeting

➤ Learn how to measure the success of your meeting

➤ Explore the return on investment (ROI) process

➤ Create your own meeting evaluation form

This chapter is about evaluating your meeting. Why have a meeting if you don't take the time to make sure it was worth it? All organizations look for ways to save money and scrutinize their expenditures, meetings included.

In Chapter 2, "One, Two, Three … Goal!" we told you that meetings need to be held with purpose and that goals and objectives are very important in the overall meeting-planning process. Here is where you will learn how to use your goals and objectives to determine the value of your meeting.

Who Cares?

You might just be surprised. Meetings take a lot of time, effort, and money. Attendees, sponsors, exhibitors, senior management, and planners care. They all have an interest in the success of any meeting with which they are associated. When you weed through all the hidden agendas and reasons for holding a meeting, the main reason is this—for the attendee.

Food for Thought

Be creative. Incorporate the meeting's message (goals and objectives) into the meeting theme, agenda, collateral material, Web site, company letterhead and envelopes, fax cover sheets, and so on. Continue the message onsite with the general sessions, signage, meal functions, tradeshow, and handouts.

The Inside Scoop

It is much easier to keep current exhibitors and sponsors than to find new ones. At your meeting, host a reception or a special meal function for your exhibitors and sponsors. They will certainly appreciate the extra recognition, and you can get to know them even better.

An organization producing a meeting has to decide whether its message was effectively communicated. If not, what other ways could the information be delivered? Would a manual have given the salespeople the same information? Was an expensive motivational speaker necessary to deliver the message? Could a video sent to their homes have taught the same thing? These are all questions that need to be answered to determine whether the meeting was a success.

Your exhibitors and sponsors have an interest, too. Did they see an increase in sales as a result of their participation in the meeting? Do they have more potential customers? Did they gain the valuable exposure to the market that they thought they would? Did they walk away feeling that the time spent was worth it?

I've Gotta *Attend* Another Meeting?

Attendees are motivated to attend meetings for a variety of reasons:

➤ Education

➤ Networking

➤ New product information

➤ Force of habit

➤ Recognition

➤ Job requirement

➤ Entertainment

➤ Just because

From their perspective, attending a meeting should fulfill their specific goals and make it worth their time and money. In Chapter 2, you learned about the SMART process for writing meeting objectives. Here is where these objectives are put to the test. Clear objectives make it easier to attract attendees.

I've Gotta *Plan* Another Meeting?

Meeting planners have an entirely different subset of motivations during the planning process. Once the goals and objectives are set, you are charged with the responsibility of producing the meeting according to those goals and objectives. You also have to deal with these contingencies:

➤ Budgets

➤ Staffing issues

➤ Office politics

➤ Economic climate

➤ Contracting issues

➤ Working with vendors

➤ Deadlines

➤ Attendee issues

You are the master communicator to all *stakeholders*. It is your job to monitor the planning process and to make sure the stakeholders stay on track.

In most situations, you will interact with senior management as well as committee members and peers. Keep in mind that, as long as you keep people on track in a nonconfrontational and professional manner, they will respect and in most cases adhere to your schedules.

Meeting Speak

A **stakeholder** is someone who has a vested interest in the success of the meeting, such as the vice-president of the company paying the bill.

I've Gotta *Fund* Another Meeting?

The financial outlay is an important part of any meeting. Someone pays, whether it is the company, association, attendee, or sponsor. The people writing the checks have an entirely different set of motivations for doing so:

➤ Educate staff

➤ Introduce a new product or service

➤ Public relations/advertising

➤ Roll out a new strategic plan

The Inside Scoop

During the past five years, a push for measuring the return on investment of meetings has moved planners into a more strategic role. In many companies, the professional meeting planner is a senior/vice-president executive-level position.

➤ Motivate staff or customers

➤ Customer appreciation

After the meeting, proving to the decision-makers that the goals and objectives were accomplished is exactly what needs to be done.

Don't Forget the Exhibitors and Sponsors

Exhibitors attend a conference to show their products and services within the tradeshow arena. They are there to gain exposure for their company or organization. Here are some of their motivations for attending:

➤ To sell products or services

➤ To educate the attendees on an issue

➤ Advertising/public relations

➤ Product demonstration

➤ To collect sales leads

➤ To showcase new products or services

Meeting Speak

In-kind means that a product or service is provided instead of cash.

Sponsors participate in a conference for the same reasons but on a different level. They give money or *in-kind* products or services to the meeting's host organization.

Make sure your accountant is aware of sponsorships. He or she will determine your tax liability regarding the goods, services, and cash given to your organization. Anyway you look at it, a donation is better than paying for it!

Meeting Speak

Return on investment (ROI) is the process of evaluating a meeting in terms of value to the stakeholders involved in it.

Measuring Return on Investment (ROI)

Some meetings have been a ritual for so long that the reasons behind having them either have changed or are forgotten. Today, organizations want to know if the resources spent on a meeting brought a return on the investment. In other words, the meeting was a success because the goals and objectives were achieved and provided a positive *return on investment (ROI)*.

A company called Fusion Productions created "The ROI Process" for Meeting Professionals International's

Foundation. It was sponsored by Marriott International and is based on Fusion's approach to meetings and benchmarking of leading meetings and conventions worldwide. Their ROI model makes it easier to justify your next meeting. For a meeting or event, the ROI process focuses you to ...

➤ Identify and prioritize your stakeholders and gain their input.

➤ Establish measurable meeting objectives and review them with your stakeholders.

➤ Design measurements for success.

➤ Design, develop, and deliver meeting content based on the objectives.

➤ Demonstrate your ROI by using the measurement results and by reporting those results to management.

Although this process may seem time consuming, do give it a try. The process gets easier once you are familiar with it, and it makes the difference between bringing value to what you do and just winging it.

Measuring Tools

There are many ways to measure the return on investment of a meeting. In most cases, a combination of measuring tools is used in ROI. It is best to customize the process for each meeting based on the goals and objectives.

Hard Dollars

Did the meeting make or lose money? This is an easy answer to obtain once the bills are paid and the revenue is accounted for. Many association meetings need to make money to support the organization. The tool for measuring this is the budget.

Has your sales meeting ever been postponed or cancelled because company revenue was down? In many for-profit organizations, meetings are looked at as cost centers. The attendees do not pay a registration fee, and there is little or no income associated with the meeting. When companies look at cutting costs, meetings are usually one of the first items to be eliminated. Many times, this decision is made without analyzing the real value of a meeting. That's when understanding the ROI is key.

Don't Drop the Ball

Learn the entire ROI process step by step at www. fusionproductions.com/resources/ roi1.htm.

Food for Thought

The meeting's budget compared to actual expenditures is how you measure the financial success of a meeting. Did you make or lose money? The answer is the bottom line.

Soft Sense

But wait, earlier you learned that objectives are based on many things besides money. What if your sales team needs to learn about new products or be motivated? In that case, having the meeting may be an investment in the company's future. It is easier to keep the meeting from being eliminated if it's presented to senior management from this perspective. In the long run, having the meeting could actually increase sales! Imagine that! If goals and objectives were not created, then a meeting could be cancelled just because it costs money and they were in a cost-cutting mode.

If your objective is to increase sales by 25 percent during the next six months, then your sales report is the measurement tool used to determine whether the goal was achieved. Create a review system and share the sales figures on a monthly basis with the team. It keeps the goal in front of everyone and is less likely to be forgotten.

Don't Drop the Ball

The time to think about your ROI is in the beginning. You need to understand what represents a positive return on investment and collect the appropriate data from the start.

The ROI is not just about money. An increase in productivity, efficiency, motivation, and education are just some of the outcomes a positive ROI can achieve.

Attendee Perspective

Measuring attendees' ROI takes more time than an internal ROI process. Sometimes you will never know what actually motivated someone to attend your meeting.

There are several tools for measuring attendee return on investment. The first, an *evaluation,* is a list of questions designed to measure satisfaction with the meeting. Here are some sample categories for questions:

➤ The program's content and educational value.

➤ The speakers and their delivery styles.

➤ Their level of understanding about key parts of the meeting—did they learn what they wanted to?

➤ A place to add comments or questions.

➤ Suggestions for improvement.

➤ Whether they will return next year.

➤ The facility.

➤ The food and beverage.

➤ Meeting location.

Written evaluations usually have a rating system for each question on a numerical scale or from excellent to poor. They are scored, and an overall summary is tabulated. Make sure you ask for the information you want to know from the attendees.

At the bottom of your evaluation, always provide instructions on how to return it. Ask that they be returned at the end of the conference. Registration-supply companies sell large, standing boxes for just that purpose. In case attendees opt to take it with them, have an address or a fax number for them to return it later.

If you have a lot of breakout sessions, consider a separate evaluation form for each one. Distribute them at each breakout session. Ask questions about the speaker and if the program was relevant to them. If you do this, you do not need to include the breakout sessions on the overall conference evaluation form.

Evaluations can be short or long and as quick or detailed as you want. Your chances of a higher return lay with the shorter forms. The longer and more involved they are, the fewer will be returned. See Appendix A, "Sample Forms and Checklists," for sample evaluations for attendees, exhibitors, and breakout sessions.

Another way to poll attendees is an audience response system conducted at the general sessions. A moderator asks questions, and the audience provides immediate answers via an electronic keyboard. The results are available before they leave the room. This is also a great lead-in to asking the audience open-ended questions about the meeting. You'd be surprised at how many people will voice their opinions if you ask them. So ask!

Don't Drop the Ball

Be consistent with the questions and the format of your evaluations, especially if you want to compare results from different meetings.

Food for Thought

Offer an incentive for returning the meeting evaluation. Either give everyone a small trinket or enter their name in a drawing for a larger prize. People love prizes!

You can also use statistical data to evaluate your meeting. Is attendance up or down compared to the past two to three years? If your registration numbers are really different, make sure you take into consideration any changes to your fee structure, agenda, meeting location, and program content.

Exhibitor Perspective

There are several ways to measure the success of your meeting from the exhibitors perspective. First, a written evaluation is important. Ask them to rate the following:

➤ Networking with attendees

➤ The cost of the exhibit booth

➤ Material received from the organizer prior to the event

➤ The overall exhibit schedule

Also ask them what they liked best and least about exhibiting at the conference. Let them know that their comments are valuable and that they will be used in making future decisions.

In addition, during the meeting or tradeshow, visit the booths and ask how things are going. Talk to them. Solicit feedback on the entire agenda. They attend many meetings each year and can give you some of the most valuable suggestions you will ever receive!

> ### The Inside Scoop
>
> Spend time talking with your exhibitors. Ask them why they attended and if they will return next time. This extra attention goes a long way. All too often, we hear about the forgotten exhibitors and how their needs often go unnoticed. They can provide great insight.

Use the Information!

Too often, organizations go to great lengths to evaluate the meeting from all angles, and then the report grows dust on the shelf.

Once the results are tabulated, distribute them to the stakeholders and schedule a wrap-up meeting. Discuss all aspects of the evaluations. Brainstorm ways to improve for next year. Write it all down. This is one of the first places you will start when planning your next meeting.

> ### Food for Thought
>
> Place the summary of your evaluations in your meeting binder. They need to be readily accessible at all times.

> ### The Least You Need to Know
>
> ➤ A meeting stakeholder is any person who has a vested interest in the successful outcome of a meeting.
>
> ➤ Return on investment is not just about money.
>
> ➤ Return on investment determines the real reason(s) you should hold a meeting.
>
> ➤ Meeting evaluations are an important tool to find out if you met the attendees' objectives.

Chapter 4

Who Ya Gonna Call?

In This Chapter

➤ Identify valuable resources for meeting professionals

➤ Discover how to find and contact them

➤ Understand what they can and cannot do for you

➤ Create your own resource network

The meetings industry has a multitude of organizations that supply a product or service to planners, but how do you know where to find them? This chapter is all about who they are, what they do, where to find them, and how to use them.

Web Sites

The Internet provides a tremendous opportunity for meetings-industry players to research, gather, and use information they have never had access to before. But, wading through thousands of Web sites can be a daunting experience. There are many solutions to your particular issue, but you have to pick and choose what is right for you. You can't use them all!

Don't Drop the Ball

The industry's most comprehensive listing of meeting-related Web sites is www.corbinball.com, and it's updated regularly.

Food for Thought

Before joining an association, really think about why you are joining. Write down what you expect to gain from being a member. Then, when your renewal notice arrives in the mail, you can make an educated decision whether or not to renew.

Understanding what is available on the Web is a good start to finding what you need later in the planning process. In the next chapter, we will discuss meeting-planning tools available on the Web. You will be amazed at what is out there.

Associations

Just like any industry, there are a variety of trade associations dedicated to providing education, conferences, books, magazines, newsletters, and other services. The meetings industry is no different.

In Chapter 1, "What Is a Meeting or Event Anyway?" we talked about three key associations—Meeting Professionals International (MPI), Professional Convention Management Association (PCMA), and American Society of Association Executives (ASAE)—so we won't review them again. But do look into them as a resource because they are on the cutting edge of our industry. All three have excellent meetings and conferences designed to help educate meeting professionals on the how-tos and what's new in our industry.

Depending on what type of planner you are, you might want to join additional associations. Each discipline (corporate, association, government, special event, medical, insurance, and so on) has its own association and focuses on industry-specific issues. They are there for you. However, don't just join for the heck of it. Really investigate what they can bring to the table and make sure it is of value to you. Membership dues are not cheap—especially if you join more than one association.

Why Join?

One thing to keep in mind is *why* you are joining. The following is a list of things you should ask yourself before signing up:

1. Are you joining for one or more of the following?

   ➤ Education

   ➤ Networking

   ➤ Access to publications

➤ A members-only Web site

➤ Conferences and events

➤ Certification

➤ Access to a resource library

➤ Dedicated to profession

➤ Credibility

➤ Job/employee search

➤ Contacts in other cities

2. Will this association help you in your job? How?

3. Will you be an active participant? How?

4. Do you plan to attend conferences and events? Which ones?

Food for Thought

The common thread for getting the most out of an association is involvement. People who are involved in one way or another feel that the time and money are worth it.

We know a lot of planners who are members of associations, and we hear about some great reasons to join. The number one reason is networking. It is great to have access to other people who do what you do, especially if you do not work with others who plan meetings in your organization.

Even if you only attend a few meetings, are involved in a committee, or just read the magazines for information, use your association as a resource. It is worth the money only if you take advantage of its benefits.

Trade Publications

Trade pubs are your vehicle for news about our industry. Keeping up with local news is hard enough, but our industry is so global that these publications are really a valuable tool for keeping abreast of the pertinent industry news. Why, you ask, should you read them? These publications often contain articles on meeting-planning how-tos, salary surveys, destination information, hotel and resort information, best practices, contracting issues, job opportunities, and information on products and services.

The list is endless, but our point is that these publications are a great resource. Some are free to planners, so you have nothing to lose. Try the following: MeetingsNet.com is a great place to start. Adams Business Media publishes more than a half-dozen publications with special focus on various industries including *Association Meetings, Corporate Meetings and Incentives, Insurance Conference Planner, Medical Meetings, Religious Conference Manager,* and *Technology Meetings.* Go to the company's Web site (www.meetingsnet.com) and click on Contact Us for subscription information.

Here are some other excellent and more broad-based publications:

➤ *Business Travel News* (www.btnonline.com)

➤ *Corporate & Incentive Travel* (www.corporate-inc-travel.com)

➤ *Meetings & Conventions* (www.meetings-conventions.com)

➤ *MeetingNews* (www.meetingnews.com)

➤ *Successful Meetings* (www.successmtgs.com)

In addition, you'll discover publications designed for special markets or regions. Here is a small sampling:

➤ *Midwest Meetings* (www.midwestmeetings.com)

➤ *Meetings West, Meetings South,* and *Meetings East* (www.meetings411.com)

➤ *Small Market Meetings* (www.smallmarketmeetings.com)

➤ *Where Magazine* (www.wheremagazine.com)

Don't Drop the Ball

Once you subscribe to the applicable trade publications, you could have well over a half-dozen magazines and newspapers rolling in each month. Don't let them pile up. If there is no time to read them all, skim through them, tear out the applicable articles, and recycle them. File the articles for future reference.

Meeting Speak

Convention and visitors bureaus (CVBs) are nonprofit organizations representing destinations. They are typically funded by a combination of membership dues and room taxes. Their members are organizations that provide products and services to planners such as hotels, restaurants, and attractions.

Convention and Visitors Bureaus (CVBs)

Convention and visitors bureaus (CVBs) are organizations that are available to meeting planners to provide information on the meeting host city or destination. They exist to put "heads in beds" and are eager to serve you. They are a valuable resource both before selecting a location and after a decision is made. They help you locate products and services available in the area and will work to make sure your experience in their city or destination is a successful one. Smaller communities may not have a CVB, so contact the local Chamber of Commerce.

Here are some services that CVBs provide at no or low cost to meeting planners:

➤ Site inspection of the destination

➤ Meeting guides about the destination

➤ Lead referrals to appropriate facilities with your meeting information

➤ Supplier contacts

➤ Attendee name badges

➤ Registration assistance

➤ Promotional brochures

➤ Arranging a welcome from the mayor or another official

➤ Assistance in wading through city red tape

➤ Welcome signage at the airport

➤ Spouse and guest program coordination

➤ Press releases about the meeting

➤ Promotion material such as photographs

Just ask, you may be surprised. (One CVB we know ordered and delivered 500 balloons for a client's awards luncheon because the client was so busy. They often will go above and beyond the call of duty!) They are a great resource for just about any question or dilemma.

Keep in mind that the meeting guides produced by CVBs are sales tools for the city or destination. They are not intended to be recommendations. Always be on the lookout for ways to garner recommendations from colleagues (join those associations!) before signing vendor contracts. CVBs have to be fair and equitable to all of their members, so you need to do some research on your own, too.

Don't Drop the Ball

All CVBs have Web sites, but the umbrella organization is the International Association of Convention and Visitors Bureaus (IACVB). This organization can be found at 1-877-GO IACVB or www.iacvb.org. From this site, you can find most CVBs worldwide. Also check out www. officialtravelinfo.com for destination information.

Destination Management Companies (DMCs)

Destination management companies (*DMCs*) are fee-based companies that provide general information and assistance in a city.

Need a tour arranged? A special event venue? Theme ideas and event coordination/management? Spouse tours? Someone to meet and greet your VIPs at the airport? Special gifts? A DMC is a second pair of hands at your meeting location. They know the city well and can recommend suppliers based on unbiased firsthand experience.

Meeting Speak

Destination management companies (DMCs) are fee-based companies that are available to help you in a destination or city. They can arrange tours, plan and manage your meeting, plan a themed event, and conduct a spouse/guest program, among other things.

To CVB or DMC?

Now, what is the difference between a CVB and DMC? A CVB is a nonprofit entity available to guide you in what a city or destination has to offer. They provide a range of services to assist you when you are there. They know the press, government officials, the mayor, and other important people. They can tout your group as the best thing to hit the area since sliced bread.

A DMC is a for-profit company with expertise in most aspects of meeting planning. They arrange airport transportation for VIPs, create themed award dinners, take spouses and guests on city tours, and hire motor coaches for the delegates' opening reception. They are hired by you and report to you, whereas a CVB is acting on your behalf in taking care of requested tasks and projects.

Look at it this way: A DMC takes on a contractual responsibility with your organization, and a CVB provides general overall needed services.

The Inside Scoop

If you are considering using a CVB, it is key to investigate what they can and can't do for you. Their services will vary depending on location and the size of the city. If you are visiting a small town, you are the big fish in the little pond and may get more services and attention. If you are meeting in a large city, you are the small fish in a very big ocean and may receive limited services. CVBs will do what they can based on the size of your meeting, your needs, and their resources.

So, if you need additional assistance above and beyond what the CVB will provide to you, a DMC may be your next phone call. Be sure to call the CVB for a list of recommended DMCs in the area or ask your hotel salesperson.

National Sales Offices (NSOs)

Most hotel chains have national sales offices (NSOs). An NSO is a sales office for one hotel company that represents all of their properties and facilities. If you book a lot of meetings, the advantage of an NSO is having one main contact versus one at each facility. For example, if you had to book 20 meetings throughout the United States, without an NSO, you would be calling 20 different hotels within the same company.

If you work with an NSO, one person can book all 20 meetings for you, saving you a lot of time.

Another advantage in using an NSO for a number of meetings is that you generate greater buying power. The NSO understands the value of your collective meetings and can help you get better rates and other concessions.

Today, there is a growing consolidation of many hotel chains within the same company; therefore, you may even be able to book more than one chain with a single call to an NSO. Do your homework and see what works best for you.

The Inside Scoop

By establishing strong NSO contacts, it becomes easier to weed through potential meeting sites. Try to book all your meetings together as a package versus one at a time. Got 20 back-to-back meetings? Call the NSO for your group, tell them your meeting specifications and desired locations, and let them do the work!

Industry Experts

Industry experts are a must-have resource for every planner. At first glance, you may think you could not possibly have access to them. You have no clue who they are! Read on and we'll show you the way. Then, you can hob-nob with the experts!

Ask The Experts

Ask The Experts is a column where you can ask advice from many leading authorities in the planning world. It is published in the *MeetingNews* trade publication and is also on their Web site at www.meetingnews.com/exp.htm. Just go to the Web site, select a category, and e-mail a question. It's that easy. You will receive an e-mail response. You can also go to the Web site for your answer and read all the other Q&As in a slew of categories.

The following are some of the categories:

➤ Special events
➤ Meeting software
➤ Return on investment
➤ Tradeshow issues
➤ Legal issues
➤ Working with speakers
➤ Hotel negotiating strategies
➤ Food and beverage
➤ Audio-visual issues

As you can see from these topics, this column covers a wide range of pertinent meeting-planning issues. Where else do you have access to questions answered by experts?

mpoint.com

Another hangout to find experts online is the mpoint discussion forum. The mpoint Web site is a central location for meeting and event planners to find valuable meeting-related resources. The mpoint discussion forum features expert moderators, and you can ask meeting-planning questions, discuss opinions, and share advice on a wide range of topics. Some of the discussion forums are as follows:

➤ Facility supplier search

➤ General discussion

➤ International issues

➤ Legal issues and negotiations

➤ Meeting management

Join the discussions at www.mpoint.com.

MeetingsCoach

MeetingsCoach is an innovative service (developed by yours truly) of Alliance LLC based in Menomonee Falls, Wisconsin. We are veteran meeting professionals who provide constructive, balanced feedback on your unique meetings-industry issues. You simply select one of the coaching options (cyber, tele-coaching, or in-person), and we'll be there to answer your questions. By using MeetingsCoach, you will …

➤ Be able to ask questions to a seasoned meeting professional.

➤ Gain a quick second opinion on an important, pending decision.

➤ Have someone help you through challenging situations.

➤ Have assistance weeding through the many issues you face daily.

➤ Discover ways to make the most of your opportunities.

➤ Learn how to set better goals so you can accomplish more.

Coaching topics include planner/supplier relationships, meeting-planning form and process review, meeting planning 101, career development, Web site development, technology in the meetings industry, and all of the topics covered in this book. We can be reached at www.meetingscoach.com.

Meeting Matters (MIMlist)

The MIMlist is an online discussion group moderated by a well-known, leading educator and expert in the meetings industry. It is a place to learn, discuss, ask, get information, and build your network of industry peers. It is a moderated discussion group where you can actively participate by asking and answering questions, or you can just lurk in the background and read the e-mails as they whiz by. This is a tremendous resource because you learn from your peers. Chances are, if you post a question, someone has an answer to it. Their Web site is www.mim.com/forum/forum.cfm.

Meeting Management Companies (MMCs)

If you are a planner and don't work for a company or association, chances are you work for a *meeting-management company* (*MMC*) or are an independent planner. MMCs are companies that provide meeting-management services to organizations. Many organizations do not have the resources to handle all their meetings in-house, so they go outside to get the work done.

You can hire an MMC for all or any part of your planning process. If you don't have time to find a meeting site, calling an MMC may be just the ticket to getting it done in an expeditious manner. Some call themselves meeting resource firms. They bring to the table experience, know-how, and their Rolodex. If you just want consulting services, they can provide objective opinions and fresh ideas.

Meeting Speak

A **meeting-management company (MMC)** is an organization that provides full-service planning assistance and management to organizations. They can plan just one component of the meeting or do the entire planning and management of the event.

You can find these companies by asking CVBs, peers, or suppliers; through trade associations and trade publications; or just by looking in the phone book.

One organization, the Alliance of Meeting Management Consultants (AMMC), is a group of experienced meeting-management business owners. One of AMMCs objectives is to be a one-stop source to locate meeting managers, consultants, and planners. You can find them at www.ammc. org or at 1-800-200-2774.

Just about any meeting-management firm will help you find a site. Fee structures vary from company to company. Some charge a flat fee, and some work for the hotel commission. If you outsource this function, work with the firm you feel most comfortable with.

The Least You Need to Know

➤ Many trade publications offer free subscriptions to meeting planners.

➤ Convention and visitors bureaus (CVBs) will help you find the suppliers, products, and services you need at no charge.

➤ You have easy access to industry experts online.

➤ Meeting-management companies can help you with any aspect of your meeting.

Chapter 5

Technology
Soft-Where?

In This Chapter

➤ Discover how planners manage their meeting data

➤ See what's going on online

➤ Learn where to find answers to planning questions online

➤ Understand how valuable the Web is to meeting planning

Data. A significant portion of your meeting management revolves around managing data—and there is *a lot* of data. You have data about your attendees, facilities, vendors, speakers, and on and on. In the old days, meaning before the Web, there were limited resources available for meeting management. Fortunately, today there is a plethora of software and Web tools available to help you track and manage your data.

This chapter just scratches the surface of what's out there in the ever-evolving field of meeting-management software. This chapter is *not* a review of meetings software, nor does it even address all the different categories—there is just too much available. We will, however, point you in the right direction and give you the lowdown on how to find a complete software review—just read on.

Do It Yourself

In the do-it-yourself toolbox, there are three key pieces of software that every planner should have: a word-processing program, a spreadsheet program, and a *relational database*. Let's elaborate.

Meeting Speak

A database is a structured set of data made up of records. A **relational database** allows data to be searched and accessed across different databases.

Food for Thought

If you are using a database for registration, give each attendee a unique registration or identification number. You just might have two people with the same name attending, and you need to keep them straight.

It's a no-brainer that everyone uses a word-processing program. Planners need to correspond, right? It's also a given that, if you need to manipulate numbers—and we all have budgets—then you need a spreadsheet, too. But what is this relational database thing?

A database is a collection of information using records. A record is a unique collection of information about a specific thing. For example, you might develop a new database for all the attendees of your upcoming meeting—BARCO 2 (the second annual meeting of the Big Association of Rare Cat Owners). The database consists of all your attendees. A record is the specific information about one attendee.

If you use a relational database, when you input a name, the database checks last year's database (BARCO 1) to see if the name exists. If it does, the record can be accessed and input into your BARCO 2 database—no retyping! That's the beauty of a relational database; you can manage, update, and use data (records) from other databases, making your work a lot easier.

For planners just starting out, on a limited budget, or working on small meetings, all you need are the three basic software applications. However, if you generate your own marketing collateral or need a polished look, desktop-publishing software makes a nice addition. You can also purchase stand-alone specialty software packages for name badges, floor diagrams, and other specific tasks. The following table gives you a sampling of the documents generated in the planning process and the software you need to do the job.

Document Type	Word Processing	Spreadsheet	Database	Desktop Publishing	Specialty Software
Budgets		X			
Calendars	X	X			
Diagrams				X	X
Evaluations	X			X	X
Floor plans				X	X
Forms	X			X	
Letters	X		X	X	
Lists	X		X	X	

Document Type	Word Processing	Spreadsheet	Database	Desktop Publishing	Specialty Software
Memos	X				
Name badges	X		X	X	X
Name tents	X			X	X
Outlines	X	X			
Place cards	X				X
Postcards	X				
Posters				X	
Press releases	X			X	
Receipts	X		X		
Reports	X		X		X
Schedules	X	X			
Signage	X			X	X
Thank you notes	X				
Tickets	X		X	X	X
Timelines	X	X			X

As you can see, you can do a lot with just three or four programs. However, as your meetings and budgets grow, you may find it more advantageous to invest in specially designed meetings-management software.

Off-the-Shelf

Just a few years ago, there were not a lot of meetings-management software programs available. Today, there are over 200 programs and more are being developed. Here we highlight three popular categories, just to whet your whistle.

Room Diagramming

Imagine sitting down with a pencil, a diagram of your meeting space, and the property's specification sheet (a list of meeting rooms and the number of people they can hold). You need to figure out if the room will hold your extra-large stage with rear screen projection, the four motorcycles (giveaways)

The Inside Scoop

An excellent compendium of descriptions and analyses of meetings-management software is *The Ultimate Meeting Professional's Software Guide,* by Corbin Ball, CMP. Go to Corbin's Web site at www.corbinball.com for details.

on the side, and an extra-wide center aisle (for the marching band). Can you do it accurately? Probably not. This is where meeting and exhibition design software comes in.

Room diagramming or design software helps you create accurate floor plans, seating arrangements, staging, and any other component you need to "fit in." These programs are fairly easy to use and provide an accurate layout of how you want your room to be set up.

Room design software lets you do the following:

➤ Quickly modify layouts (over and over if need be).

➤ Provide clear instructions to venue staff.

➤ Work with the venue to be more creative.

➤ Update diagrams from prior meetings quickly and easily.

You can change your specifications, and the diagrams immediately update. They allow for customized shapes (to draw tables, chairs, stages) and are printable so that all users can have a copy. Some also create a detailed inventory report that keeps track of how many tables, chairs, podiums, and so on that you need. Wow!

Want to learn more? Check out these programs:

➤ Expocad (www.expocad.com)

➤ MeetingMatrix (www.meetingmatrix.com)

➤ Optimum Settings (www.optimumsettings.com)

➤ Room Viewer and Event Sketch (www.timesaversoftware.com)

Name Badges

Once an immaterial detail, name badges now take on a new light. Since meeting people, both formally and informally, is part of the meeting ritual, it is important to have name badges that stand out.

To the rescue are stand-alone name badge printing programs. These applications import registrant data from your source (word processing, spreadsheets, or even certain databases) or let you input data directly. They produce badges that are easy to read and very professional looking. They allow you to use different fonts, manipulate text, and add logos. Since they use a database structure, you can print all, one, or a subset of badges as well as find, sort, and update records. The applications also have templates for certificates, place cards, name tents, and tickets.

It's also nice to be able to take the software onsite and print badges for new attendees or redo existing ones. Attendees appreciate it, and it promotes a higher level of service and professionalism to your meeting.

Here's a different twist to printing name badges onsite. Instead of asking a registrant to fill out a form, ask for his or her business card. Using a special scanner and software from a company called CardScan, you can extract the business card information. (CardScan is designed to export business card information into electronic address software.) You can then export this information into your name badge program and print badges lickety-split. What a time-saver! CardScan claims its software can be incorporated into any software application, so you can have business card information exported directly into your registration database, too.

Want to learn more? Check out these programs:

➤ BadgePro (www.badgepro.com)

➤ CardScan (www.cardscan.com)

➤ PC/Nametag (www.pcnametag.com)

Food for Thought

If you want high-quality name badges but don't want to purchase the software, contact PC/Nametag at 1–800–233–9767. For very reasonable fees, they will prepare great-looking name badges, alphabetized and assembled. Done!

Turnkey Management

As your meetings get larger and you have more information to track, you might want to purchase a comprehensive meeting-management package.

These all-inclusive software suites integrate all your essential tasks such as budgeting, registration, housing management, session scheduling and room layouts, travel arrangements, and more. These packages also provide attendance tracking (from past meetings); allow complex registration processes and payment options; track food and beverage and audio-visual sets; handle exhibitor and vendor details; design and produce correspondence, confirmations, mailing labels, receipts, name badges, certificates, and tickets; and produce a dizzying array of reports.

The upside of these types of software packages is that, 90 percent of the time, they really *do* everything you need. With all the information in a database, it is easy to track just about anything you can think of. You can also have multiple users working on the software simultaneously.

The downside is that they can be pricey, may take a while to get the hang of, and are not completely customizable. Most packages do allow for a lot of customization, but if you have significant or really unique requirements, you may need to latch on to a programmer.

Don't Drop the Ball

Be sure to save your files and back them up frequently. Also, keep hard copies of everything important. Databases do crash and data is lost. Be prepared!

Want to learn more? Check out these programs:

➤ Complete Event Manager (www.ekeba.com)

➤ Event Planner Plus and Meeting Planner Plus (www.certain.com)

➤ MeetingTrak (www.psitrak.com)

➤ PeoplewarePro (www.peopleware.com)

Lots of Online Stuff

You may be asking, what happened to registration and housing? Aren't there a lot more resources available for these two key elements? Yes, Virginia, you are right. We haven't forgotten. You see, it turns out that, in the world of the World Wide Web, these two important functions have migrated online, and there are a number of terrific tools available.

Site Selection

One of the hottest areas in online meeting resources is site selection. First, let's point out that there are thousands of venues: hotels, resorts, conference centers, convention centers, and numerous unique venues. Since these facilities are in the business of selling space, they always need to have available specific and accurate information about their venues, and the Internet is the perfect mechanism to communicate this information.

Meeting Speak

A **request for proposal (RFP)** is an outline of all pertinent meeting specifications. It includes contact info, dates, tentative agenda, description, history, special needs and requests, and the date of decision.

Enter the site-selection companies. They have developed extensive searchable databases of meeting facilities and suppliers to the industry. They want you to use their site to find the right location for your meeting. Some even go beyond just providing venue listings; they have developed a *request for proposal* (RFP) feature that makes it easy for you to outline your specifications. The RFP process makes sure you don't forget important details when communicating your needs to a venue. These companies also track the status of your RFP and offer assistance in the booking process if you want it.

These companies will continue to add more venues, making your site-selection process even easier. Many also offer expanded features to help planners, such as articles, checklists, discussion forums, tips, and more.

Want to learn more? Check out these sites:

➤ AllMeetings.com (www.allmeetings.com)

➤ EventSource.com (www.eventsource.com)

➤ mpoint (www.mpoint.com)

➤ Starcite (www.starcite.com)

Registration and a Whole Lot More

Registering your attendees is one of the most challenging parts of your job, right? You need to decide what information to collect, how to store it, and how you want to use it. Also, factor in the lost time spent trying to read handwriting, contacting someone who did not answer key questions, or solving payment problems. ARGHH!

What about housing and transportation? Even if your attendees are responsible for their own, they still need to know what is available. It's your responsibility to select vendors, determine services offered, and clearly communicate this information.

Look at it from their perspective. They need to know dates, rates, location, directions, special discounts, and payment options. They also have questions about attire, food choices, disability access, family programs, social events, and on and on. Do them a favor—make it easy. Do yourself a favor—check out management resources online.

Several companies have developed efficient and very comprehensive online attendee-management programs. These programs take care of meeting/event registration (including signup for sessions and social events), housing reservations, flights, ground transportation, tours, printing name badges, confirmations, and tickets. They allow basic customization to your meeting specifications; generate up-to-date, accurate reports; offer password protection; and allow attendees to register 24/7 (24 hours a day, 7 days a week).

Don't Drop the Ball

When using an online RFP Web site, stick with just one. Sending your RFP using several online RFP services can create extra work for venues (and you) because they could easily receive two or more of the same RFP and not know it. It's also good professional manners to let the venues know that they were not selected and why.

The Inside Scoop

If you want to take advantage of the benefits of an online attendee-management program *and* want to merge it with your existing system, consider a full-scale custom design by the provider. For a fee, their programmers will work with you to make sure their front end captures and delivers your specific attendee data exactly the way you want it.

Not all companies provide the same services across the board, so you will have to do some research to determine what features best meet your needs.

Want to learn more? Check out these sites:

➤ b-there.com (www.b-there.com)

➤ bluedot.com (www.bluedot.com)

➤ cvent.com (www.cvent.com)

➤ Event411.com (www.event411.com)

➤ Passkey.com (www.passkey.com)

➤ RegWeb (www.regweb.com)

➤ seeUthere.com (seeuthere.com)

➤ ViewCentral (www.viewcentral.com)

Food for Thought

As you collect useful meeting and event Web sites, organize them under your browser's Favorites or Bookmarks menu. Be sure to categorize them for easy reference.

Everything Else

Well, maybe not *everything* else. There are a ton of online resources to choose from, and we can't possibly cover them all. As you investigate the Web sites listed in this chapter, you will discover additional links to many other valuable Web sites.

Here's just a sampling of some interesting and useful Web resources for the meeting professional in all of us:

➤ **all-hotels.com (www.all-hotels.com).** A compendium of over 60,000 hotels worldwide. Also includes availability checks and discounts.

➤ **EventWeb (www.eventweb.com).** This resource consists of two e-mail newsletters that cover Internet and technology developments impacting meeting/event planners.

➤ **Guide to Unique Meeting and Event Facilities (www.theguide.com).** This site references over 5,000 nontraditional facilities in the United States and Canada.

➤ **Meetings Industry Mall (www.mim.com).** An extensive listing of meeting-related Web sites and resources. Includes the MIMList (an e-mail discussion forum) and a job board. Check it out.

➤ **Meeting Planners Survival Guide (www.meetingsnet.com/mpsg).** This listing has checklists, tips, timelines, and lots of how-to info.

➤ **OfficialTravelInfo.com (www.officialtravelinfo.com).** Contains over 1,000 official tourism organizations worldwide.

> ➤ **Room Size Calculator (www.mmaweb.com/meetings/roomcalc.html).** Enter the number of people or exhibit booths, and this program calculates the square footage for various sets.

> ➤ **Successful Exhibiting (www.tradeshowresearch.com).** A good resource for tradeshow trends, reports, and tips.

Trends of the Trade

With all the technology tools available, planners have oodles of choices. How is this technology improving the meeting-planning process? Let's take a look at some of the trends.

The Registration Process

Old way: Collect hard-copy registration forms and input (retype) information into a spreadsheet or database. Communicate lists to interested parties (venues, decision-makers, speakers, and so on). This process is labor intensive and does not lend itself to providing timely information.

New way: Attendees register electronically with an online, full-service, registration-management company. No retyping! Their data is instantly downloaded into a customized database. The group's housing inventory, sessions, and social event counts are automatically updated. Interested parties have access to real-time data on demand.

Site Inspections

Old way: Pore through directories and hotel brochures. Call venues to arrange for a site visit. Get on a plane. Get off a plane. Tour the site with a sales representative. Collect lots of material about the site. Possibly do this for several sites in different locations.

New way: Get on the Internet. Use one of several online site-selection companies and submit an electronic RFP. From your desk, do virtual site inspections on the Internet. More and more venues have Web cams that provide 360-degree views of their facilities. Pick a site. If you then want to visit, you'll have a better understanding of the site before you arrive.

The Inside Scoop

One of the hot industry issues is the lack of standardized planning documents (agendas, event orders, floor diagrams, and so on) that both planners and venues can share and work on electronically. Several organizations are working to create standards and software just for this purpose. When adopted industry-wide, this will have a huge impact on the way we communicate with venues.

Online Auctions

Old way: There is no old way.

New way: You have a meeting to book. You are ready to commit. You go to an online site that offers venues the ability to bid on your meeting—auction style. You're intrigued. Yes, this site found prequalified venues that meet your specifications. You sit at your computer and watch them bid on your meeting in real time. This is fast, easy, and offers competitive rates. You thank your lucky stars.

There's much more ahead as innovative companies and creative people discover better ways to help meeting professionals do their job.

The Least You Need to Know

➤ Go to www.corbinball.com for the best listing of meetings-industry Web sites.

➤ Meetings technology software makes planning more efficient.

➤ Save time by using online, full-service, meeting-management packages.

➤ The Internet is changing the way planners and suppliers do business.

Chapter 6

An Event by Any Other Name

Quick, what is the difference between a meeting and an event? Tick ... tock ... tick ... tock ... tick ... tock ... tick .... Give up? It's a hard question, and there is no right answer. For the most part, meetings are congregations of individuals for a specific purpose—usually educational- or business-related. The word "meeting" implies work or seriousness. An event, on the other hand, is a collection of people for a variety of purposes. Events are fun, social, and interesting.

There are a number of components that both meetings and events have in common: setting goals/objectives, selecting a site, marketing, food and beverage, timelines, staffing, working with vendors, and so on. However, events also include additional considerations that meetings usually do not have. Because the line between meetings and events can get blurry, you'll need to evaluate your needs based on each situation. In fact, some of the following items apply to a meeting as well as an event.

The Smorgasbord

We touched on the various kinds of events in Chapter 1, "What Is a Meeting or Event Anyway?" including anniversaries, award ceremonies, auctions, bar/bat mitzvahs, birthday parties, concerts, fairs, festivals, fundraisers, galas, golf outings, ground-breaking ceremonies, graduations, holiday parties, parades, political rallies, reunions, road shows, school functions, sports competitions, theme parties, tradeshows, and weddings, among others.

Food for Thought

Events can be private or public, large or small, lavish or frugal. Just like meetings, they have goals and objectives, budgets, agendas, and many of the other components that a meeting has.

Food for Thought

If you do not have an event logo, use clip art appropriate to the event to add a creative touch to the promotional pieces. For example, use a golf ball and tee for a golf tournament or fire-crackers for a company anniversary celebration.

Think about what these events have in common. Many are festive, special occasions that last a day or maybe just a few hours. Of course, there are special events like the Olympics or county fairs that last several days. Even events like concerts, expositions, and festivals can span more than one day. However, one thing is certain: No matter what your event size, it takes a lot of time and resources to organize it!

Who are the people that create and produce events? Meeting planners plan meetings and events; event planners plan events and meetings. Large festivals, fairs, and parades, to name a few, often have executive directors and additional staff members who do the planning.

You will find some professional-planning companies that specialize in either meeting planning or event planning. They may define their specialization one step further by specializing in corporate events. Don't get confused about the difference between meetings and events. You'll know an event when you see one.

Identity Crisis

One thing to think about when planning an event is your event's identity. After you create your goals and objectives, the next step is to create a memorable identity. Think of a large event in your area. Does it have its own personality? A logo? A catch phrase? Would you recognize the event just by its colors, logo, or jingle? If you can, then it has an identity. Also consider whether the event is a one-time occurrence or if it will be held again in the future.

For example, your company may decide to hold a one-time golf tournament as a fundraiser. Your event's identity may be as simple as putting your corporate logo on all promotional pieces and marketing it as a community fundraiser. This works for some events. Others need a true identity to survive and ensure longevity.

Think about the future. Is there the possibility that this one-time event could be held again? If there is, get the creative heads together to develop an identity for the event. You may find a talented local freelancer by talking to other organizations in your area.

It's More Than Drink Umbrellas

This is the fun part. Events often need to deliver a festive, fun, and unique experience. Events need to motivate and engage your participants as well. For example, an annual event can have the same theme every year, or you can change it depending on the message you want to convey. Here are some of the more popular themes:

➤ Carnival

➤ Casino night

➤ Celebration

➤ Festival

➤ Game show

➤ Island adventure

➤ Jailbreak

➤ Mardi Gras

➤ Picnic in the park

➤ Sports

➤ Western BBQ

➤ 1950s or any other era

Think Outside the Box

Here is where you can really get your creative juices flowing. Themes can be tied to current events, popular movies, or a historical event. You might even come up with a new theme idea that ties into your organization's mission. Keep your theme simple, relate it to your message, and weave it throughout the entire event. If your theme involves activities, try to include those that appeal to a broad range of people. Incorporate entertainment and a variety of food choices if appropriate. Even the follow-up correspondence after the event should tie into the theme.

The Inside Scoop

Big events often have professional event planners managing them. If you have a large or complex event, consider hiring an event planner or destination management company (DMC) to help. In the long run, their contacts in the industry can save you money on props, food, and other supplies. See Chapter 4, "Who Ya Gonna Call?" for more information on how to find these organizations.

Not Under One Roof

Events are often held at locations other than hotels, conference centers, convention centers, and self-contained facilities. If you hold events in parks, festival or company grounds, churches, or other similar locations, you need to bring in all the equipment and food for the events. You also need to comply with city ordinances and other local and municipal laws. Here is a list of items that need to be considered as part of your planning process:

tables, chairs, stage	sound/video equipment	decorations
vendors	food/beverage	cooking equipment
eating utensils	permits	toilets
waste/trash removal	security	fencing
alcohol sales/ liquor permit	traffic control	parking
street closures	local public relations	ticket sales
lost and found	lost people	wheelchairs and strollers
ATMs	accessible services	pricing
logo item sales	volunteer staffing	ambulance/medical aid
overnight accommodations	insurance (both you and all contractors)	protection from inclement weather
power	evacuation procedures	kids area/games for family events
readmission procedure	telephones	refund procedure
public transportation	stops and schedules	

The event facility may provide some of these components but not always. Before you sit down with the site manager(s), prepare a list of questions or develop your own checklist. Be sure to get full contact information for all individuals who provide services you need. Some venues have lists of vendors that they prefer to work with or with which they have exclusive contracts. You can usually work directly with these vendors or ask the site manager to handle arrangements for you. In either case, stay on top of the details because, ultimately, it's your responsibility.

If the site does not have a preferred or exclusive vendor list, look into the catering companies first. Obtain at least three proposals. Ask them for referrals to other vendors. Hiring contractors that frequently work together can make things easier and run smoother. Find out what permits and any other contractors the catering company will be responsible for.

Staging big outdoor events takes a different set of knowledge and skills. How do you know the rules? The best resources are the CVBs, city officials, and other companies you contract with. Many cities have an instruction handbook for holding public events. They have requirements for everything from the number of toilets to who provides the liquor license.

A Marriage Made in Sponsorship Heaven

Sponsorships are in. It is big business. Companies spend billions of dollars each year sponsoring meetings and events. If you find the right sponsors, it is a huge opportunity for both of you because it gives them exposure to a targeted audience and gives you additional resources to produce your event.

Sponsors should understand the event's goals and objectives and should be approached from the standpoint of creating a long-term strategic partnership. Don't approach them just because they have something you want. Understand what they need from the relationship and then build a sponsorship package.

Before you begin, you need to understand what you need from your sponsors. Sponsorships often are a way to defray costs. What do you currently buy that could be donated? Make a list and target these items first. Here are some places to start:

➤ Airline tickets

➤ Bus transportation

➤ Entertainment

➤ Food and beverage for a volunteer tent

➤ Hotel rooms

➤ Kids games

➤ Phones/communication equipment

➤ Receptions/specific meal functions

➤ Signage

Don't Drop the Ball

Make sure all contractors you hire have adequate insurance. Get a copy of their coverage and ask them to add you as an additional insured for the event. Look for a minimum of $1 million to $2 million in liability coverage.

The Inside Scoop

The local CVB is an excellent place to begin. Get its member directory (see if it is online, too) and inquire about local ordinances. Use the CVB directory as a resource to find contractors for other services.

➤ Speakers

➤ Specific food and beverage

➤ T-shirts

➤ Tote bags

Don't Drop the Ball

Consult your accountant before you start soliciting sponsorships. He or she will tell you how it affects your tax situation and what verbiage to include in your sponsor correspondence.

Your organization obviously wants money, too. You need to decide whether sponsorship items will support your current budget and defray costs or will they enhance your event by providing items that weren't initially in your budget.

With everyone looking for sponsorship dollars, the best way to find them is to match the opportunity with the sponsor. Do your homework. What organizations are potential sponsors? First, look at exhibitors and other organizations that do business with you.

Next, look at your audience and determine what companies are looking for the same audience. Create sponsorship opportunities that meet the needs of the sponsoring organization. Are they looking for recognition? Access to participants onsite? Marketing opportunities before, during, and after the event?

In other words, *customize*. Sponsorship is give and take. Each company gives something in exchange for a benefit. Some companies want their name in front of your participants. Others want more interaction with participants. Here are some ideas to give your sponsors exposure:

➤ Recognition in front of participants onsite

➤ Pre-event mailings

➤ Logo on items such as hats and T-shirts

➤ Web site banner ads

➤ Promotional materials

➤ Signage before, during, and after

➤ Fax cover sheets

➤ Mailing list

➤ A booth at the event to promote the company or to sell products or services

Don't just create one sponsorship brochure with stock benefits. Personally contact potential sponsors and ask them to be a part of your event. Then send a letter outlining your discussion and confirming participation.

"Fun"-Raising

Events are also frequently used to raise funds for a charity, organization, person, or a multitude of other reasons. These are different from sponsorships because the monies you collect at a fundraiser are donations to your selected cause.

Ways to raise funds include designating that a portion of ticket sales will go to the cause, staging a *silent auction*, selling raffle tickets, selling other items, you name it. Brainstorm. Anything (legal, that is) that people will pay money for can be used to raise money.

Your target audience are those who hold your cause *du jour* near and dear to their hearts. Match the right audience with the right cause and half the battle is won—high attendance, great exposure for your sponsors, and money raised for the cause.

A good resource for fund-raising questions is the National Society of Fund Raising Executives (NSFRE). They have a resource center available to members (for free) and nonmembers (a fee applies) to have your questions answered and have information sent to you on your topic of interest. They can be reached at www.nsfre.org.

You will need to solicit giveaways or prizes if you sell raffle tickets (don't forget the raffle license) or have a silent auction. You solicit giveaways like you solicit sponsors. Decide who can benefit by being affiliated with the event and ask them for a donation. Give them what they need in return such as recognition or access to your participants in some way.

Meeting Speak

A **silent auction** raises funds by displaying items up for bid. The participants provide their bid via a form displayed in front of the item. At the end of the specified time period, the person with the highest bid buys the item. You solicit the auction items, so there is usually no cost to you. All proceeds go to your cause.

Food for Thought

The tax-deductible portion of any ticket is the difference between the ticket price and the fair market value of the ticket. The event organizer determines the fair market value and communicates the tax-deductible amount in writing to the participant.

The Final Four

There are many things to plan for when organizing an event. This section discusses the key areas you need to pay special attention to.

Master Plan

Every event needs a master plan. This is a written document with all the details for the event. It includes a complete diagram of the site including placement of all activities, a list of contractors, a list of responsible parties, any required permits, staff training and work schedules, an event schedule, emergency phone numbers, security procedures, and much more.

During your event you need to be mobile, and carrying around binders or folders is not practical. If you consolidate the important event information onto a few sheets of paper, you'll have the right info at your fingertips when you need it.

Contingency Plans

Contingency plans provide the details of what to do in an emergency. Emergencies include, but are not limited to, the following: earthquakes, tornadoes, floods, hurricanes, fires, medical emergencies, inclement weather, and violence. Training for all volunteers and staff is a must. They should know who to notify and what to do in case of an emergency. Work with your site managers and vendors in preparing this document. They probably have one in place and can help you customize contingency plans for your unique event.

Meeting Speak

Contingency plans are written documents prepared in advance that address every conceivable emergency and other urgent issues.

Joe Q. Public can also be a huge challenge when you consider the things human beings are capable of. Potential onsite problems include disorderly conduct, drunks, theft, medical problems, and littering. Include dealing with these situations in your contingency plan workup.

Another consideration with regard to weather is what you will do if your outdoor event is rained out. Will it be cancelled or postponed, or do you have a backup site? For a large event, you may consider contracting with a convention center or other indoor venue as an inclement-weather backup. Think of the rental fee as a kind of insurance policy. Be sure to have a plan in place to change venues at the last minute. This includes keeping your vendors in this loop, too.

Entertainment

If your event includes entertainment, and most do, you are responsible for the care and feeding of the entertainers and their entourage. You will need a secure area where they can rest and stay throughout the event. You may need to provide dressing rooms, showers, and other special accommodations. If you hire a really big name, he or she will require even more services and amenities. Read your entertainment contracts thoroughly to make sure you can accommodate any requests.

Volunteers

Most events require a large number of staff, and many of them will be volunteers. They may be volunteers from within the company or organization planning the event, they may be drawn from the local community, or both. Some volunteers have experience working on events; others don't. The best thing you can do for them is provide solid training.

You also need to establish procedures for them to eat, take a break, and have some fun. Provide an area stocked with food, beverages, and a place to rest. Remember, they are volunteering their time. If you take care of them, they will take care of your event.

The Least You Need to Know

➤ Events take on a broader array of details and considerations.

➤ Sponsorship packages should be customized to each organizatior

➤ Raising funds needs to appeal to the emotions of the particir

➤ Volunteers are critical to the success of any event, and t^

Chapter 7

Supplier Secrets No More

In This Chapter

➤ Learn what happens when you call a hotel, resort, or conference center

➤ See why booking a meeting is a two-way street

➤ Understand the "passing off" of your business

➤ Know what makes your business profitable

➤ See your meeting under a supplier's microscope

Suppliers or vendors are the folks who provide you with the products and services necessary to plan and execute a meeting or event. They include, but are not limited to, the following: hotels, airlines, ground-transportation companies, decorators, destination management companies, name badge and other supply companies, registration companies, software suppliers, speakers, and entertainers.

In this chapter, we explore the sales process and how your meeting is evaluated and booked. Just because you call a hotel and request meeting space and sleeping rooms doesn't mean you'll get it. The facility booking process is really a business decision based on experience and predetermined calculations. This process will vary depending on the type of facility and the business plan of the owners. This chapter primarily addresses hotels and similar facilities. Your meeting is carefully evaluated, and a decision is made about whether it is a viable "piece of business" for the property.

Walk a Mile in My Shoes

One of your first tasks is to call the hotel to book space. This is called an *inquiry* call.

Every hotel sales manager is assigned a market segment. Here are some typical assignments:

➤ Corporate

➤ Association

➤ SMERF (social, military, entertainment, religious, fraternal)

➤ Any meeting with fewer than 50 total guestrooms (small meetings)

➤ Territories by state or region

Most hotels have booking parameters for assigning inquiries to salespeople. A typical standard is that all inquiries with 10 or more sleeping rooms are booked by the sales department. Inquiries with less than 10 sleeping rooms are booked by the catering department.

Meeting Speak

An **inquiry** is your initial contact with the hotel. Each sales office assigns these calls to the appropriate sales manager based on sales territories. Some offices assign a person each day to be dedicated to handling these inquiries, or your first contact could be with an administrative assistant who is trained to ask you initial qualifying questions. Be sure to ask whom your sales contact will be before you end the call.

When you call a hotel, here are some questions you will be asked about your meeting. If these questions are not asked, you should provide the information to the hotel.

➤ What are your goals and objectives for the meeting?

➤ Who are your attendees?

➤ Where do they come from?

➤ What are the dates?

➤ Are the dates flexible?

➤ What is the meeting agenda?

➤ What are the food and beverage functions?

➤ What is the required guestroom block?

➤ What reservation method will you use?

➤ What is your guestroom and food budget?

➤ Where was the meeting held the past three years?

➤ What did you spend last year for rooms?

➤ What did you spend last year for food and beverage?

➤ What mode of transportation will they use?

➤ Do they have any free time?

➤ Will you be planning any outside activities?

➤ Do you plan on having all the functions at this hotel?

➤ Is this a required or optional meeting?

➤ What other facilities are you looking at?

➤ What will your location decision be based on?

➤ When will your decision be made?

➤ Who makes the location decision?

➤ What did you like best about last year's meeting?

➤ What is one thing you would change about last year's meeting?

Don't Drop the Ball

It is important to understand hotel profit calculations. Ordinarily, hotels have a 70 to 80 percent profit on rooms and a 20 to 30 percent profit on food and beverage.

These are all important questions that help the sales manager qualify and learn about your business. The more he or she knows about you, the better he or she can service your group. It is a good sign if you are asked a lot of questions.

Once the sales manager understands the details, he or she checks availability. The sales manager then analyzes whether or not it is good business for the hotel. For example, if you ask for a really low rate in peak season, some properties may not book your meeting. If you are not getting the space and dates you want, start asking questions. These work well:

1. What space *is* available over those dates? At what rate?

2. What could I do with my program to fit it into your facility? Change the agenda? Change the dates?

3. How many group rooms can you give me over those dates? At what rate?

4. Is this business you want to book into your hotel during this timeframe?

These questions will, at the very least, start a dialogue about space availability and your needs.

Food for Thought

If you are not making progress with a facility, ask the sales manager what would make it a better piece of business for them.

Don't Drop the Ball

Groups that are flexible on their check-in and check-out patterns have a better chance of getting the room rates they are looking for. The hotel then can fill the "holes," and it is a win-win situation.

Most hotels have a group target rate that they aim for on any given date. A target rate is calculated based on the hotel's budget and supply and demand. Your meeting will also be evaluated for total room revenue, food and beverage revenue, and the amount of meeting space required. Groups are allotted a specific amount of meeting space based on the number of rooms/room revenue and food and beverage revenue. Every hotel is different based on the number of guestrooms in its inventory and the amount of meeting space available, so there is no standard calculation figure. This will also vary according to season, the day of check-in, and group history.

Do a little research in the destination city before setting your budget. Don't go to a major city in October if you want a downtown hotel for $75 a night and the going rate is $250. You can call the reservation department and see what rates it is quoting during your dates. This will at least give you a ballpark figure. Be aware of the business climate and know what is reasonable and what is not.

Hotels know when they need group business. For example, groups that meet on Sunday through Tuesday, Thursday through Sunday, and holiday periods may be the perfect group for hotel X and not so good for hotel Y. These are called *booking patterns*. The booking patterns vary at each property because of *transient demand*.

Why don't hotels sell all their rooms to groups? You will find that most hotels have a maximum group block or ceiling. Transient customers pay a higher rate, so hotels are careful about not turning them away too many times because they may never return. Every night has a transient-demand, guestroom-usage projection. The difference between transient demand and the total hotel room inventory is the group room inventory available to sell to groups.

Hotels have an annual budget and marketing plan. These documents serve as the road map for selling group, transient, and catering business. From these documents, sales and catering managers create their own goals and objectives for selling to their market segment.

Meeting Speak

A **booking pattern** is the arrival and departure days for a group or individual. All meeting facilities determine what pattern they need for groups during each week of the year. Booking patterns vary depending on **transient demand,** which is the demand of the individual traveler. When transient demand is high, group blocks are kept to a minimum. When transient demand is low, groups are needed to fill the hotel.

Your Business Under a Microscope

Not only are you asked about every single meeting detail, the hotel also does some investigative work on its own. It conducts what is called a history check. Unless it is a first-time meeting, your meeting has a meeting history. The sales manager contacts past meeting facilities and asks for some statistics about your meeting. He or she wants to know the dates, how many guestrooms you used each night, the agenda, food and beverage functions, and any other pertinent issues about your meeting. The only thing he or she can't ask about is your room rate (because of anti-trust laws). Meeting history information is frequently shared among hotels and is a requirement at most hotels before a contract is sent to a client.

If the sales manager finds any discrepancies in the meeting history and the space you are trying to book, he or she will ask more questions. Be prepared to support the space you need. If your room pickup last year was 90 rooms for three nights and this year you are asking for 150 rooms for three nights, the hotel will want to know why there's such a big difference. Support the difference with a solid reason, such as you hired more salespeople or experienced a big increase in membership.

Food for Thought

Keep your own meeting history. Track all statistics including revenue and expenses associated with the meeting. Ask the hotel to supply this data after you have checked out. With this information, you have more bargaining power when you book your meeting in the future. See Appendix A, "Sample Forms and Checklists," for a sample history form.

Meeting Speak

A **cutoff date** is the date on which the hotel releases your room block back to general inventory. It is typically 21 to 30 days prior to arrival.

Be aware that hotels will also internally cut your block (called blind cutting). For example, if you are holding 100 rooms for one night, the hotel may internally only hold 85 rooms. They will take a look at your meeting history and make a decision on how much to blindcut your block, if any. Not all groups will sell their entire block, so blind cutting usually works in their favor. When your *cutoff date* appears, rooms that have not sold in your block (if any) are turned back over to the hotel's general inventory to sell. Request that any rooms sold after your cutoff date be at the group rate and counted in your block. If the hotel agrees, make sure it is in the contract. Also consider adding a damage clause to your contract that protects you from blind cutting. This clause should state what you get if the hotel cannot fulfill their room block commitment prior to the cutoff date.

The following is an example of room pickup statistics. Let's take a look at some important calculations.

Group Pickup Report

Pickup Timeframe	Day/Date	Day/Date	Day/Date	Total
Contracted room block	90	95	85	270
Room pickup five weeks out	40	44	39	123
Room pickup three weeks out	85	88	84	257
Room pickup one week out	89	90	87	266
Room pickup two days out	88	89	88	265
Room pickup arrival day	88	89	88	265
Actual room pickup	85	87	86	258

The time increments for tracking room pickup can vary depending on your situation. Some larger conventions start tracking a year or more prior to the arrival date. Smaller corporate meetings may only track pickup three to four weeks out. Ask the hotel to provide you with weekly pickup reports as your meeting draws near so you can get a handle on your group. Ask who will be providing these reports and set a schedule for when you will get them.

From the preceding report, you need to know the following:

➤ The contracted room block is 270 room nights.

➤ The room pickup one week out is 266 room nights.

➤ The room pickup on the day of check-in is 265 room nights.

➤ The actual room pickup after group checks out is 258 room nights.

➤ The peak night is the second night (the night with the most rooms picked up).

➤ If you qualify for one complimentary guestroom for every 50 paid for on a cumulative basis, then $258 \div 50 = 5.16$. Five complimentary (comp) room nights will be given to your group.

➤ Calculate total room revenue by multiplying the actual room pickup minus comps by the room rate: $258 - 5$ comps $= 253$; $253 \times \$110 = \$27,830$.

➤ Your room pickup percentage is the total number of rooms picked up divided by the contracted room block: $258 \div 270 = 95.5$ percent. You picked up 95.5 percent of your group block.

➤ The difference between the room pickup for the day of check-in and the actual room pickup is the number of *no-shows* or cancellations you had on the day of check-in: $265 - 258 = 7$ rooms. Ask the hotel if these were cancellations or no-shows.

Meeting Speak

A **no-show** is a person who has a reservation for a guestroom and does not show up. There are two kinds of no-shows. One is someone who has a reservation guaranteed until a specific time, for example, 4 or 6 P.M. the day of arrival or 24 to 72 hours prior to arrival. If a person does not show up or guarantee the room, the room is released and is available for sale again. The second type of no-show has a guaranteed reservation. This means the person has guaranteed to the hotel that he or she will pay for the room. If the person is a no-show, the hotel charges his or her credit card or keeps the deposit.

You need to know how many no-shows and cancellations your group typically has because it helps you block properly in the future. You also should know whether anyone on your rooming list that you are paying for was a no-show. This affects your pocketbook.

A form for tracking your meetings is located in Appendix A. Make copies and start today. You may want to expand and customize this form so it fits your specific needs.

Hotel Tag Teams

After you've booked your meeting at a facility, your file is turned over to the convention services and catering department. Either a *catering manager* (CM) or a *convention services manager* (CSM)—or both—will handle the details from this point forward. A convention services manager handles the meeting details such as meeting room setups and meeting production. A catering manager handles the food and beverage arrangements. Sometimes a catering manager or a convention services manager does both.

Don't Drop the Ball

If you have a very small meeting, some hotels have what they call a "one stop shop." The sales manager actually keeps the file. Usually it is 10 to 50 total guestrooms or less, but this varies by property. Ask if the hotel has this program. It will save you time to work with just one individual throughout.

Put everything in writing to the catering and/or convention services manager. When you discuss the details, a written document provides a place to take additional notes and is a reference when the actual hotel documents are written. It also provides a record of what you told the hotel and makes it easier to review the hotel documents.

The Details, Please

Once your file is assigned to a catering and/or convention services manager, you should schedule an appointment to discuss the details. Try to visit the hotel again; however, sometimes you'll have to do this over the phone. Before the appointment, ask for an updated packet with new menus and other applicable information. Make sure the information is consistent with what is in the contract.

The Inside Scoop

One of the biggest pet peeves of sales and catering managers is not being kept in the loop on changes. Don't need all the meeting space? Release it back to the hotel. Did your dinner drop from 500 to 250? Tell them, so they block space accordingly. The time to tell them about changes is not right before the meeting. It is an ongoing process. This kind of reputation gives you big points when you work with them on a consistent basis. They will know your information is timely and accurate.

The catering and/or convention services manager will take the meeting details and create internal documents for staff members. You'll learn more about this in Chapter 19, "You Gotta Feed 'Em, Too."

Use your sales and catering managers as a resource. They see hundreds of meetings each year and know what works. Ask them for ideas and suggestions that might work for your meeting.

Sales Managers Just Wine and Dine—Not!

Once your meeting has been passed off, your sales manager is still a contact for you; however, his or her job is to move on and keep booking business. This person should check in with you occasionally to find out how things are progressing and to see if there is anything else you need. In some hotels, it is his or her responsibility to get the rooming list from you.

One of the best ways to have a successful meeting is if both the sales manager and the meeting planner take the time to continually communicate with each other about the meeting. It is their job to help you have a successful meeting, and you need to give them the information they need to do just that. It is a two-way street.

The Least You Need to Know

➤ Pay attention to the venue's business climate to negotiate better deals.

➤ Flexibility with your meeting specifications can save you money.

➤ Track your own meeting history to help you with future planning.

➤ Always keep the hotel informed about changes to your meeting.

Part 2

First Things First

Okay, so you're ready to start plannin'. Before you can get into the details, however, you need a timeline, a budget, and a request for proposal to distribute to potential meeting facilities.

Once that's out of the way, you can begin negotiations with vendors, and you are finally ready to sign a contract. Whoa! But are you? Especially with hotel contracts, there are tons of things you need to know. But don't worry, we've got the scoop on hotel contracts from one of the leading meetings-industry attorneys. He is a guest author and is here to share the tips you need to stay out of trouble. (Thank heaven for lawyers!)

Will exhibits be part of your next meeting? Pay attention so you can decide whether exhibits are right for your meeting. You'll also learn a bit about marketing and how to find the right people to market to. It's a never-ending battle. You need to know what to tell people so they will want to come to your meeting. Stay tuned and read all about it here.

Chapter 8

Creating and Following a Timeline

In This Chapter

➤ Create your meeting road map

➤ Understand the importance of milestones

➤ Identify important tasks for any timeline

➤ Discover that a timeline is one place to capture many of your details

Developing a timeline for your meeting is an important early step in the planning process. You already know that planning a meeting or event involves scads of details and that most planners are married to their to-do lists. However, a timeline is not just one big to-do list. In fact, it's different. A good timeline will identify key tasks and dates. It will keep you on track, and most importantly, it will factor in time you need to make sound decisions.

Timelines are as unique to an individual meeting as the people who create them. Your planning tasks differ from meeting to meeting. They are also different depending on whether you are planning a corporate, association, nonprofit, or business meeting, and event, and so on. Effective timelines must be customized to your unique situation. This chapter looks at what goes into a timeline and offers suggestions for using timelines efficiently.

Timeline Types

Timelines, just like every component in meeting planning, will vary depending on your special circumstances. When thinking about your timeline, consider these questions:

➤ Who is the timeline for? The planner? Staff? Committees?

➤ Who will be the keeper/modifier/checker of the timeline?

➤ How frequently will the timeline be looked at?

➤ Do you need task due dates?

➤ Do you need task completion dates?

➤ Do you need to assign responsibility for tasks?

➤ What type of software, if any, will be used to manage the timeline (word processing/spreadsheet/project management)?

Some people prefer timelines that list only key dates or *milestones*. Examples of milestones are room block review dates, deposits due, publication dates, mailing dates, registration deadlines, housing cutoff dates, and meeting start dates. Since this type of timeline focuses on hard dates, it is usually short. Planners who use this type of timeline just want to make sure they don't miss a critical date or decision.

Meeting Speak

A **milestone** is a significant point in a process or development. Missing a milestone usually has significant consequences.

Other planners like an exhaustive listing of every task including who is responsible for the tasks, the dates by which tasks should be completed, and even the actual completion dates (for future planning purposes). These timelines resemble large to-do lists and that's okay. These types of timelines still identify milestones and can be useful tools when working with large events or staff.

Still others like a combination of the two. Some planners find that creating a timeline that outlines the milestones plus some of the major tasks works best. They use a modified timeline to focus on major planning activities and use their own methods to handle specific action items.

Key Elements, Key Dates

One important question is "When do I begin working on my timeline?" A common answer is "When you have a confirmed site." This is because your dates and location determine almost all of your other decisions such as marketing, selecting speakers, budgets, and so on. Before we go any farther, however, realize that there are instances when you know for a fact you are doing a meeting, you just don't know the exact dates or location. You can and should develop a timeline that includes your RFP process, site selection, and the associated decisions. This is especially important for annual meetings when you are preparing for them years in advance.

Whether you are developing a milestone timeline or a lengthy timeline, you need to incorporate the key tasks and key dates. The following is a (far from complete) task listing of timeline items to get you started:

➤ Develop meeting goals and objectives.
➤ Determine decision-makers and chain of command.
➤ Assign responsible parties.
➤ Draft program topics and an agenda.
➤ Prepare the budget.
➤ Determine policies and procedures.
➤ Do venue research (sites, weather, social activities).
➤ Prepare a site request for proposal (RFP).
➤ Establish site contacts (host committee, CVBs, and so on).
➤ Conduct site visits.
➤ Negotiate site contracts (hotel, convention center, other).
➤ Research and select speakers.
➤ Negotiate speaker contracts.
➤ Prepare RFPs for other vendors (audio-visual production, exhibition, airline and ground transportation, exhibit company, and so on).
➤ Negotiate vendor(s) contracts.
➤ Obtain insurance coverage.
➤ Decide whether you need music licenses.
➤ Develop a marketing plan.
➤ Schedule committee meetings.
➤ Determine/order promotional materials and *giveaways*.
➤ Create communication/marketing pieces for attendees.
➤ Decide on a registration process (in-house, outsource, and so on).

The Inside Scoop

Don't underestimate the value of a timeline. It keeps everyone on track, and most important, deadlines are not missed if the timeline is created right. Don't be afraid to spend a day perfecting your timeline for an important meeting. As you gain planning experience, timelines become second nature.

Meeting Speak

A **giveaway** is any gift-like item given to attendees at a meeting, usually for promotional purposes.

➤ Implement the registration process.

➤ Make meeting room assignments.

➤ Make VIP housing/staffing sleeping room assignments.

➤ Print onsite materials.

➤ Decide on food and beverage.

➤ Decide on audio-visual equipment.

➤ Decide on meeting room sets.

➤ Review banquet event orders/meeting resumé.

➤ Handle VIP requests.

➤ Prepare evaluations.

➤ Prepare contingency/emergency plans.

➤ Train staff members.

➤ Determine/order onsite supplies.

➤ Determine onsite office needs (setup, communication, security, and so on).

➤ Review the rooming list (on a periodic basis).

➤ Ship materials to the site.

➤ Meet with hotel staff.

➤ Distribute tips.

➤ Send thank you letters to all vendors.

➤ Review and approve all vendor billing for payment.

➤ Evaluate the meeting, including ROI.

Clearly, this list does not cover all components of a meeting. In fact, some of the tasks really are a group of tasks. For example, before you print materials to be provided at onsite registration, you must know what the materials are. Tickets, name badges, agendas, programs, attendee lists, and maps all are important information for the attendee. You may decide to add each of these items as individual tasks with a due date as part of your timeline.

When you want more breadth in your timeline and have many details, it is a good idea to apply a category to each of your tasks. Here is a sampling of categories:

➤ Audio-visual

➤ Budget

➤ Communications

➤ Exhibits

➤ Hotel or site

➤ Mailings

➤ Marketing

➤ Printing

➤ Programming

➤ Public relations

➤ Registration

➤ Speakers

➤ Supplies

➤ Transportation

➤ Vendors

Don't Drop the Ball

At the very least, have a timeline that identifies can't-miss dead-lines such as room block review dates. A good place to look for can't-miss dates is in your vendor contracts.

The use of categories makes it much easier for you to view like tasks (by using a sort function) and to delegate responsibilities for specific categories. For large timelines, categorized tasks are easier to understand and manage. Here are examples of timeline tasks that fall under the registration category:

➤ Develop a registration procedure.

➤ Create registration policies (cancellations, name changes, no-shows, and so on).

➤ Decide on registration deadlines.

➤ Decide on in-house or Web-based registration.

➤ Develop registration forms (paper version).

➤ Develop registration forms (Web site).

➤ Develop accompanying registration documents (housing info, travel info, session selection, confirmations, receipts).

➤ Print accompanying registration documents.

➤ Put accompanying registration info on Web site (if appropriate).

➤ Hire/train registration coordinators.

➤ Test the registration procedure.

➤ Milestone: Registration system ready [date].

Remember that your milestones need a specific date that should be fairly fixed. Dates for other tasks are optional but recommended. You can identify important dates by talking with your vendors. Find out from them when they need something from you. Take a look at products you need to order and factor in enough lead-time. Also look to internal organizational criteria for deadlines or decisions. The end of your fiscal year or a change in management may impact your timeline.

Begin at the End

A good technique for developing a timeline is to use your meeting date as a starting point and work backwards. To do this, write a listing of the major tasks (use the list we just provided for help) and pencil in due dates. If you are unsure how much time is needed for a task, use your best judgement—which is what we do.

Here is an example. The annual In The Know (ITK) management conference is one year away in August. The three-day conference is for 120 people. There are general sessions and breakouts but no exhibits. A sample timeline (created backward) listing just the milestones might look like this:

Food for Thought

Identify your hard versus soft deadlines on your timeline. Many deadlines have some wiggle room, but the hard deadlines don't. It's a good idea to be able to tell the difference when looking at your timeline.

August 23 to 26	ITK Meeting
August 18	Ship materials to site
July 30	BEOs/resumé due
July 23	Housing cutoff date (hard date)
July 15	Program mailed to attendees
June 30	Earlybird registration deadline (hard date)
June 18	Final program to printer (hard date)
June 15	Make staff/VIP housing reservations
June 15	Meeting room sets, F&B, A/V to property
May 30	Deadline for ordering giveaways (hard date)
May 15	Room block review (hard date)
April 30	Second meeting brochure out
January 15	Registration open (hard date)
January 15	First meeting brochure out
December 15	Speakers hired
November 15	Site decision due
October 23 to 29	Site visits—three sites (hard date)
October 11	Site RFPs due back (hard date)

October 1	Finalize budget/agenda
	Prepare site RFP
September 15	Initial meeting to determine goals and objectives
	Tentative agenda
	Tentative budget

As you can see, the closer you are to your meeting, the more deadlines you have and the more work you must do. This is true for all meetings and events. When working backward, consider the task and ask yourself whether you can schedule it farther from the meeting start date. If so, do it. Every meeting has last-minute changes, problems, or unexpected issues. You will be swamped with requests, questions, and fire drills that only you can handle, and time—your time—is limited. It is essential that you schedule tasks away from the meeting due date whenever you can.

Another timeline-development suggestion is to identify a milestone first and then add the specific tasks about that milestone. For example, decide when your first promotional marketing piece needs to be mailed. Then determine what kind of mailer it is, what it says, what it looks like (logos, colors, printing), how many other promotional pieces you need, their mailing dates, and so on. By placing the critical element on the timeline before scheduling the associated details, you can ensure that you have allowed enough time to get them all done.

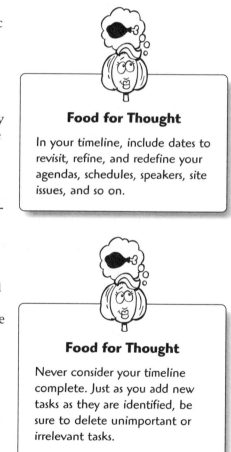

Food for Thought

In your timeline, include dates to revisit, refine, and redefine your agendas, schedules, speakers, site issues, and so on.

A timeline does not end with the start of your program. There will be important details to follow up on after your program is completed. You must write thank you letters to all vendors, helpful site staff, sponsors, committee members, planning staff, and many more in a timely manner. You will need to review all bills, see that they are paid, and review/tabulate your meeting evaluation(s). Be sure to schedule these tasks so they are completed as soon as possible after your meeting.

Food for Thought

Never consider your timeline complete. Just as you add new tasks as they are identified, be sure to delete unimportant or irrelevant tasks.

Keep on Track

Now you have a great timeline. You've covered every detail and identified every deadline. You've left no stone unturned. Now what? Well, make sure it is in a format that you understand and can

Don't Drop the Ball

Look at milestones at least one week before their deadline, especially if you have a deadline that requires a decision. Your decision-makers may be busy, out of town, or need time to make an informed decision.

easily modify. A timeline is a work in progress, and you will change it as your situation changes.

Sometimes, how a timeline visually looks is important. If you have several pages of items and they all look alike, it may be hard to identify key tasks at a glance. Use colors, check boxes, bold, larger fonts, whatever makes it easy for you to identify the key tasks. Maybe your milestones are red, your less important tasks are blue, and your supporting tasks are black. Some people like to cross items off their timeline or leave a space to write in the date the task is completed.

Still others like to use software products that offer scheduling features. These products integrate many planning components such as contact management, budgeting, and to-do lists. They cross-reference tasks and allow prioritization. Many are Web based, too.

Last but not least, meet with your staff or colleagues who are working on your meeting fairly regularly. Follow up, ask questions, and make sure they are getting their work done. Just having a written document to which you can refer not only helps you see the big picture, but if you have to rattle some cages to get things done, you can whip out the timeline to reinforce the importance of your deadlines.

The Least You Need to Know

➤ Successful planners use a timeline to stay focused.

➤ Schedule your to-do tasks around your can't-miss milestones.

➤ Your timeline is an important planning tool. Share it with all appropriate stakeholders.

➤ Updating your timeline is a must; it will help you improve future meetings.

Chapter 9

Dollars and Common Sense

In This Chapter

➤ Find out why a budget is so important

➤ Identify what goes into a budget

➤ Understand the value of fixed versus variable costs

➤ Check out useful cost-saving tips

One of the first things to do after outlining your meeting's goals and objectives is to prepare a budget. This is a key step because your budget is an essential tool that you will refer to frequently. Once prepared and approved, your budget is your blueprint for planning your meeting. Your budget will also help you make educated decisions and ensure you don't lose sight of your meeting's purpose.

In this chapter, we take a look at budget components, discuss the importance of fixed versus variable costs, and review some nifty cost-saving budgeting tips. Are you ready?

Everything Has a Price

Exactly what should you include in your budget? Answer: everything. Meetings cost money—more than many people realize—so putting down every anticipated cost (and all revenues) is essential. To give you an idea, take a look at the following list of items frequently found in budgets:

Activity fees (golf, theater, and so on)	Administrative overhead
Audio taping (sessions)	Audio-visual equipment
Audio-visual production services	Communications (cell phones, copiers, pagers, radios)
Complimentary registrations	Computing onsite (data lines, equipment, licenses, personnel, supplies)
Decorations	Entertainment
Equipment	Food and beverage
Freight and shipping	Gifts (speakers, sponsors, others)
Giveaways (to attendees)	Gratuities
Insurance (liability, meeting cancellation)	Labor costs (including overtime)
Marketing and promotion (ads, envelopes, letterhead, posters, materials)	Meeting room rental
Office/meeting room furniture rentals	Personnel (salaries, benefits)
Phone and fax	Photography
Postage (U.S. mail, overnight)	Printing
Public relations	Registration materials
Rental cars/vans (for staff)	Security
Service fees and taxes	Signs (banners and posters)
Speaker costs (fees, expenses, travel)	Staff costs (salaries, fringe benefits)
Staff travel and lodging	Supplies
Tickets (for social activities)	Transportation (shuttles to/from airport, other)
Venue rental (for other sites)	Web site (design, maintenance, registration)

Of course, you may have additional expenses. When you look at the preceding list, you see that these are really expense categories and that each category can and should be broken down to describe specific budget line items.

When developing your budget, also consider current industry trends and how they impact your meeting costs. Tap into your industry's publications, your colleagues, the newspaper, TV, and so on. For example, just a few short years ago, no one even knew what the World Wide Web was. Today, Web site registration is gaining acceptance. This trend might impact your budget because you might decide to move the majority of your registration resources to your Web site and only offer paper registration upon request.

Food for Thought

Don't use a miscellaneous category. You will always wonder exactly what it includes.

Up for Bid

Developing a budget takes quite a bit of work, and you probably won't be able to do it in one sitting. After you develop a list of anticipated expenses, figure out which categories will benefit from obtaining competitive bids. For example:

➤ Audio-visual

➤ Catering

➤ Equipment and furniture rentals

➤ Meeting venue (primary and additional venues)

➤ Speakers (especially keynoters)

➤ Transportation (bus companies, shuttles)

The Inside Scoop

For first-time budgets, many planners will take the time to get pricing for most categories. Once you have a feel for the general costs, you can estimate them for future meetings. However, do bid out high-ticket items—every time.

These are major categories, but you can get bids for any expense, no matter how minimal. Whenever you are selecting vendors, also consider the quality of their product or service, their ability to meet your deadlines, and their willingness to make good if there is a problem.

Where do you find vendors once you have selected a meeting site? The best place to start is at the venue. They usually have in-house audio-visual and food and beverage services; many even require that you use them. Otherwise, ask the venue for a list of preferred vendors. Also contact the local area CVB, do Web searches, or tap into your meeting-planning network for recommendations.

Food for Thought

Unless you have extraordinary audio-visual and/or food and beverage requirements, it usually makes sense to use the in-house services. They have the experience at the facility and the resources onsite.

Don't be afraid to negotiate with vendors. In most cases, their bids are not cast in stone. Most vendors welcome the opportunity to work with you. There may be long-term business in store for them.

Building a Budget

Every meeting or event has a financial objective. Are you trying to make a profit? Will the sponsors and organizing body pay all the bills? Or, will your meeting just break even?

Your financial objective plays an important role in how your budget is structured. If you are trying to make a profit, then you should be very cost conscious and need to get the most bang for your buck. You will also want to work hard to bring in revenue from sponsors or ticket sales. If your organization is footing the bill, let's say for an extravagant awards banquet, you will want high-end, excellent-quality (read: more expensive) products and services.

Spending Money

When preparing a budget, we recommend that you first figure out what your expenses will be before you tackle the process of generating revenues. This is especially important if you need to determine a registration fee, but you'll learn more about that later.

To help illustrate the budgeting thought process, let's look at an example of a first-time meeting.

Meeting name:	The Toofers Conference
Meeting sponsor:	Toofers—Dentistry for Toddlers
Dates:	March 11 to 13 (3 days)
Location:	Dallas
Estimated attendance:	100
Goal:	To promote advancements in toddler dentistry
Planning/host objectives:	Get press coverage in at least three dental journals
	Develop a core attendance that will attend next year's meeting
	Raise $30,000 as seed money for next year

Program agenda:	Day 1: Keynote in A.M., three breakouts in P.M., reception
	Day 2: Breakouts in A.M., lunch, poster session (30 posters) in P.M., reception
	Day 3: Breakouts in A.M., lunch with keynote, end

Wow, even with this information you still have a ton of questions. Where do you start? Well, based on your goal and objectives, you will have to make some assumptions that will impact your spending:

1. **The quality of your program is key.** Identify well-known and respected industry speakers who are good at speaking and teaching, as well as being subject matter experts.

2. **You want this to be an annual conference.** Don't skimp on food. Offer breakfasts and break food but remember that your audience is a group of dentists.

3. **End on a high note.** Shoot for a whiz-bang keynote, maybe from outside the field. Make the Day 3 lunch fun and memorable.

4. **People like to talk.** Give them opportunities to network and meet new colleagues.

5. **As a new conference, you will be looking for an audience.** Brainstorm creative ways to market and promote your meeting.

It's a natural part of the process to guess and make assumptions. The important thing is that you get your budget started. You'll be able to modify it as your program develops so that it truly meets your needs.

What are your anticipated expenses? Start with the expense categories previously listed. Ask yourself if you will have any expenses in these categories. You will be surprised to see how things add up.

If possible, prepare your budget using a spreadsheet; it will change several times before it's all over, and you won't want to do it by hand. Learn how to set up your budget so that most of your numbers are automatically calculated when you add raw information.

The Inside Scoop

It's a good idea to generate a draft budget before you sit down with others to hammer out details. It's much easier for a group to work from an existing document than to prepare it from scratch. Plus, when working with the decision-makers, it is always easier to take something out than to add it in after the meeting is over.

Don't Drop the Ball

When calculating the amounts for any expense or income, show the formula used to arrive at the number. Always provide as much detail as possible so that others will understand the thought process.

Making Money

Up to now we have discussed expenses, but there are two sides to every budget: expenses and revenues. Now we will take a look at revenues.

How are you paying for your conference? It will depend on the type of organization sponsoring it as well as your financial objectives. In most cases, corporations will use internal funds from one or several budgets. However, associations and other nonprofit organizations depend on a combination of registration fees, grants, sponsorships, exhibition fees, product or ticket sales, host underwriting, and in-kind donations.

Fixed vs. Variable Costs

Understanding the difference between fixed and variable costs is useful. With any meeting, there are some costs that you will pay for regardless of the attendance. Those are known as fixed costs (FC). There are also costs that will vary according to the number of attendees. These are variable costs (VC). The following table compares some common expenses. Almost any fixed cost can turn into a variable cost if the meeting grows substantially or there are add-ons.

Expense	Fixed	Variable
Audio-visual equipment	X	
Food and beverage		X
Giveaways		X
Ground transportation		X
Insurance	X	
Lodging		X
Marketing	X	
Meeting room rental	X	
Office equipment	X	
Registration materials		X
Signage	X	
Speakers	X	
Shipping and freight		X
Staff travel and expenses	X	

You could argue that some of the fixed expenses are variable and vice versa—and you would be right. If your attendance soared and you needed more space, your meeting room rental might increase (variable cost). And you still have to ship all of your stuff whether you have 10 or 100 people (fixed cost).

But now to the big question: Why should you care about fixed or variable costs? Well, if you need to calculate a *break-even point,* you need to know what your fixed and variable costs are.

If your meeting needs to turn a profit and you are deriving much of your income from registration fees, you need to know how many attendees you need to break even. Then, for all attendees above that number, your meeting will make money. Using the Toofers Conference as an example, we need to calculate the break-even number of attendees if we want to fund the conference strictly using registration fees.

First, determine the fixed cost (FC). Add up these costs, including meeting room rental, speaker fees and expenses, marketing costs, audio-visual costs, and so on, for a total expense number. Let's assume the Toofers Conference has its total fixed costs set at $75,000.

Meeting Speak

A **break-even point** is the point at which your meeting neither makes nor loses money.

Food for Thought

Most items that are consumable would be considered a variable expense.

Then determine the variable cost (VC) on a per-person basis. Remember that we don't know how many people will attend, but we can determine how much we'll need to spend per person on food and beverage, registration materials, giveaways, and so on. Let's assume the Toofers Conference has a variable cost of $200 per person.

To do the break-even attendee calculation, we must assume a registration fee (RF), so let's estimate we want to charge a registration fee of $500 per person. Now, to calculate the break-even number of attendees, use this formula:

FC ÷ (RF − VC) = Number of attendees

Let's run the numbers:

$75,000 ÷ ($500 − $200) = 250 attendees

We will need 250 attendees paying $500 to cover all of the meeting costs. Don't believe us? Let's reverse the calculation.

Don't Drop the Ball

Factor in the cost of complimentary and reduced-fee registrations from speakers, sponsors, VIPs, and staff. These are expenses for the meeting.

The fixed cost ($75,000) plus the variable cost (250 × $200 = $50,000) brings the total cost of the Toofers Conference to $125,000. If we charge all 250 attendees $500, we get a revenue of $125,000. Bingo!

Doing a break-even calculation is beneficial. Initially, the Toofers Conference anticipated 100 people. Now that we know the total costs, we see that keeping the registration fee at $500 requires an attendance of 250 people. If we really just want 100 people, the registration fee will have to be $950 just to break even. Take a look:

100 people × $200 = $20,000 (VC)

$20,000 + $75,000 = $95,000 ÷ 100 = $950 (RF)

Remember, however, that one of the planning/host objectives was to make $30,000 profit. So to do that, the registration fee for 100 people would need to be a whopping $1,250!

$95,000 + $30,000 = $125,000 ÷ 100 = $1,250 (RF)

Armed with this information, we can choose to do some or all of the following:

➤ Increase the attendance.

➤ Increase the registration fee.

➤ Solicit sponsorships.

➤ Reduce expenses (both fixed and variable).

➤ Solicit in-kind donations.

Each individual situation will dictate which option(s) you choose. Registration fees may not matter, and the attendees will pay whatever is asked of them. (You are lucky!) Or, sponsorships may be a natural solution to your budget issues. Discuss the options with the appropriate stakeholders and make a decision that is best for you.

Cost-Saving Ideas

This topic could take up a chapter in itself, but alas, we've come to the end of this chapter. Below we leave you with 10 tips to help you stretch your meeting dollar:

1. Negotiate complimentary services when selecting a site (such as free parking, airport shuttles, free local calls, free freight storage, and so on). If it comes out of your budget, try to get the venue to provide it for free.

2. Order food and beverages in quantity, not per person.

3. When appropriate, order *on-consumption*. You won't pay for unused/uneaten food and beverage (sodas, packaged food such as granola bars, and so on).

4. Bring your own LCD projectors and laser pointers if possible. Big savings! Address security and labor issues.

5. Reconfirm your speaker's audio-visual needs at least one week prior to the program.

6. If you are tax-exempt and are reimbursing certain attendees anyway, put their housing on your master bill to avoid taxes.

7. Ask the venue if it charges a service fee for taking care of special requests (offsite tours, purchasing supplies). If it does, handle the details yourself.

8. Look into entertainment booked by other groups at your venue or in town. Try to piggyback with another group to get reduced fees and/or travel.

9. Use your general session room as a breakout room to save on audio-visual and/or meeting room fees.

10. Ask for a cash discount if you pay your bill immediately after the meeting.

Keep your eye on expenses at all times and never lose sight of your budget. Meeting expenses add up quickly.

Meeting Speak

On-consumption means you will only be charged for the items you consumed; this mostly applies to food and beverage items.

The Least You Need to Know

➤ A realistic budget says a lot about the feasibility of your meeting.

➤ Use a spreadsheet's formula functions. Let the spreadsheet do the math and calculations.

➤ Put every expense and revenue item into your budget and keep it updated.

➤ There are hundreds of ways to stretch your meeting dollar. Be creative and negotiate.

Inn Sites
and RFPs

In This Chapter

➤ Discover how site selection contributes to achieving goals and objectives

➤ Learn how to write a request for proposal (RFP)

➤ Know what information to provide and ask for in your RFPs

➤ Explore the important aspects of a site inspection

Selecting the right location sounds easy, doesn't it? It is, if you do it right. Picking a location because it looks good or sounds like fun is not the best way to make a decision.

In this chapter, you will learn how to figure out the right site and the reasons behind the selection process. You will also learn how to write a request for proposal (RFP) and ways to conduct a site inspection.

Location, Location, Location

You've heard the cliché—location, location, location. Just as a retail store needs the right real estate to sell its wares, a meeting needs the right site to accomplish the goals and objectives you have worked so hard to establish.

When you select a site, you are really buying service and an experience for meeting attendees. Make the right decision to support your goals and objectives.

Don't Drop the Ball

No matter what type of meeting you are planning, the attendees have to get there. Is transportation abundant and reasonably priced? Keep this in mind during the initial planning stage. It may or may not be a factor.

The location sets the tone for the entire meeting. Common venue types include airport hotels, conference centers, convention centers, cruise ships, downtown hotels, gaming casino hotels, resorts, suburban hotels, and universities.

Is the main purpose business, pleasure, or both? There are no definitive rules for matching sites with meetings, but think about the goals and objectives before you sign on the dotted line. Book business meetings at facilities that cater to business travelers and meetings. Book pleasure-related groups at resorts and other places that have activities and lots to do. Book larger meetings and events at convention centers and large convention hotels. Conference centers are designed for smaller, education meetings and retreats. Make sense?

Here are some questions you need to think about when selecting a site:

➤ What kind of facility will help you achieve your meeting's goals and objectives?

➤ What type of facility has the available services and accommodations you need?

➤ Which location and facility would best fit your meeting budget?

➤ Is the meeting space sufficient for your agenda?

➤ Does weather matter?

➤ What are the average airfares to the site?

➤ Are there plenty of flights to and from the attendees' points of origin?

➤ What is the distance to the meeting facility from the airport?

Don't Drop the Ball

Don't pick a venue just because you got the best deal. If a site is a mismatch (inappropriate space, poor service, too difficult to get to), it will ultimately reflect on the success of your meeting.

➤ Is there transportation from the airport to the meeting facility? What is the cost?

➤ Is the facility easily accessible for people driving to the meeting?

➤ Are there nearby area attractions and restaurants for attendees and their guests?

➤ What activities and services are available onsite?

➤ What other groups and/or activities will be in the city or in the facility?

Make sure you book the facility or location for the right reasons because it plays an important role in your overall meeting experience.

Write the Right RFP

Once you have determined your goals and objectives and have outlined your agenda, you are ready to write a request for proposal (RFP). In other words, you determine what you need from a meeting facility and ask facilities to bid on your requirements.

We recommend putting your meeting needs in writing. For smaller meetings, a call to a facility is probably okay, but a written document serves as a reminder of what you need and ensures that you don't forget anything. With a phone call, there is no record of what was discussed. Putting it in writing can actually save time because facilities can assign a sales manager and check space before a conversation even takes place.

> **Food for Thought**
>
> Your RFPs should be concise, detailed, and include everything you need from the facility. Making changes after the facility has sent a proposal can actually change the bid.

An RFP can be as basic or as detailed as you deem necessary, but the more detailed, the better. Why? Because the meeting facility can only help you if it understands your requirements. The more a facility knows about your meeting, the better service you will get in the long run.

Meeting Scoop

A meeting RFP covers many aspects. Good RFPs should identify the following components:

➤ The name of the meeting

➤ Its dates and days of the week

➤ The flexibility of the dates (with alternate dates if possible)

➤ The goals and objectives of the meeting

➤ An attendee profile (who the attendees are including the percentage of men and women and their age ranges, where they are coming from, and their transportation methods)

➤ The sleeping room block (your estimate)

➤ *Commissionable* or *net* guestroom rates

➤ A meeting agenda with exact space needs (start/stop times, number of people, and room setup style)

➤ A meeting history, if any (total attendance, guestroom pickup, number of people served/meal function and rooms, and food/beverage revenue)

➤ The meeting budget (only share what you are comfortable with; you will be asked this question so be prepared)

➤ Food and beverage requirements

➤ Special needs such as dietary and accessibility issues

➤ High-tech needs such as Internet access in the meeting rooms

➤ The proposal due date, decision date, and process

➤ Request that space be held on a tentative basis if applicable

➤ Where to send the proposal

> **Meeting Speak**
>
> A **commissionable rate** is a guestroom rate in which the hotel agrees to pay a specific percentage back to a designated organization. A **net rate** is void of any commissions.

Also ask that a complete information packet be sent to you. Include the date a decision will be made and consider letting facilities know how the decision will be made (by you, committee, supervisor, and so on). Some want to know that information.

> **The Inside Scoop**
>
> When sending your agenda, make sure to note whether you need a meeting room past 5 P.M. If your meeting is from 8 A.M. to 5 P.M. but you need to keep materials in the room overnight, you need the room on a 24-hour hold. If you don't tell them, they could rent the room to another group in the evening, and your binders could end up in the dumpster.

You should also have a list of questions for the facility to answer in your RFP. The following are some sample questions:

➤ What is your room tax? Are there other taxes?

➤ Do you have airport transportation? What is the cost? How long does it take, during rush hour and nonrush hour?

➤ Do you have a business center? What are the hours?

➤ Ask for a set of banquet menus, and an audio-visual price list.

➤ What company provides the audio-visual equipment? Does the company have an exclusive contract? Can outside audio-visual companies be brought in? Is there a cost to bring in an outside company?

➤ Do you have any exclusive agreement with outside vendors?

➤ What are the self- and valet-parking fees? Are there in-out privileges for overnight guests?

➤ What are room service hours?

➤ Do you have a health club? What is the cost?

➤ How is the facility in compliance with the Americans with Disabilities Act, and the local or federal fire safety codes?

Food for Thought

Almost every facility has a Web site, and many include fairly detailed information about the property and services. Do some research online before you submit an RFP.

The questions you ask will depend on the needs of your group, so adjust them accordingly. Also, be sure to take notes as you receive responses to your RFPs. When suppliers call to get clarification on your requirements, you should update your RFP accordingly. You might need to send it out a second time.

By Fax, Snail Mail, E-Mail, or Online

A big question these days is how to submit an RFP. The most common way is to submit RFPs by fax or e-mail. Less common is using the old-fashioned U.S. mail. However, the up-and-coming method is to submit online RFPs. In Chapter 5, "Technology Soft-Where?" we discussed online RFP services. Planners are still getting used to this process, and it may take some time to reduce the paper trail. Be aware that it does take some time to enter the information into online forms, and some forms may not allow you to describe all of your requirements, but try it to see how it works for you.

Another thing you need to decide is who to send it to. Use Chapter 4, "Who Ya Gonna Call?" as a guide to make this decision. You can use the following routes:

1. Hotel(s) and conference centers directly
2. Convention and visitors bureau (CVB)
3. National sales office (NSO)
4. Online RFP services (see Chapter 5)
5. Meeting-management company

Meeting Speak

A **concession** is something you get over and above the standard offering. An **amenity** is an item placed in a guestroom such as food and beverages or some other gift. In-room amenities are also shampoos, bathrobes, and stuff!

Now, before you go off and start sending your RFP, it is best to have a contact name. If you send it without one, it will be more difficult to follow up. Once you have a name or e-mail address, it will be much easier to track someone down if no one calls you.

Ask and You May Receive

Booking a meeting is a two-way street. Each party brings something to the table, and it needs to be a win-win situation to have a really successful meeting. In the past, items such as complimentary rooms and complimentary meeting space were industry standards. Now, what you bring to the table also determines your meeting facility costs.

The following is a list of potential *concessions* to ask for if they apply to your situation:

➤ One complimentary guestroom for every X number paid for on a cumulative basis (ask for 1 per 50, 40, or even 30), often referred to as the comp policy

➤ Upgrades to suites or to concierge or club floors at the group rate

➤ Complimentary meeting space

➤ VIP *amenities*

➤ Complimentary newspaper for all in-house guests

➤ Complimentary airport transportation

➤ Complimentary parking

➤ Complimentary refreshment break (be specific)

➤ Complimentary transportation to offsite events

➤ Refreshments and cookies for your registration area

➤ Three-week cutoff date (standard is four weeks)

➤ Use of radios onsite (state the number needed and dates for use)

➤ One complimentary microphone in each meeting room

➤ Complimentary welcome reception

➤ Staff rooms at a reduced rate

➤ Late checkout for VIPs and staff

➤ Free local calls from guestrooms

➤ Free parking for VIPs and staff

➤ Waive package receiving/shipping fees

➤ Food and beverage discount

➤ Audio-visual equipment discount

➤ Complimentary use of sign easels

➤ Complimentary health club passes

Be prepared to support your requests with solid business that warrants the concessions. If you don't ask, you can't get.

Also talk to the local CVB or sponsors about assisting with some of your meeting costs. Sometimes they are able to provide transportation to offsite events or provide other services at no cost. You may also be able to negotiate with the hotel a dollar amount per room night as a credit (also known as a rebate) toward some of your meeting expenses. It always pays to ask.

Special Accommodations

Special accommodations are items or services that you or the meeting facility provide to attendees. These can include dietary, medical, and other personal requests. If you know of any special needs in advance, make sure they are included in your RFP.

The Americans with Disabilities Act (ADA)

The Americans with Disabilities Act (ADA) calls for "reasonable accommodation" for people with disabilities. As a meeting planner, you need to be aware of the law and provide for such accommodations. Your meeting site also has to be in compliance with these laws. The definition of a reasonable accommodation is the subject of debate. Depending on the situation, you may be required to provide sign-language interpreters, assisted-listening devices, or closed-caption systems. For more information about ADA, go to www.usdoj.gov/crt/ada/adahom1.htm.

Bon Voyage!

We can't emphasize it enough; if you can visit the site in advance, do so. Brochures, videos, and virtual site inspections are good tools to help you narrow down the potential sites, but they don't take the place of experiencing the facility in person. You cannot experience what the service is like or see what the property's condition is unless you go and see it for yourself. Also consider taking a video or digital camera along. This way, you can record the details for the staff or committee back at the office.

Food for Thought

Prepare in advance by making a list of what you need to learn on your site inspection. If you don't prepare, you will have a tour based on what the sales manager wants you to see and learn about the property—not what you need to know.

Meeting Speak

A **familiarization (FAM) trip** is hosted by a destination or a CVB and its members for the sole purpose of showcasing the city as a meeting location. Warning: Only partake if you have a need for the city. Going on a FAM trip for the heck of it is unethical.

Guided Tours

Any hotel, conference center, CVB, or NSO can arrange a site inspection for you. These are scheduled in advance and are usually private, individual tours. You may tour just one or two hotels on a trip arranged by you, or you can go on a CVB-scheduled site visit to multiple hotels, a convention center, area attractions, and potential reception facilities.

Most CVBs periodically have *familiarization (FAM) trips* for meeting planners. Typically, a CVB hosts a group of meeting planners and provides a one- to three-day area tour. Virtually every minute is packed with need-to-see sites in the city. These trips are complimentary to planners and usually include airfare, a hotel room, and all meals. The CVB wants to make a positive and lasting impression.

Another bonus when scheduling a site visit through a CVB is that all of the scheduling is done for you. You just show up and take the tour. They usually drive you from site to site and can add last-minute additions to the itinerary if needed.

Surprise! Go It Alone

Another option for conducting a site visit is to do it unannounced. Make a reservation if needed, check in, and explore the facility on your own. You learn a lot just by wandering around the meeting space and experiencing the property from a regular guest's point of view. The drawback to this is that you may not be able to see all of the features or ask questions.

When you are on a scheduled site visit, you get treated like royalty, and your room is flagged as a VIP! In other words, when you call room service, of course the service is great because they know who you are! If you do it incognito, you will really see what kind of experience your attendees will have.

Front of the House

Front of the house refers to all the space accessible to the public: lobby areas, meeting space, food and beverage outlets, and the like. Carefully look at the entire facility. How well do they keep it clean? Are the employees you come in contact with friendly? Are the rooms and suites acceptable for your meeting?

Back of the House

Back of the house refers to the areas accessible only to the staff (oh, really?) and includes hallways behind the meeting space, kitchens, laundry areas, and the like.

On your site visit, ask to have a tour of these areas, too. How properties take care of them is a good indication of their pride in the facility and their attention to detail. Are they clean or dirty? Neat or messy? Safe or hazardous? It is also good to know where the convention services and banquet offices are located. (They are frequently located in the back of the house.) In a pinch, going to find them onsite is quicker than trying to locate them by phone.

The Inside Scoop

Take notes during your site visits. Create a checklist with items that are important to your organization and meeting. Some lists have planners checking for dust bunnies under the beds. Use your time wisely.

Site Checklist

You need to be prepared for your site inspection. All site visits are unique because each meeting has its own goals and objectives. Be sure to evaluate the properties based on their ability to help you achieve them.

In Appendix A, "Sample Forms and Checklists," we have included a sample site visit checklist. Fine-tune it to your specific needs.

Virtual Inspections

If you absolutely cannot conduct a site visit, find out if the facilities have a Web site with a virtual-tour capability. At the very least, ask for a video. Obviously, these will only show the good stuff, but it is better than nothing. A virtual tour in advance of your site visit is also helpful to prepare for your tour. Brochure pictures can be very deceiving!

Decisions, Decisions, Decisions

The site decision is not that difficult if you have carefully laid the groundwork for the meeting. Look at it from this perspective:

➤ Is the facility conducive to achieving the meeting's goals and objectives?

➤ Which site do you feel most comfortable with?

➤ Does the preferred site have an acceptable bid?

➤ Can the attendees easily travel to the site?

➤ Can you work with them? Do they listen to you? Do they understand your needs and concerns?

➤ If you conducted a site visit, was the service good? Was the facility in good condition?

➤ Whom can you call that recently met there? Ask for the names of recent planners who held a meeting there and call for a reference or two.

Sometimes the decision to pick a site will fall to someone who did not participate in the site tours—a boss or committee, perhaps. It's easier for them to look at hard numbers (rates, concessions, and so on) than it is to understand other important factors (service, quality of rooms, and so on). In these cases, you must prepare a very thorough report and list the pros and cons. If you really like a specific site, be prepared to defend your position. Otherwise, the best site (in your professional opinion) may lose out to a site that looks better on paper.

Inform the Suppliers

Once you make a site decision, don't forget to inform all the properties that sent a proposal. Tell them in writing the reason your group is not selecting their facility, send them a thank you note, and move on. This is good business etiquette (we're sure you were taught good manners!) and they will remember your follow-through next time you send them an RFP.

Announce Your Decision

Finally, tell all your stakeholders of the site selection. These are the first people who should know because they can start talking it up!

Also tell your staff as soon as you know. Once your site is determined, they (or you) can begin working on other important aspects of your meeting that hinged on the dates and location.

The Least You Need to Know

➤ Carefully match your goals and objectives with your meeting location to make your meeting more successful.

➤ Ask for what you want in the RFP because the facility's bid is based on your needs.

➤ Site visits are a valuable tool for making a location decision.

➤ Always let the bidding facilities and all stakeholders know your decision and reasons in a timely manner.

Chapter 11

Negotiating the Best Deal

In This Chapter

➤ Identify the vendors you need to plan a meeting

➤ Learn what is and is not negotiable

➤ See how to protect your organization during the negotiating process

➤ Learn the common items that are often overlooked when negotiating contracts

➤ Understand meetings-industry insurance issues and how to get proper coverage

---

Everyone is looking for the best deal and the meetings industry is no different than any other. The meetings industry uses a variety of vendors, and we can't possibly cover them all in one book. We can, however, list the most widely used vendors and discuss how to negotiate with them. We will also focus on the big one—hotel negotiations.

In Chapter 10, "Inn Sites and RFPs," we discussed the RFP process for site selection, but you can and should consider submitting RFPs to your other vendors. This chapter focuses mostly on the negotiation stage after you have received proposals or quotes from your vendors.

Vendors You Need

Make a list of the vendors you need for your meeting. To help you identify them, let's look at a list of common meeting vendors:

➤ Airlines

➤ Awards and promotional-gift companies

➤ Copying services

➤ Decorating companies

➤ Desktop-publishing companies

➤ Destination-management companies

➤ Entertainers

➤ Exhibition-services companies

➤ Ground-transportation companies

➤ Insurance brokers

➤ Meeting facilities

➤ Meeting-supply companies

➤ Production companies

➤ Speakers

➤ Temporary help providers

➤ Web site providers

Finding these vendors is easy. You may have already located all or some of them when you prepared your budget and sent out RFPs. If not, ask your meeting venue or the local CVB for recommendations. Also check out meeting trade magazines, browse the Web, and ask your colleagues.

Needs, Wants, and Everything Else

The key to negotiating is to do some homework before making any inquiries. Here are some things to think about:

➤ Know the value that your business brings to each vendor.

➤ Think long-term vendor relationships.

➤ Understand the business/economic climate.

➤ Buy for multiple meetings, not just one (if possible).

➤ Network and ask for vendor recommendations.

The best rule of thumb is to first understand your goals and objectives, then prioritize your needs, and then determine your "wish list" of products and services. This list should contain items that would be great to have but are not deal breakers.

When inquiring about vendors and their services, ask them what they need to give you a proposal. You can gain valuable insight by asking a few questions. Whether you ask for quick quotes or full-blown proposals, get everything in writing.

Everything's Negotiable (Almost)

Once you have proposals/quotes in hand, review them carefully. Do they address all your needs? Don't be afraid to go back to a vendor and re-address your important issues. If a proposal does not address an item from your RFP you should find out why. Then select the finalists. Be honest and up front. Tell your first-choice vendor how they can get the business but only if you are prepared to give it to them!

Occasionally, a vendor will approach you with the question, "If I give you what you want, will you definitely give me business?" That is being refreshingly direct. Your answer should be up front and honest. Tell them the decision-making process and when they will have an answer. Then follow through.

Don't Drop the Ball

If you plan meetings in more than one city, look for vendors that have branch offices in those locations. Then you can give them more business and save time and money in the process. Network! Network! Network!

Attrition

It is imperative you understand *attrition* when negotiating contracts. If you have attrition, you must pay the facility a sum (also called damages) to recoup its lost profit. See Chapter 12, "Contracts: Signing on the Dotted Line," for more detailed information on attrition in contracts as it relates to both rooms and food and beverage.

According to attorney and former hotel director of sales, John S. Foster, Esq., CHME (you will meet him in Chapter 12), "The sole purpose of an attrition clause is to shift the risk of low pickup or underperformance from the facility to the meeting sponsor." This can apply to guestrooms, food and beverage covers, or both.

Meeting Speak

Attrition is a reduction in numbers from what you promised the meeting facility. The numbers are the guestrooms and food and beverage meal covers from which the facility forecasts its potential revenue and profit. Attrition is also called slippage or drop off.

Don't Drop the Ball

Facility attrition calculations can be vague, tricky, wrong, or all three. You must learn as much about them as you can. Go to classes, buy books, read articles.

Attrition calculations are usually proposed by the facility and can be calculated many different ways. It is your responsibility to understand and negotiate attrition calculations that are agreeable to you and the hotel. Make sure the calculation uses "lost profit" instead of "lost revenue" and stipulates that your damages will be reduced by any guestrooms or food and beverage that the hotel resells. Also make sure you have the opportunity to reduce your room block up to an agreed upon percentage of the total room block at specific intervals prior to arrival. The reduced block now becomes the number of rooms you are liable for.

Say, for example, your room block is 1,000 rooms and you are allowed to reduce it up to 15 percent prior to arrival. If necessary, this would allow you to reduce your total block by 150 rooms down to an 850-room block by the predetermined dates stipulated in the contract. Now if attrition occurred, it is based on 850 rooms and not 1,000. So, if you picked up 800 rooms, you pay the hotel for 50 rooms times their lost profit.

If the group rate was $100 and their profit margin is 70 percent, you would pay $70 times 50 rooms or $3,500 in attrition. Make sure the profit percentage is stated in the contract.

Meeting-Room Rental

Sometimes a facility may charge you meeting-room rental based on room pickup. For a meeting with a total of 1,000 room nights and a maximum of $15,000 in meeting-room rental, a meeting room rental calculation might look like this:

Meeting-Room Rental Requirements

Percentage of Room Block Picked Up	Total Meeting-Room Rental
85 percent or higher	Complimentary
75 to 84 percent	$5,000
65 to 74 percent	$10,000
64 percent and lower	$15,000

The Inside Scoop

According to former hotel director of sales and industry attorney, John S. Foster, Esq., CHME, the contract should provide for either attrition fees or meeting-room rental based on a sliding scale but not both. They are both intended to accomplish the same objective: compensating the hotel for a group's low pickup. There are two exceptions to this: if the group needs more meeting space than it is entitled to receive on a complimentary basis from the hotel or if the group insists on a specific meeting space that the hotel would not normally give to the group based on the group's attendance.

Understand that setting up your meeting in a facility is not free. Staff members have to be paid to set up the chairs and tables and prepare the meals. They also clean the public spaces, answer the phones, direct meeting attendees, park cars, and serve food. You will be asked to pay meeting room rental at some point. Your job is to negotiate the best contract for your group and you should work to reduce or eliminate meeting room rental, but depending upon your specific circumstance, meeting room rental may be necessary.

Unexpected Charges

During negotiations, many items can be overlooked that have an impact on your bottom line. Read the contract with a fine-tooth comb so you are not surprised when your bill arrives. Any items that you are required to pay for should be incorporated into your RFP and contract.

If there are any "automatic fees" (such as gratuities, porterage or luggage handling, resort fees, shipping charges, and service charges) associated with a vendor, they should appear in the contract; otherwise, you should never pay them. Ask to review the facility's standard contract in the beginning so you will understand all the issues in advance.

Food for Thought

During the negotiating stage, ask for a copy of the vendor's standard contract. The contract is where many miscellaneous charges are itemized. Then you can clarify any issues in advance of finalizing a contract.

Items Often Overlooked When Negotiating Contracts

Vendor	Items Often Overlooked
Hotels	Attrition fees
	Automatic housekeeper gratuities or other service charges
	Box storage fees
	Cleaning fees
	Computer-usage charges
	Cutoff dates
	Deposits
	Electrical and mechanical services
	AV equipment setup fees
	Copying charges
	Easel rental fees
	Fax sending and receiving charges
	Guestroom phone call access fees
	Hanging banners and signs
	Health club fees
	Internet access fees
	Late checkout fees
	Meeting-room key charges
	Meeting-room rental
	Package-delivery fees
	Package shipping and receiving charges
	Parking
	Per-person service fees
	Security
Convention centers	Most of the items listed for hotels plus ...
	Doormen/electricians/engineers/maintenance
	Stagehands
	Labor to change a room set
	Loading dock access
	Staging, risers for meeting rooms
	Tablecloths, table skirting
Other vendors	Deposits
	Gratuities
	Excessive shipping or rush charges
	Labor or setup fees
	Special service fees
	Transportation and other expenses

Written Documents

Once you have the proposal or quote and the contract in hand, carefully compare the two and note any differences. Make sure you include a statement in your contract that says any miscellaneous charges not stated in the contract will not be paid for unless agreed to in writing by both parties.

Nonnegotiables

There are a few items you will not be able to negotiate (but you can always try!). The meetings industry has taxes, license fees, insurance, *service charges,* and *gratuities* to contend with. These are a necessary part of planning a meeting. These costs need to be included in the budgeting and execution of the meeting.

Music licensing, insurance, and other fees may be a surprise for your committee, boss, and other people outside our industry, but they are very important to safeguarding the outcome of the meeting itself.

Music Licensing

Music is protected under U.S. copyright law as intellectual property just like books, movies, photos, and articles. Any time music is played to third parties via CD, cassette, video, and so on, a music license is required. Copyrighted music cannot be played or performed in public without permission from the copyright owner.

There are currently three organizations that charge and collect the fees associated with playing music in public:

➤ Broadcast Music, Inc. (BMI) (www.bmi.com)

➤ American Society of Composers, Authors, and Publishers (ASCAP) (www.ascap.com)

➤ Society of European Stage Authors and Composers (SESAC) (www.sesac.com)

Depending on the music you play, you may need a license from one or all three organizations. Contact them for more information.

Meeting Speak

A **service charge** is a mandatory charge added to a service. For example, hotels often charge a flat service charge for food and beverage and audio-visual services. A **gratuity** is a voluntary amount of money given in exchange for a service performed. This is also referred to as a tip.

Don't Drop the Ball

If you are playing music at your event, you probably owe music license fees. Check out the Web sites for BMI, ASCAP, and SESAC to determine how to proceed in your particular situation.

Service Charges, Gratuities, and Uncle Sam

We all have to pay them, so always take them into consideration when planning budgets and looking at potential meeting sites.

Service charges are taxable but gratuities aren't to the meeting sponsor. Most hotels keep a portion of the service charge and disburse the rest to the service staff. You may be able to negotiate to have the portion that goes to the staff billed separately and not taxed. This gets a bit complicated, so consult an attorney for the appropriate contractual language if you take this route! For large meetings, it may be worth the effort.

Food for Thought

Service fees, gratuities, and taxes can total upward of 20 to 30 percent of your bill. Understand the hotel's formulas for each and incorporate them into the budget and conference fees.

If your organization is tax exempt, tell your vendors early on and provide a copy of your exemption certificate. Not all states allow organizations that are exempt from taxes on the federal level to be exempt from state and local sales tax. To determine whether your group qualifies, contact the sales tax division of the state government where your meeting is held. If your group qualifies, the state sales tax office will issue a certificate stating that the state exempts your organization from sales tax. Be aware that cities and counties are separate taxing authorities from the state. They must be contacted as well if you want to avoid tax assessments on this level.

Remember that it is your responsibility to obtain and furnish your exemption certificate(s) to the hotel. Without the certificate(s), hotels have no authority not to collect taxes from your group. Check with your host facility for more information but don't expect it to be fully knowledgeable on this. It is the planner's responsibility to do the footwork.

Insurance

You have to have it. Your vendors need to have it. You need to understand it. Find an insurance broker or attorney who understands the meetings business and make sure you are covered in case of an incident. There are so many potential situations that could result in a claim against you and/or your organization that it can make you dizzy. These include liquor and/or host liquor liability, personal injury, convention/meeting cancellation, fire, property damage, and theft.

Kinds of insurance policies include, but are not limited to, the following:

➤ **Commercial general liability** (CGL). This covers bodily injury and property damage. Host liquor liability is included, which protects you if you have alcohol served at your event by another party such as the hotel or caterer.

➤ **Convention cancellation and interruption.** This protects your organization from any disruption that results in a financial loss for your event or meeting. This could include fire, earthquake, strike, destruction of a meeting facility, and other causes.

➤ **Directors and officers (D&O).** This covers volunteers, trustees, employees, officers, and committee members conducting business on behalf of the association in case of a lawsuit.

➤ **Professional liability/error and omissions.** This is a policy for independent or third-party planners who need coverage while they provide their services to other organizations.

➤ **Liquor liability.** This protects against claims if your organization serves alcoholic beverages and is sued for some reason.

The Inside Scoop

Many professional associations offer insurance programs that address the many issues meeting planners face. You need someone well versed in the meetings industry to help you determine your exposure and risk and to determine the amount of coverage you need. Call today.

Have all vendors and exhibitors provide you with complete certificates of insurance prior to the meeting. These certificates should include general liability and workers compensation. You can also ask to be named as an additional insured on their policy for liability, property, and medical payments. Make sure you understand your own policy so you know when and if you need to obtain additional coverage.

Once you find the right insurance agent or attorney, review your meetings and events with him or her and ask for an analysis of your potential exposure to lawsuits or claims against you and your organization. Every year or two, review your policy with your insurance agent. Things change and your policy should be kept current.

The Least You Need to Know

➤ Demonstrating the value of your business to each vendor is crucial to successful negotiations.

➤ Make sure attrition calculations are based on lost profit and not lost revenue.

➤ Hidden charges that a facility imposes while onsite are important to address in the negotiation stage.

➤ Music licensing fees, service fees, gratuities, taxes, and insurance are often unexpected and unavoidable costs.

Chapter 12

Contracts: Signing on the Dotted Line

In This Chapter

➤ Define the items that should be in a hotel contract

➤ Learn the difference between canceling and terminating a meeting–facility contract

➤ See what indemnification means to you as a planner

➤ Understand the difference between damages and penalties and which are enforceable

➤ Know how to sign contracts on behalf of an organization

Since we are not legal eagles, we have asked John S. Foster, Esq., CHME, a meetings-industry attorney and former hotel director of sales, to help us out with the important topic of hotel contracts. John is an attorney and counsel whose Atlanta-based firm—Foster, Jensen and Gulley, LLC—specializes in the legal aspects of meetings and conventions, trade shows and events, and association management. He has been named one of the 25 most influential people in the meetings industry by *MeetingNews*. Many thanks to John for authoring this chapter.

Recent disputes and lawsuits between meeting sponsors and hotels continue to emphasize the principle that it's better (and cheaper) to *stay* out of trouble than to have to *get* out of trouble. If you are involved in a lawsuit, as a plaintiff or defendant, there is no guarantee that your side will prevail.

The best way for meeting sponsors and suppliers to avoid controversies and lawsuits is to write a successful contract that clearly specifies the intent of the parties. This chapter provides guidelines and suggestions to assist both planners and suppliers in avoiding expensive and time-consuming lawsuits.

It's More Than Dates and Rates

It used to be done with a handshake. Not anymore. Just when you think selecting a meeting site is the challenging part, you get to jump one more hurdle.

Food for Thought

To avoid ambiguity, it is preferable to call the final agreement a "contract" instead of using generic names such as "letter of agreement," "letter of intent," or "confirmation letter." However, documents that meet the requirements of a contract are still valid regardless of what they are called.

Meeting Speak

The meetings-industry term **comp** is short for "complimentary," or no charge.

You know the dates and have agreed to the rates, but the success of your meeting hinges on the performance by you, the meeting sponsor, and the hotel. A well-written, fair contract is essential to create the rules by which both parties must abide. A meeting represents significant financial gains, but it also carries significant risks. To sufficiently cover both parties, a contract must address numerous issues. Many non-lawyers on both sides believe that a short contract is better than a longer contract. This is not necessarily the case. If your shorter contract fails to address an issue that later becomes the subject of a messy and expensive dispute, your shorter contract has failed one of its essential objectives—to be a road map for the meeting and to steer the parties around pitfalls that lead to future disputes.

In order to thoroughly describe the components of a hotel contract, the remainder of this chapter is a bunch of lists. Remember that we're talkin' the big "L"—legal stuff. So, go get your favorite beverage and read on. It is what you really need to know.

General Provisions and Guestroom Issues

The following 16 items address general meeting information including guestrooms, reservations, *comp* rooms, and other room-related stipulations that should be addressed in your contracts.

1. **Identity of parties.** Use legal names, if known, which include the names of the owners of the property.

2. **Purpose statement.** Include language stating that the parties intend the document to be a contract and intend to be bound by the terms.

3. **Conference name and dates.** State the official conference name and conference dates.

4. **Authorized contacts.** Specify the name, title, address, and phone number of the contact(s) for each party who has the authority to negotiate and amend the contract.

5. **Guestroom block.** State arrival/departure patterns, the type of rooms/suites, and the number of each per night. Specify number of rooms per suite.

6. **Room block review dates and attrition:**
   - ➤ Adjustment date(s) for reviewing the group's history.
   - ➤ Formula for determining the revised block.
   - ➤ Final review date(s) when the block will be reviewed and adjusted for the last time without liability to the meeting sponsor.
   - ➤ The percentage of slippage or block reduction the group is allowed at the final adjustment date(s).
   - ➤ Formula based on lost profit for determining damages or a sliding scale for meeting-room rental owed to the hotel, if any.
   - ➤ Requirement that the hotel will take affirmative steps to resell the unused rooms and apply the number to reduce any attrition damages.
   - ➤ Establish when money owed to the hotel, if any, will be paid.

7. **Check-in/out times.** The time a guest can check in the hotel and the time by which a guest has to check out.

8. **Room rates:**
   - ➤ Specify rates by room type such as single, double, standard, or deluxe.
   - ➤ If the meeting is more than one year out, set the date when the hotel will quote definite rates.
   - ➤ Specify the formula to be used in setting definite rates for meetings one or more years out: percentage cap on current rates, guaranteed percentage off definite future rack rates, or change in consumer price index (urban) for the hotel's city or region.
   - ➤ Specify if the hotel offers lower "promotional" rates over the meeting dates and some of your attendees receive them. Those rooms get counted in your room pickup. Also try to get the hotel to agree not to offer lower rates during your meeting dates.

➤ Specify all suite types, arrival/departure dates for each, and rates. Specify the number of bedrooms with each suite included in the rate and the rate for additional bedrooms.

➤ Specify current sales tax and hotel bed tax, and how the group will be notified if and when taxes increase.

9. **Meeting planner/agent of record.** If the group is represented by an independent meeting planner or a travel agent, spell out what authority the planner/agent has and whether the planner/agent has the authority to contractually represent the group. If a commission arrangement is involved, spell out the commission rate and when it will be paid.

10. **Complimentary rooms and staff rates.** Set the formula for determining the number of comps. Specify whether comps will be figured on a cumulative or per-night basis and whether they can be applied to a master account in an equivalent dollar amount. Specify whether additional comp rooms will be extended to convention staff and/or guest speakers or whether a percentage discount will be given.

11. **Reservations:**

➤ Specify whether the meeting's sponsor, a third-party housing bureau, or the hotel is handling housing.

➤ Specify the method: reservation cards, call-in, rooming list, bureau form.

➤ Dishonored reservations: Determine what compensation the hotel will make for guests that are *walked* (that is, free sleeping room at comparable hotel, free transportation to and from the substitute hotel, long-distance phone calls to office and family).

➤ Cutoff date: Specify the last date the hotel will hold the block of rooms before releasing the unsold rooms (if any) back into the hotel's general inventory.

➤ Specify whether the organization will be compensated for reservations the hotel is unable to accept before the cutoff date due to hotel overbooking. This is a reverse attrition clause.

➤ Specify when the hotel will send out confirmations and whether the planner is to receive copies.

Meeting Speak

A **walk** (also called a dishonored reservation) is a term used for a person who has a guaranteed reservation but is moved to another hotel because the hotel is overbooked. If you are walked, the hotel will compensate you by taking you to another hotel and paying for the room and a phone call home.

12. **Deposits.** Specify the hotel deposit policy and spell out any conditions under which deposits will be refunded, within what timeframe, whether deposits will be placed in escrow, and the terms of the escrow.

13. **Billing arrangements.** Specify what is paid individually and what goes on the master account (M/A). Identify who is authorized to sign the M/A. Specify credit information required by the hotel and whether an advance deposit is required (specify dates, amount, and escrow requirements). If certain functions are to be sponsored by third parties, specify procedures.

14. **Report of meeting.** Specify whether the hotel will furnish the meeting planner with actual group revenue, including rooms picked up, food and beverage, and other income, at the conclusion of the meeting.

15. **Suites.** Specify whether all requests for suites are to be approved by the planner.

16. **Parking.** What is the cost? How is VIP parking handled?

Meeting Space Provisions

Make sure you understand how the hotel is charging you for any meeting-room rental fees. Calculations can be very complicated, and you must understand them. Here's a list of what you need to know:

1. **Meeting and function space requirements.** Be detailed about initial space requirements. Agree on and specify the date that the final program will be submitted. If group needs a *hold all space,* determine the hotel's policy. Is a 24-hour-space hold needed? Specify the date when the hotel will provide definite meeting-room names. Does the hotel reserve the right to move the group to another space? Can this be negotiated? Will the hotel agree to pay for reprinting programs if the group is moved to an alternate space? What is the hotel's policy on releasing reserved function space to affiliate groups? Will the hotel seek approval from the meeting sponsor first?

Don't Drop the Ball

It's important to understand where you are in the negotiation process. This is John's Golden Rule of Contract Negotiations: If you ask for something from the other party before you have a contract, it's called "negotiating." If you ask for something after you have a contract, it's called "begging."

Meeting Speak

Hold all space means that all meeting space in the hotel is being held by a group. If you have a hold all space, it should be stated in the contract along with a date when your agenda is due.

115

Food for Thought

A lawsuit is a process in which you go in as a pig and come out as a sausage. In other words, the process is never neat, clean, or simple, and both parties come out a different shape than when they went in.

2. **Function space rental.** Specify the hotel's criteria for waiving rental. (Note: In most instances, a room rental clause is not applicable if the hotel also includes an attrition clause.) Agree on sliding-scale formula, if applicable. Set a firm price for function space, if applicable.

3. **Services and equipment.** Specify whether the hotel charges for setup and teardown of meeting rooms. Specify what equipment the hotel provides on a complimentary basis and a cutoff date for ordering equipment.

4. **Signage.** Determine whether the hotel will provide signage for the group and at what cost. What are the hotel's rules for displaying signs?

Food and Beverage

Are you having fun yet? It isn't over until it's over. Keep paying attention. We are halfway there:

1. **Food and beverage functions.** Give the hotel preliminary figures for anticipated attendance. Determine a date for the final guarantee and for what percentage over the guarantee the hotel will prepare for. Determine how far in advance firm F&B prices will be confirmed. Will the hotel guarantee a certain F&B percentage maximum rate increase?

2. **Taxes/gratuities.** What is the hotel policy and formula for each? Does state law require the hotel to tax the service charge? Can the group agree to pay a gratuity and therefore avoid paying tax on the gratuity?

3. **Bartender and waiter charges and training.** Determine hotel policy on these. Does the hotel have a minimum charge for F&B functions? What are their procedures in place to minimize liquor liability?

4. **Attrition.** If the hotel insists on including an attrition clause for food and beverage functions, include an original estimate of catered food and beverage (F&B) revenue that the meeting sponsor will spend. Also include a review date or dates when the parties will establish a final figure for catering food and beverage revenue that the group will spend at the hotel. It should include a percentage of attrition allowed to the group from the figure previously projected. The industry average is currently 20 to 25 percent. Get the hotel to agree to reduce any damages by any food and beverage functions it resells or any business the hotel is able to book after the notice of reduced attendance at food and beverage functions is received by the hotel. (The same criteria should be used if a food function is cancelled.)

The Inside Scoop

Sometimes a group cancellation is beneficial to a hotel because it allows the hotel to accept a more profitable piece of business that wants the rooms and space. If this occurs, the hotel has not been damaged by the first group's reduction or cancellation. In your contract, make sure you have clearly stated the resell provisions and have a mechanism to calculate the reduced damages.

The food and beverage attrition formula should state the final amount of catering food and beverage revenue guaranteed by the group, minus the actual catering food and beverage revenue spent by the group, minus revenue from resold functions or space. The resulting figure should then be multiplied by an agreed upon percentage to represent lost profit. Industry average is 20 to 30 percent. The resulting amount represents the damages for catering food and beverage attrition, subject to an audit by both parties. (See "audit provision" in Appendix C, "Glossary.")

Exhibit Space Provisions

Contracting for exhibit space is a different process than booking meeting space. Read on for exhibit-specific info:

1. **Exhibit space.** Includes move-in/out dates, rental price, and what is and is not included: signage, carpet, pipe and drape, general daily maintenance, HVAC to the group's satisfaction, and so on. If floor sales are allowed, do exhibitors have to obtain a sales license and pay sales tax?

2. **Discuss special requirements.** Includes items such as insurance certificates, hold-harmless clauses, licenses or permits needed, security personnel, the hotel's policy on concession sales, fire safety, rules of the house such as prohibited activities and health code requirements, and medical personnel onsite.

Don't Drop the Ball

Pay attention to the special limitations of the exhibit area such as floor load limits, dock space, storage space, and union jurisdictions, if applicable. Determine when union contracts expire so you aren't caught in the middle of union negotiations.

117

3. **Have exhibit floor plan approved by fire marshal.** Have the facility sign a statement that, during the dates of the meeting, the facility and exhibit space will meet or exceed all local fire safety and health code regulations.

4. **Payment terms for rental charges.** What are the criteria for waiving rental (flat fee basis versus per booth basis)?

Bye-Bye

Although you never plan to cancel a meeting, you need to agree with the property on how to part ways. Every contract should contain reciprocal provisions for cancellation by either side. If you get this right in the contract, if you ever need to cancel, your life will be a little easier. Here is what you need to address in the contract:

1. **Termination and excuse of performance.** Under what terms can the agreement be terminated without either side incurring damages to the other? (This might include acts of God, acts of third parties not under the control of either party to the contract, change in management or chain affiliation, foreclosure or bankruptcy, and so on.)

Don't Drop the Ball

Understand the difference between termination and cancellation. If a contract is "terminated" for acts of God or other similar circumstances, neither party has any obligation to the other. If a contract is "cancelled," it means one party has breached or defaulted on its performance and owes the other party damages unless otherwise stipulated in the contract.

2. **Cancellation by the group:**

   ➤ Define the term "cancellation" to differentiate it from "attrition" and "termination."

   ➤ Establish the right of the parties to cancel or modify the terms by mutual agreement at any time.

   ➤ Establish that, if cancellation by the group occurs for reasons other than those outlined in the termination clause, a cancellation fee or liquidated damages are due to the hotel.

   ➤ Establish the sliding scale or fixed amount applicable for determining the cancellation fee owed to the hotel based on when the cancellation occurs. The cancellation fee should be based on a percentage of the anticipated revenue, not to exceed the departmental profit margin of the hotel for the anticipated revenue sources specified in the contract. If the formula or flat fee is a reasonable approximation of actual damages and not a penalty, it is called a liquidated damage clause.

➤ Establish how anticipated lost revenue is calculated. The formula should explain exactly what revenue sources are included in "lost revenue," and it should exclude sales tax unless required by state or local law.

➤ Unless the damages are a reasonable and valid liquidated damage provision, establish the duty of the hotel to reduce its damages and credit those room nights and revenues against the cancellation fee.

➤ Establish when the cancellation fee is due and payable. Payment can be set to be at the time of cancellation or after the anticipated meeting dates to determine whether the hotel has recouped any business. Note that if one party breaches a contract, the other party is entitled to damages but not penalties. Damages are defined as lost profit, not 100 percent of the revenue. Penalties are not allowed in contract law. Penalties exist if the nonbreaching party would come out farther ahead if the contract was enforced as written rather than if the contract was actually performed by the other party.

3. **Cancellation by the hotel:**

➤ Define the term "cancellation" by the hotel to differentiate it from "termination." It should include: a) failure to provide facilities, or b) failure to give reasonable assurances of its ability and intent to provide facilities after notice of foreclosure or bankruptcy.

➤ Establish the right of the parties to cancel or modify the terms by mutual agreement at any time.

➤ Establish the group's right to damages if cancellation by the hotel occurs for reasons other than those outlined in the termination clause.

➤ Establish how damages will be calculated to compensate the group either as: a) a sliding scale based on percentage of revenue and when the cancellation occurs, b) a specific sum, or c) actual out-of-pocket expenses and lost profits. Expenses you would incur if the hotel cancelled your contract include expenses to research alternate facilities (airfare, long-distance phone calls, and so on) and the difference in the increased cost of the alternate facility (room rate, F&B prices, meeting-room rental, additional mailings, and so on).

➤ Specify when damages will be paid by the hotel to the meeting sponsor, either at the time of cancellation or after actual amounts are incurred.

➤ Establish the hotel's duty to return deposits within a specific timeframe.

Beyond Your Control

The following clauses protect you from things beyond your control. The last thing you need is a jackhammer on the other side of the wall during your meeting.

1. **Other meetings at the hotel.** Determine if it's appropriate for the group to restrict the hotel from booking competitors' groups over the same dates. Specify the terms of this restriction and the procedures for releasing function space.

2. **Construction, remodeling, and noise control.** The hotel should advise the group of any construction or remodeling to be performed in the hotel or in the vicinity over the meeting dates. Determine and specify whether group wants the right to terminate the agreement if the construction will be detrimental to the meeting.

   Specify that, if noise becomes an issue to the extent that the meeting is impaired, the meeting sponsor will be due compensation in the form of a credit on the master account. The parties will have to negotiate what a reasonable amount is based on the circumstances.

3. **Deterioration in quality.** For all bookings, the facility should warrant that the quality of its service and the condition of its physical facilities will be the same or better at the time of the meeting as they were when the contract was signed.

People Provisions

Here are some other things to think about:

1. **Use of outside contractors.** Specify whether the meeting sponsor wants, or will be allowed, the right to use outside contractors for services not specifically reserved to the hotel, and if there are any additional fees to be paid or provisions to be made. (This also applies to convention centers, and may apply to any other facility you use, including museums, restaurants, clubs, etc.)

2. **Staff and staffing.** Specify specific performance standards, and the hotel's duty to assign an adequate number of personnel to handle the meeting.

3. **Ownership and management changes.** Require the hotel to notify the group if this happens. Specify the effect of ownership or management changes on the contract.

More Legal Mumble Jumble

You really need a lawyer to sift through the gook in a contract. However, to get you started, the following are often standard clauses in most vendor contracts.

1. **Mutual indemnification and hold harmless.** Each party should agree to indemnify each other for its own negligent acts or omissions. Specify that the hotel will specifically indemnify the sponsoring organization for alcohol-related claims, defects in the facilities, and defects in equipment provided by the hotel.

Don't agree to indemnify other people or entities for their negligence. If someone asks you to sign an *indemnification* clause, make sure you understand what risks and responsibilities you are being asked to assume or seek legal counsel.

Meeting Speak

Indemnification is an agreement in which one party agrees to protect the other party from liability, damages, or out-of-pocket expenses that may occur in connection with a particular transaction. **Mutual indemnification** means that each party will be responsible for its own negligent acts or omissions if it causes a loss to the other party or causes the other party to defend itself against an asserted claim in connection with a particular transaction.

2. **Insurance.** The hotel and group should both agree to carry adequate liability insurance that protects both parties against claims arising from activities in the hotel. Stipulate the amount of insurance and specify that the group and the hotel are responsible to each other for property damage only up to the amount of insurance.

3. **Warranties, duties, and responsibilities of parties.** The hotel should warrant compliance with all federal, state, and local fire-safety and health codes, including compliance with the Americans with Disabilities Act (ADA) and the Hotel and Motel Fire Safety Act. The meeting sponsor also should warrant its compliance with the ADA in the areas it controls. Include provisions for hotel security and deterioration in quality.

4. **Costs to enforce agreement.** The contract should provide that, in the event the parties must resort to a dispute-resolution method, as previously outlined, the party prevailing in the action shall be entitled to attorney's fees and costs in bringing the action.

5. **Procedure for notices.** Stipulate where legal notices or notices about termination or cancellation should be sent. This usually corresponds with the names listed as contacts at the beginning of the contract.

6. **Restrictions on assignment by either side.** Stipulate that neither party may assign this contract to a third party without written permission from the other party to this contract.

7. **Counterparts.** Stipulate that the final contract may be executed in one or more counterparts, that each counterpart shall be considered an original, and that all counterparts taken together shall be considered one and the same instrument. Stipulate that facsimiles and photocopies are as valid as originals.

8. **Waiver and severability clause.** If any provision is found to be unenforceable, the remainder of the contract is still valid. No right or remedy specified in the contract shall be waived by either party except in writing.

9. **Dispute resolution/choice of law/venue and jurisdiction.** The parties should determine how disputes will be handled: arbitration, alternative dispute resolution, mediation, or litigation. If arbitration is chosen, parties should reserve the right to use the courts for equitable remedies. Specify the jurisdiction, venue, and choice of law.

10. **Effect of agreement.** Stipulate that the contract does not create a joint venture or agency relationship.

11. **Paragraph headings.** Stipulate that paragraph headings, numbers, letters, and emphasis marks have been inserted for the convenience of reference only, and if there is any conflict between any such headings, numbers, letters, or emphasis marks and the text of this agreement, the text shall control.

12. **Merger of terms and modification.** Stipulate that the contract contains all the terms and conditions agreed to between the parties and that no changes may be made to the contract except in written form signed by the parties.

13. **Coauthorship of contract.** If the contract is negotiated and prepared jointly by both parties, stipulate that, in any dispute in connection with this contract, ambiguous terms shall not be construed against either party.

The Inside Scoop

In our legal system, you can sign contracts in only one of two capacities, as the principal or as the agent. If you sign as the principal, you are personally liable for performance. If you sign as the agent, your acts are imputed to the principal as long as your acts were authorized by the principal. If you signed as an agent but weren't authorized or if you don't indicate your agent status, you become the principal. If a contract is valid when signed, it remains valid even if the parties that signed it, including agents, are no longer employed by the principal.

14. **Authorized signatures.** Who is authorized to sign? Make sure titles are used and make sure the parties warrant and represent that they are signing individually or on behalf of their organizations.

Food for Thought

Hotel, facility, and other meeting vendor contracts are getting more complicated and are covering more ground. In meetings-industry circles, legal issues and contracts are always hot topics. If you educate yourself about the items described in this chapter and incorporate them into your hotel contracts, you increase your chances of a successful meeting. For more information, buy one of John Foster's books on meeting and facility contracts. Contact John at 404-873-5200 or jsfoster@mindspring.com. To find out more about hospitality industry attorneys, contact the Academy of Hospitality Industry Attorneys at www.ahiattorneys.org or 303-892-6966.

The Least You Need to Know

➤ Make sure everything your organization needs from the facility or vendor and vice versa is included in the contract.

➤ Attrition can be applied to both guestrooms and food and beverage. Make sure all sliding scales use a formula for calculating attrition damages.

➤ Always sign contracts as an agent on behalf of your organization. Otherwise, you are personally liable.

➤ Penalties are not enforceable in contract law. The correct term is damages, which means lost profit and/or out-of-pocket expenses incurred.

Chapter 13

Marketing, Marketing, Marketing

In This Chapter

➤ Understand that meeting or event goals and objectives contribute to your marketing campaign

➤ Find out what to put in a marketing brochure

➤ See how technology can enhance marketing efforts

➤ Understand that the timing of your marketing pieces makes a big difference

---

Marketing your meeting is serious business. Marketing and promotion are necessary if you want strong attendance. Good marketing allows potential attendees to understand why they need to attend and what's in it for them.

Once again, your goals and objectives play an important role. If they are clear and provide the right message, your promotional campaign should be easy. In this chapter, we will explore what goes into your marketing pieces and your marketing strategy, and we'll take a look at how to deliver your message.

The Marketing Message

Whoever is responsible for marketing and promotion needs to understand the reason for the meeting. You need to demonstrate to the decision-makers, sponsors, exhibitors, and especially the attendees that you have a meeting people want to attend.

It's marketing's role to take your goals and objectives and repackage them into a positive campaign that gets attention and creates interest in your meeting.

To help you define your marketing message, start by answering the following questions:

➤ What is the goal of the meeting?

➤ What are the meeting objectives?

➤ What is your financial objective?

➤ Who should attend?

➤ What are the benefits to the attendee?

There may be other issues that factor into your marketing direction. Even if you are having a mandatory company meeting, your marketing message should still focus on the goals and objectives to build excitement. After all, everyone is so busy that they really need to understand the benefits of being away from work or family. They want to know what's in it for them. Nothing is worse than having a boring sales meeting and knowing it is going to be boring ahead of time!

Marketing Philosophy

Your marketing message depends a lot on your target audience. Let's take a look at two different scenarios. You will see that each scenario has a very different audience, but both want the same end result—a successful meeting. There are many ways to deliver your message, but first you need to determine what the message is and how to package it.

Scenario 1: You Have to Attend the Sales Meeting

Pretend you work for a corporation that is planning a sales meeting. There is no need for a meeting brochure because a memo or company e-mail will do the trick. You have a captive audience and you just need to tell the sales team the dates and give them airplane tickets. How motivated will they be when they hear a directive telling them they have to attend? They already know that.

The Inside Scoop

Marketing is not just about getting attendees; it's also about getting buy-in from sponsors and vendors. Determine a realistic attendance goal and communicate it to your stakeholders.

The Inside Scoop

Many companies waste thousands of dollars on meetings that accomplish nothing. You need to let the employees (attendees) know the agenda in advance and why the meeting is important to them. You also need to build some fun into the meeting. Unhappy attendees bring down the morale of the entire crew, and an entire meeting can be sabotaged.

How about a little motivation? Create a theme, and put some fun into it. Add excitement by getting them involved in the theme. Let them in on the agenda ahead of time, promote your fabulous keynote speaker, and pique their interest with some fun, teambuilding exercises. Don't just send out the mandatory meeting memo and leave it at that. Generate some "buzz" and create posters, games, or whatever gets your crew interested. By promoting the meeting again and again, attendees will start to look forward to the meeting instead of dreading it.

Scenario 2: Please Come to This Meeting

Now you work for a large trade association and are planning an annual conference. Attendance is usually around 1,000 people, but competition for attendees is tough. You really need to appeal to the attendees' needs. Promotional material must grab their attention and provide detailed information. An agenda is very important. Include information on the speakers; they bring credibility to the meeting and are one of the key motivators to attract an audience. You need to answer the question "What's in it for me?" and get people to take action by registering.

Also consider that meeting costs play a significant role in the decision to attend meetings. Your attendees may have to get approval from supervisors or others to pay for these costs, or they may have to pay for it themselves. Either way, your audience must justify the value of being away from work, families, or community obligations as well as the financial cost. Other barriers that prevent people from attending meetings are too many meetings, too little time to attend meetings, and too much time out of the office.

When considering your marketing philosophy, you must take many issues into consideration. For example, you want to hold your meeting in an interesting location, but depending on your audience, promoting all of the fun things to do (say, in Las Vegas or Orlando) may backfire if the meeting sounds like a vacation. If your program is too much like your last one or is too similar to a competing program, you need to figure out a way to make your meeting different and better.

> **Food for Thought**
>
> Give potential attendees a dozen reasons why they should attend the meeting by using words such as "how to," "learn," "increase," "identify," "improve," "discover," "understand," and "find out" to describe why they should attend.

Don't Shoot the Messenger

Once you know your audience, you can use the following methods to reach out and "touch" them:

➤ Advertisement

➤ Current customer

Don't Drop the Ball

Mass mailings without researching your potential audience are a waste of money. Spend the time up front qualifying your target audience before you go to the post office. The key is offering what the potential attendees need.

Food for Thought

Offer discounted registration fees to attendees who bring in new people to your next meeting. The more new people they bring in, the greater the discount. Also consider giving discounts to multiple participants from one organization.

➤ E-mail blast

➤ Fax distribution list

➤ Mailing list

➤ Networking

➤ Partnerships with other organizations

➤ Past attendee

➤ Press release/media

➤ Referral

➤ Web site

➤ Word of mouth

Create a marketing plan using a combination of the preceding distribution methods. Understand your potential audience and make sure you have determined the best way to reach these people. Add a question to your registration form and meeting-evaluation form that asks how they heard about the meeting. This can tell you where to advertise more.

Review your marketing plan every year and for every meeting. What is effective today may be obsolete tomorrow. Pay careful attention to what advertising vehicle gave you the most attendees. It is your responsibility to get the word out in the right places.

Hard Copy

Brochures are expensive, but they set the image for the event. Plus, many people just like something they can touch. Brochures need to have visual impact. Professional, well-written brochures or flyers are a must. Use color if possible and a good-quality paper.

Before you set your sights on a specific brochure design, paper, color, size, and so on, determine the costs. You may even want to hire a desktop publisher to design the pieces. It will most likely cost more money than doing it yourself, but the expertise is worth it. A designer will know how to design a brochure that fits your budget and will also understand design techniques that will capture your audience's attention.

Brochures also need strong content. Be sure your promotional materials include the following:

➤ Meeting title

➤ Meeting days of the week and date(s)

➤ Meeting agenda including times

➤ Speakers with brief bios

➤ Location, address, phone, fax, e-mail, Web site

➤ Who should attend

➤ Benefits of attending

➤ Goals and objectives (from the attendees' perspective)

➤ Testimonials from previous attendees, if applicable

➤ Registration fees and deadlines

➤ Special incentive offers for early or multiple registrations

➤ Sponsors

➤ Exhibitors if applicable

➤ *CEUs*, if applicable

➤ Housing information (name of facilities, address, rates, and a URL) and cutoff dates

➤ Spouse/guest activities

➤ Airline and ground transportation information

➤ Complete registration form

➤ Online registration information

Don't Drop the Ball

U.S. mail has certain size and weight restrictions. Before you spend a lot of time and money printing beautiful announcements, take a mockup to the post office and have someone sign off on your mailing.

Meeting Speak

CEUs are continuing education units. Many professional associations require that individuals earn a specific number of CEUs to maintain their original certification status. Check with your industry trade association on how your attendees may qualify/earn them at your meeting.

Cyberspace

Technology is making it easier to promote your meetings and events. Today you can advertise, register, customize, and keep track of attendees online. There are some really cool ways you can reach your audience.

If your organization has a Web site, put your meeting information on it. Meeting information is dynamic, and should be updated frequently. When attendees know they can get current, accurate information about the meeting on the Web—they will. It's cost effective and efficient.

Another efficient communication tool these days is the e-mail distribution list. Who doesn't have an e-mail address anymore? You can easily create distribution lists of your targeted audience and e-mail people short and sweet informational notes. Use this method to tell them to "save the date," to point them to your meeting Web site, and to send them important meeting updates.

Up and coming in online meeting and event marketing are some new Web sites that help you get the word out. They are companies that help you create customized e-mail, announcements, and invitations online. They work as follows.

Go to their Web site, and complete templates about an upcoming meeting. They even allow you to use your logo. You provide an e-mail address list of potential attendees, and the software creates a personalized e-mail from "your organization." One of the great features is that the software allows you to require, track, and manage RSVPs. If you need to send reminders, you can do that, too. These programs offer a lot of features and flexibility, more than we can describe here.

Check out Senada.com (www.senada.com) and Cvent.com (www.cvent.com) to see what we mean. There will be more of these cool tools coming down the pike.

Food for Thought

Don't just announce your meeting once or twice, do it several times. With Web and e-mail technology, it's easier than ever to get the word out and send gentle reminders.

Ads

Advertise in your trade publications and other regional or local publications. Newsletters are also a good place to reach potential attendees. For example, if your audience were CPAs, then the local, regional, and even national CPA associations would be a great place to find attendees. Print ads can be expensive, so be sure you are reaching the right audience.

Media

Keep an up-to-date list of appropriate media in your area. Send press releases to announce your meetings. Also use the CVB for media contacts in the city where you are holding the meeting. In some cases, the CVB will even send the press releases for you.

Be creative. Is there an innovative way to announce your meetings? The media is more apt to give you ink if it is unique and newsworthy. In other words, make it exciting!

If You Can't Beat 'Em, Join 'Em

Is there a way to partner with other industry organizations and hold joint meetings? If there are two similar meetings taking place, does it make sense to join forces and have one meeting together? In the long run, both organizations just might benefit. Your attendees will love it because they don't have to choose between the two, and pooling resources allows you to create a stronger program and reach a larger audience.

The Inside Scoop

Meetings are on the rise, and there is a tremendous amount of competition for attendees. Give them many opportunities to learn about your meeting. Market early, market often.

Timing Is Key

Start early. Some organizations announce their annual meeting dates 5 to 10 years in advance. Do what makes sense in your situation, but the earlier you get on people's calendars the better. You also need to avoid scheduling over other meetings, so it helps to know when the key meetings in your industry are held.

For employee meetings, you may have a particular month in which it makes sense to hold the meeting. For example, an annual sales meeting may be held in the first or last month of the fiscal year for planning purposes. It also helps the sales staff plan personal trips because they know the first or second week of a certain month will be the sales meeting.

Meetings that are scheduled during the same days/dates every year make it easy for people to plan ahead.

The Least You Need to Know

➤ You must demonstrate the benefits of attending your meeting to your audience.

➤ Clearly written, easy-to-understand marketing materials are best.

➤ Web software allows you to reach a much broader market at a fraction of the cost.

➤ The earlier you can announce your meeting, the greater the chance you will attract your desired audience.

Chapter 14

Exhibits and Expositions: Should You Do It?

In This Chapter

➤ Recognize the difference between an exposition and a tradeshow

➤ Learn how to determine whether exhibits make sense for your meeting

➤ See where to turn for help in finding potential exhibitors

➤ Discover what an exhibitor prospectus is

➤ Learn how to get attendees to the show

A successful exhibit tradeshow means getting the right buyers and the right sellers together in the same room. How do you do this? You have to create the show, demonstrate to both attendees and exhibitors that it is worth their time and money, market it, sell booths, get attendees, and produce it. Did you know that an exhibit tradeshow can be a revenue generator for associations and other organizations? It also can be very time consuming, expensive, and if not done right, a flop.

In this chapter, we will walk you through these issues. You will understand what it takes to be successful in the exhibit tradeshow arena. You will also learn how to keep exhibitors and attendees happy so that they achieve a return on their investment of time, money, and effort.

Exposition or Tradeshow

An exposition is a show that's open to the public, whereas a tradeshow is open to members of the meeting's organization. Got that?

Every year, in many cities across the country, local builders and remodelers have home-remodeling shows. These expositions are open to the public, and you pay a fee at the door. This is different from a tradeshow that's only open to registered attendees. This chapter is about tradeshows and does not deal with the issues of public shows, which usually are larger and more complex to plan and manage, although there are similarities.

Confusing Considerations

So, someone suggests you need exhibits at your meeting. Before jumping on the bandwagon, ask yourself the following questions:

➤ Why is it beneficial to have exhibits?

➤ When will the attendees have time to look at them?

➤ Will they be several hours long or one or more days?

➤ Will they be scheduled in parallel with other sessions?

➤ Will they provide value to both attendees and exhibitors?

➤ Is there sufficient space for them?

➤ What is a reasonable fee to exhibit?

➤ What impact will exhibits have on the meeting's budget (both income and expense)?

➤ Who would be interested in exhibiting? Are there enough exhibitors?

➤ Will the exhibitors receive a return on their investment?

Exhibiting in a tradeshow can cost thousands of dollars. Costs include the booth and materials (and shipping them), travel expenses, promotional brochures and giveaways, time out of the office for one or more people, and booth registration fees. To keep exhibitors coming back year after year, they need to show a return on their investment to their organization.

Tradeshows should be considered only if both your attendees and exhibitors will really benefit from them. Refer to your meeting's goals and objectives. (This is a perfect example of why you need them.) How does a tradeshow fit into the scheme of things? Does it make sense?

If you decide to go the tradeshow route, here are some ideas for incorporating exhibits into your agenda:

➤ Have the opening reception in the exhibit hall.

➤ Schedule continental breakfasts, breaks, and lunches in the exhibit hall.

➤ Have a demonstration stage in the exhibit hall. Invite exhibitors to demonstrate their latest product or to give short presentations on how their services can help attendees.

➤ Have a grand-prize drawing in the exhibit hall at the end of the conference.

➤ Schedule a window of time during the morning or afternoon for exhibits only when there is not a conflict with sessions or other official program activity.

Food for Thought

Your tradeshow floor can be open all day, but at least a portion of the day should be dedicated only to exhibits. Consider having some of the meals and breaks in the exhibit hall.

Location, Location, Location (Again)

Convention centers are specifically designed to hold expositions and tradeshows, but in some cases, you can use a hotel. (Conference centers are not used for tradeshows or exhibits. Their size and purpose differ from convention centers.) It's really an issue of space availability and the complexity of your show that determines your location decision. Here are some things to consider when deciding which to use:

➤ Building regulations

➤ Facility rental fees

➤ Insurance

➤ Loading dock access

➤ Security

➤ Shipping procedures

➤ Space needs

➤ Union jurisdictions

Don't Drop the Ball

Locate the nearest freight elevator to your exhibits. Inform your exhibitors of the location and let them know where, when, and how they can bring their materials into the facility.

Here are some other considerations: Can you charge enough to cover your costs? Will the attendees have easy access to the show? Can the exhibitors move in easily? What additional fees will the exhibitors be charged by the facility? Can you plug in your own electrical cords, or are there union restrictions? Is there an open-dock policy, or do the exhibitors have to hire someone to carry their exhibit material

Meeting Speak

Net square foot (**NSF**) is the method some facilities charge for exhibit space. Net square footage is the space the exhibitors actually use and does not include aisles, pillars, food stations, and seating. The **gross square footage** of an exhibit hall is the total square footage of the room (length × width of the room).

The Inside Scoop

If you want to have exhibits but on a smaller scale, try tabletop exhibits or displays. You provide each exhibitor with a draped and skirted table. Each exhibitor is allowed to bring in brochures and small displays. You generally do not need an exhibitor services company for these small shows.

in for them? Can your exhibitors exhibit what they want to? For example, if your exhibitors are car manufacturers, can they display a car? What are the building policies on it? What is the floor load capacity? Will some of the exhibits be too heavy?

How Facilities Sell Exhibit Space

Facilities charge for exhibit space in a variety of ways. Take a look:

➤ Flat fee per day

➤ Flat fee for length of show

➤ Per booth

➤ Per *net square foot* (for length of show)

Usually it is the convention centers that charge on an NSF basis. Typically, hotels will rent you the space for a flat fee, although this is not always the case. Be aware that facilities charging you on an NSF basis will have different calculation methods.

Exhibit booth sizes typically rented to exhibitors are 8 × 10 feet (80 square feet) or 10 × 10 feet (100 square feet).

If you have 100 exhibitors all using 10 × 10 exhibit booths, then the net square footage being used is 100 exhibits × 100 square feet each, or 10,000 NSF. If the facility charged 80¢ per net square foot, then your charge would be 10,000 × 80¢ = $8,000.

How You Sell Space to Exhibitors

You sell booths to exhibitors in a booth package. Typically, a booth includes an eight-foot pipe and drape back wall, three-foot-high side rails, a table, and two chairs. Anything else is extra and is paid for by the exhibitor. You can create a package according to your tradeshow needs.

In addition to selling a booth to exhibitors, you can sell them ad space in the program and sponsorship opportunities. Also think about charging a premium for the best booth locations, corners, near food stations, in front of the main door, island booths, and other unique configurations.

Exposition Services Contractor (ESC)

Who provides the booth package? The *exposition services contractor* (sometimes called the decorator). Exposition services contractors are vendors that specialize in a variety of services including booth design and setup, furniture rental, floor plan diagramming, and signage. They also handle the delivery and setup of the exhibitors' show materials, the teardown and shipping back to the exhibitors' offices, as well as acting as a subcontractor for other services.

Meeting Speak

The **exposition services contractor** (or decorator) is the company that provides the booth, signs, setup, and other services needed for a tradeshow or exposition.

There is a unique relationship between you (the meeting host), the exhibitor, and the exposition services contractor. You hire the exposition services contractor and design the show (with his or her assistance). Once you have decided what your standard booth includes, the exposition services contractor quotes you a per-booth fee that you collect directly from the exhibitors. The exposition services contractor prepares an exhibit services kit that outlines all of the services provided. If an exhibitor needs additional services such as electricians, furniture rental, florists, audio-visual technicians, security staff, plumbers, sign makers, and photographers, the exhibitor contracts with the exposition services contractor directly. The exhibitor pays for additional services not offered in the booth package.

The following table looks at the responsibilities of the meeting host and the exposition services contractor:

Responsibility	Host	ESC
Select show location	X	
Determine standard booth options	X	
Create/mail exhibitor prospectus	X	
Design floor plan and flow	X	X
Determine exhibition fee	X	
Collect exhibition fee	X	
Create exhibitor kit	X	X
Mail exhibitor kits	X	X
Make booth assignments	X	
Provide additional exhibit services		X
Collect fees for additional services		X

Don't Drop the Ball

Before you sign a contract with an exposition services contractor, read all of the company's materials, ask lots of questions, and check references for shows similar to yours. Understand your responsibilities as well as theirs. Get all costs in writing and make sure you budget for them.

A budget for an exhibit tradeshow is much different from a typical meeting budget without exhibits. When it gets right down to it, the rules, regulations, contractors, and other issues can be very confusing even to the most experienced planner. Some costs are absorbed by the exhibitor, others by the meeting sponsor.

If you are considering a tradeshow, call an exposition services contractor and discuss the services and fees. Two nationwide contractors are Freeman Decorating (www.freemanco.com) and GES Exposition Services (www.gesexpo.com).

Other items you may need from the exhibitor services contractor are registration booths, furniture, and additional pipe and drape. Registration booths are floor-standing booths you can use for your registration area. Furniture can be used to create a more relaxing lounge area in the exhibit hall or other areas. Make sure to negotiate on these items. Depending on your show's size, registration booths are often provided at no charge. The pipe and drape can be used to hide office areas and to drape off sections of the exhibit hall.

Determining Potential Exhibitors

Before you can invite potential exhibitors to show their wares, you have to know what the attendees want and need to see. What products and services do your attendees use? Make a list of vendors they use on a regular basis and add those they use on a less frequent basis. Also think about which companies would like to access your audience. This is a good starting point.

Don't Drop the Ball

When looking for potential exhibitors, look in your own backyard. Who are your attendees currently doing business with? Don't overlook the obvious!

Do a little research before jumping in with both feet. Ask potential exhibitors if they would exhibit in your show. Ask previous attendees if it would benefit them to have a tradeshow. You will learn a lot just by talking to a few people about the idea. If you already have a show, reexamine it. Do some research. What would make it more beneficial to both sides?

Exhibitor Prospectus

An exhibitor prospectus and application form contain all the information a potential exhibitor needs to know to make an informed decision about exhibiting.

These can be two different documents or can be incorporated into one. Here are some things to include in the prospectus:

1. Information about the show's location
2. The dates of the show including move in/move-out and exhibit hours
3. Why they should exhibit
4. An attendee profile
5. Rules and regulations
6. A floor plan (draft)
7. Statistics on last year's show if available (number of attendees, testimonials, and success stories)
8. How booth assignments are made (first-come, first-served; random; or lottery)
9. The booth fee and when deposit/payment is due
10. The cancellation policy
11. Exhibitor services contractor information
12. Music licensing information

Here are some things to include on the application:

1. The organization's name
2. A contact name/title/address/phone/fax/e-mail for correspondence and the program
3. Exhibitor names for name badges (state how many are included) and if they are a full conference or exhibit only registration
4. A statement to sign saying that they understand the show rules and regulations and will abide by them
5. Booth number and location preference (ask for top three, if applicable)
6. How the booth sign should read—be sure to specify how many characters and spaces are allowed
7. What products and services are being exhibited
8. When and where to return the application
9. Twenty-five words or less about the product or service (if you need this information for the attendee program)
10. Liability waiver
11. Insurance statement (they need to have insurance)

Determine early on how you are going to market and communicate information about the show to potential exhibitors. Make sure complete information is available on your Web site.

The Inside Scoop

Most booth packages include two or three complimentary registrations. Sometimes exhibitors are invited to all meal functions, and in other cases they are not. Establish guidelines and communicate them to the exhibitors. Try to include them in as many events as you can. They want to network, too.

Food for Thought

Save other tradeshow brochures when they come to you in the mail and search the Web for ideas on how you can create your brochures and prospectus. Ask your exposition services contractor for samples from other successful shows.

Rules and Regs

Every show must have rules and regulations. You need to communicate with the exhibitors regarding move-in procedures, move-out procedures, security information, liability waiver, insurance requirements, shipping and storage, booth construction and obstructions, the booth assignment procedure, and the procedure for enforcement of rules and regulations. Each tradeshow will have rules that pertain to its specific industry. For example, a food show may require that visqueen (plastic sheeting) be laid on top of carpet if cooking is done in the booth. You get the idea. The booth-assignment procedure can be first-come, first-served or at your discretion. Always reserve the right to reassign booth space if necessary and pay attention to competitors. In certain industries, you will need to ask them if there is any organization they do not want to be near on the floor.

Issues Onsite

If you use an exposition services contractor, your exhibitors will check in directly with this company. Exhibitors will also need to check in with you to receive their conference packet and other information. Sometimes the meeting host places a registration table next to the exhibitor services company on the show floor so that the exhibitors can check in with both at the same time.

Move-In

Moving in can be a lengthy affair depending on the facility and the number of exhibitors. Publish specific move-in hours that must be adhered to. Depending on the facility, only so many exhibitors can use the loading dock at the same time. Sometimes exhibitors are allowed to "carry in" their stuff through the front doors as long as they do not need carts and other assistance. Other times, they are required to use the loading dock. Ask the facility about these rules.

When a loading dock is very busy, some facilities require a *marshalling yard.* This is an area away from the facility where exhibitors wait to be called to the dock in an orderly fashion. Unless your show is really big, you won't need one. But now at least you know what one is.

Meeting Speak

A **marshalling yard** is an area away from the facility where exhibitors wait to be called to the dock for unloading. It is "take a number" and wait.

After all the exhibitors are set up, you may be required to do a walk-through with the facility manager and/or fire marshal. They will determine if all the facility's rules and regulations are being followed and that there are no municipal code violations. For smaller shows, you probably won't see the fire marshal, but he or she could drop by at any time!

The Hook

Your show is open. Congratulations! But no one is visiting the booths! This is a show sponsor's worst nightmare. Here are some things you can do to lure them in.

Have a fun theme in the exhibition hall. Encourage all exhibitors to join the theme and decorate their booths accordingly. Have the attendees vote on their favorite booth. Make it a contest. They have to go into the hall to see which booth they like best!

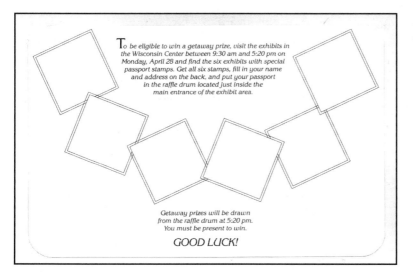

To be eligible to win a getaway prize, visit the exhibits in the Wisconsin Center between 9:30 am and 5:20 pm on Monday, April 28 and find the six exhibits with special passport stamps. Get all six stamps, fill in your name and address on the back, and put your passport in the raffle drum located just inside the main entrance of the exhibit area.

Getaway prizes will be drawn from the raffle drum at 5:20 pm. You must be present to win.

GOOD LUCK!

An example of a game to encourage booth traffic.

Some organizations create games that offer prizes for attending booths in the exhibit area. For one show, an Exhibit Passport Getaway was created. Attendees had to find the six different booths with special stamps and get their passports stamped. Once they did that, they placed their passports in a raffle drum, and they were eligible for drawings at the end of the day. The prizes were hotel and restaurant certificates. The following figure is an example of this type of passport (courtesy of the Workplace Learning Conference and designer Pete Manesis).

Outside cover of passport game.

(Courtesy of the Workplace Learning Conference and Pete Manesis)

There are a number of neat ideas like this to provide incentive to your attendees. Ask your exhibitors in advance to provide prizes and to solicit local companies as well as organizations involved in the conference to provide prizes.

Move-Out

What goes in must come out. Make sure you state in the rules when teardown can begin. If just one exhibitor packs up early, then others will follow, and you run the risk of having your entire show shut down early.

The rules that applied for bringing stuff in still apply when taking it out. Before the show is over, the exposition services contractor will have instructed the

The Inside Scoop

Most shows do not allow direct sales on the floor during show hours. If you want to allow this, check into the local sales tax regulations. Your exposition services contractor or the local CVB can tell you where to call.

exhibitors how to get their boxes shipped out. Exhibitors can even hire the exposition services contractor to tear down, pack, and ship the items for them.

If you have a tabletop show, be prepared with a list of phone numbers for the major shipping companies. The exhibitors can then arrange for the company to pick up the booth and/or boxes at the meeting facility.

Food for Thought

Interested in learning more about exhibit management? Check out the International Association for Exhibition Management (IAEM) at www.iaem.org.

The Least You Need to Know

➤ Have valid reasons and plenty of market research to support having a tradeshow.

➤ An exposition services contractor provides booth packages and is the sub-contractor for other services such as additional labor, florists, electricians, plumbers, and shipping.

➤ The exhibitor prospectus contains all the details of the tradeshow including who the audience is, why exhibitors should participate, the dates and times of the show, rules and regulations, and other details.

➤ Tabletop shows are smaller and are managed by you. They are great if you do not have the space or enough exhibitors to have a full-fledged tradeshow.

Part 3

Care and Feeding

You need to learn about taking care of your attendees. How should you set up the meeting rooms? What kinds of giveaways and amenities should you order? What about name badges? Are there really any decisions about putting a name on a piece of paper? You bet there are!

You'll get the scoop on how to find and hire speakers, make travel arrangements, and order food, beverages, and audio-visual equipment. You'll also learn about the registration process and what software programs you need to investigate.

The Setup

> ## In This Chapter
>
> ➤ Learn how the meeting room set plays a big role in education delivery leading to attendee satisfaction
>
> ➤ Understand why your audience and your program must be in sync
>
> ➤ See how room sets, speakers, audiences, and floor plans fit together for successful meetings
>
> ➤ Define meeting ground rules and understand their importance

How your meeting rooms are set up can make the difference between a successful meeting and a less memorable one. The placement of chairs and tables is just as important as the other details. Don't leave this up to the facility. In this chapter, you will learn how room-diagramming tools can help you and which room sets are conducive for effective learning.

It is also important to set a few ground rules for your meeting. The world is full of electronic intrusions and impolite people, and you don't want either at your meetings. Take a seat and get ready to set the stage for great performances!

Seating Is Important

People learn more when they can interact with other people. A session that allows for networking among peers is often more valuable than just one speaker talking to an audience all day.

You should face your audience to the long wall in any room. That way, you expose more people to the front/stage area. This is especially important if you have a long and narrow room. Also consider the direction from which people are entering the room. Try to have them enter from the back. You do not want people entering from the front when the speaker is talking.

Don't Drop the Ball

Schedule breaks that allow enough time for the attendees to interact with each other. Fifteen to thirty minutes is the norm.

Let's see how the room sets can affect your entire meeting. Here we will explain exactly how each room set works in a meeting situation. (Thanks to MeetingMatrix [www.meetingmatrix.com] for providing the diagrams.)

➤ **Classroom or schoolroom.** This set consists of rows of tables with chairs. It is a true "school" setting and allows the participants to take notes and spread out other materials. Classroom tables are 18 or 30 inches wide and 6 or 8 feet long. The 18-inch tables are often referred to as "skinnies." Place two people per 6-foot table or three people per 8-foot table. You need to specify your desires, or facilities could place three people per 6-foot and four people per 8-foot table.

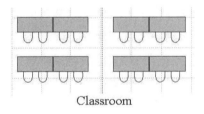

Classroom

➤ **Theater.** This is just like a classroom but without the tables. It is a good set when you have to maximize the amount of people in the room and when notes are not likely to be taken.

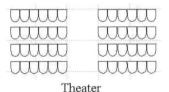

Theater

➤ **Chevron or herringbone.** These are used with classroom and theatre sets. All the rows are angled, giving attendees a better view of other participants and the front of the room. You can also curve the rows.

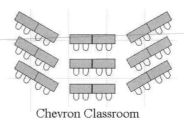

Chevron Classroom

➤ **Conference, T-shape, U-shape, or hollow square.** These are used for smaller (up to 30-person) meetings such as board, committee, and staff meetings. Tables are 8 feet long and 30 inches wide and can be placed together to make any configuration. As a rule of thumb, allow 2 to 3 feet of table space per person.

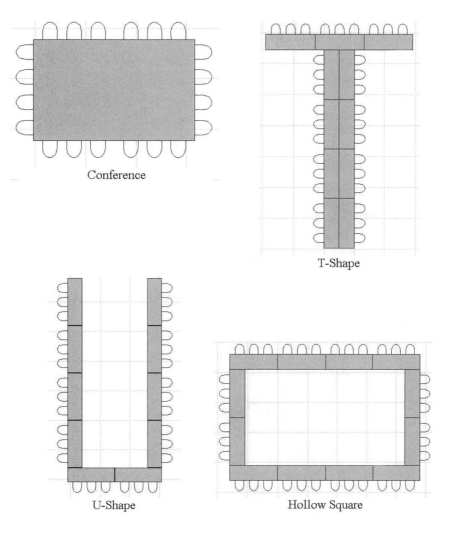

Conference

T-Shape

U-Shape

Hollow Square

➤ **Crescent.** (This is sometimes called one-half or three-quarter rounds.) Round banquet tables are set with chairs around half to three quarters of the table, facing the front. This is used for meetings at which networking and note taking are both important and allows speakers to design interactive activities. It allows for good interaction between participants.

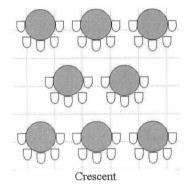

Crescent

➤ **Banquet rounds.** This configuration is used for food functions. The tables generally come in 60-inch or 72-inch diameters and seat between 8 and 12 people each.

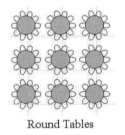

Round Tables

➤ **Reception.** This setup has rounds and smaller cocktail rounds, as well as bars throughout a room.

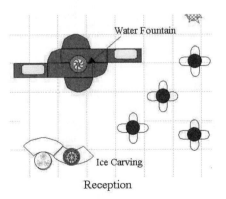

Reception

It is recommended that you go see the facility before designing the room set. If you don't see the room, you are relying on the pictures and floor plan given to you by the facility. Their idea and your idea of a good meeting set for your group could very well be two different things.

One of the best ways to set a meeting room is crescent style. The attendees can network, take notes, and have plenty of space to spread their stuff out. So, don't get in the rut of using theater or classroom style all the time. The crescent set takes up more space than theater or classroom, but it provides a better networking and learning atmosphere.

Math for Meetings

All meeting facilities have meeting-space charts (sometimes called specs) that explain how many people can fit into the meeting rooms for each setup style.

The Inside Scoop

Where do people sit when they enter a room? In the back. Some savvy planners place rope and stanchions across the back rows in a room to force people to the front. You can also put reserved signs on rounds. It also helps to have staff stationed throughout the room to help fill in the seats up front.

The only way to make sure the space is adequate is to create a diagram to scale. Companies such as MeetingMatrix described in Chapter 5, "Technology Soft-Where?" make all planners' lives easier by creating room diagrams, which use industry-standard calculations and fire codes.

As a rule of thumb, take the total square footage of the room divided by the approximate square footage needed per person to arrive at the number of people that will fit in a given room. Here are the approximate calculations:

Room Set	Space Calculation
Classroom—18-inch tables	14 to 15 square feet per person
Classroom—30-inch tables	17 to 18 square feet per person
Theater	9 to 11 square feet per person
Banquet—60-inch rounds	12 square feet per person
Banquet—72-inch rounds	13 square feet per person
Reception	10 to 12 square feet per person

The Inside Scoop

Facility meeting-space charts are not all created equal. They usually tell you the maximum number of people for each set. The maximum number typically does not include staging, aisles, audio-visual, refreshments in the back of the room, and so on.

So, if you have a 1,200-square-foot room and want to set it theater style, divide 1,200 by 9 to 11 square feet (let's say 10). The answer is 120 people, give or take.

Next you have to allow for head tables, audio-visual, staging, pillars, and other space hogs. See why we encourage the use of room-diagramming software? It eliminates the guesswork and provides a floor plan that will work. Then you simply give the diagram to the facility so that there is no miscommunication about your set—and you look so professional!

Additionally, if you really want to know how a setup will work in any given meeting space, talk to the convention services manager or audio-visual personnel. They work with many meetings on a daily basis and have probably seen it all.

Generation What?

Remember the old overhead presentations? They are being used less and less because audiences are now requiring better educational methods and more interaction. These days, it helps to understand a bit about the various generations sitting in your audience before planning your program. Many thanks to Joe Guertin, a professional speaker from Oak Creek, Wisconsin, for this information. Here's the short list:

Generation Type	Who They Are
Veterans (pre-Boomers)	As attendees, they will pay attention but need to relate. Refrain from using new terms and catch phrases. Give them respect.
Baby Boomers (born 1948–1964)	They like programs that mix education and fun, such as golf. They will ask for clarification on issues they don't understand. Q&A time is important.
Generation X (born 1965–1980)	Grew up on MTV and technology. They like interaction and movement. Static presentations are boring to them. Sessions with personal relevance pique their interest.
Generation Y (also called Nexters or Millennials)	Short attention spans and time constraints will play a role in the meetings they attend. They are impatient. Family is important. Sessions need to be shorter with a hands-on approach and possibly include family programs, too.

Your audience may also be ethnically or religiously diverse. People also have different styles of learning. Most learn best by seeing (visual learning), but others learn by hearing (auditory learning), and some like the hands-on approach and need to experience it (experiential learning). Make sure you provide a combination of all three learning styles to reach your audience. In other words, use handouts, exciting visuals, and hands-on experiences throughout the meeting.

Interactive Sessions

The speakers have a lot to do with the amount of interaction that goes on between attendees. Ask speakers how they get the audience involved and what you can do to help them create a great program.

Since your speakers will have a big impact on you reaching your goals and objectives, make sure you review these items with each speaker and provide them with an audience profile.

Also ask your speakers to integrate questions and responses throughout the session. It is important for the audience to be able to clarify the information presented and to be able to speak directly with the presenter.

You can also build in time for small discussion groups. Assign topics or areas of discussion and have each group report back to the large group on the outcome of the discussion. Getting everyone involved is a key to successful learning.

Go with the Flow

Have you ever been to a meeting and found that some of the breakout sessions were not well attended? What can you do to avoid this? To begin with, make sure you figure out in advance the number of seats you will need in each breakout.

Food for Thought

Many of the room-diagramming software companies have already produced standard floor plans for thousands of hotels across the United States. Check out their Web sites (see "Room Diagramming" in Chapter 5).

Food for Thought

If your audience is older, make sure your handouts and visuals have a larger font.

Food for Thought

Place standing floor microphones throughout the room or pass handheld wireless mics so the audience can ask questions and everyone can clearly hear the questions.

153

The Inside Scoop

If there is a shopping mall or other interesting attractions or activities nearby, it is inevitable that you will lose some people before the day is over. Plan on having a few empty seats but don't overset the rooms. Too many empty seats look bad for you and the speaker. Don't assume that everyone registered for the meeting will attend every session. It just ain't true!

Meeting Speak

A **monitor** introduces the speaker, keeps the meeting on track, gets help with audio-visual equipment if needed, and distributes and collects the evaluations (if applicable). The monitor is often a volunteer.

If you have 200 attendees with four breakout sessions, theoretically, each session should seat 50 people. If one breakout topic is more popular than the others, you should adjust it accordingly. In some cases, you just won't know, so get out your crystal ball.

Set what you need but do not overset the rooms. In the previous example, if your breakout rooms seat 75 but you only need 50, make sure the hotel sets to your needs and not the maximum set. You can always have more chairs brought in if needed. Just make sure you keep an eye on it.

Session Monitor

A meeting with various breakouts should have a *monitor* in each session. A monitor helps keep the sessions running smoothly since you can't be everywhere all the time.

Provide monitors with instructions to tell them what they are required to do. Also prepare a form for each monitor to complete. This form includes the number of attendees at the session, comments about the session, and a few feedback questions about being a monitor. Always try to improve the process for the next time!

Floor Plans

When finalizing the agenda and assigning sessions to specific meeting rooms, carefully look at where the meeting rooms are located. Are they near one another? How long will it take participants to walk from session to session? Where will the refreshment breaks go? Are the meeting rooms easy to find? Are the signs sufficient, or do you need to make additional ones? Do they need an elevator to access some sessions? Take note of the locations of phones and restrooms. Do a walk-through to experience firsthand any issues you may encounter onsite.

Also take into consideration the room sets for each session. Assign sessions with similar sets and A/V to the same rooms throughout the day. You do not want to change or flip room sets midday because it takes time and often incurs an additional labor fee.

Plan to have any general session room setup changes occur in the evening after the programs are over. Think about this especially if your lunch or dinner is in the general session room. In this case, use rounds all day.

Setting the Ground Rules

There are usually a few important items all attendees need to know. This information can be in the registration materials, the onsite brochure, a welcome packet, or some other appropriate place.

Don't ya just hate the words "It's our policy"? People just hate rules these days, but without a few of them, your meeting is headed for disaster.

Create a policy for smoking and alcohol consumption. For company meetings, policies may already be in place. If this is the case, a gentle reminder is all that is needed. State that company policies apply at your meetings, just like in the office. For other meetings, adopting these policies can reduce and eliminate problems onsite. Sample policies can look like this:

➤ **Smoking.** "Inferno Explosives Company meetings are designated as nonsmoking. Outside the meeting rooms, we adhere to the facility smoking policy." (Make sure the facility has one—usually there are designated smoking areas.)

➤ **Alcohol.** "Please drink responsibly and don't drink and drive."

➤ **Electronic intrusions.** To make sure all attendees have an interruption-free meeting experience, please turn off your phone or pager (or use the vibrate mode).

We encourage you to establish your own policies based on your situation. These are guidelines to get you started.

Food for Thought

Have a backup plan for volunteer monitors. If there are any no-shows, having an alternate that can step in at the last minute is a plus.

Don't Drop the Ball

Ask the meeting facility for its policy on smoking and serving alcohol, and tell them your organization's policies. Find out about the training provided to employees and the policy-enforcement procedures.

The Least You Need to Know

➤ Seating that allows interaction with other attendees promotes a better learning environment.

➤ Understand your audience so you can create the right learning environment.

➤ Session monitors help keep your sessions on track and let you know if something needs attention.

➤ Establish policies on drinking, smoking, and using electronic devices for your meetings.

Chapter 16

The Stuff Meetings Are Made Of

In This Chapter

➤ Check out the selection of gifts and giveaways

➤ Learn how to make your name badges stand out

➤ Make your attendees feel special with amenities

➤ Identify vendors who provide the "stuff"

We all go to meetings, and most of the time, we leave with more "stuff" than we had when we arrived. We're not referring to just the notes, handouts, and programs. What about the other items we acquire throughout the meeting—the gifts, goodies, treats, and giveaways?

As a planner, you need name badges, badge ribbons, supplies, awards, certificates, and lots of other materials. This chapter looks at the world of supplies, gifts, giveaways, and the "stuff" that makes your meetings memorable. Beware, however, there is a lot to choose from.

The Players

Before we launch into what is out there, we want to identify the players. The meetings industry has a number of vendors that supply planners with promotional products and supplies. Some call themselves promotional products companies, advertising specialty companies, or meeting-supply companies, while others focus on incentives and awards and others on corporate or business gifts. When doing searches on the Web, you can search the following topics or keywords and pull up a lot of info:

➤ Advertising specialties

➤ Business gifts

➤ Corporate gifts

➤ Promotional products

➤ Incentive gifts

➤ Meeting supplies

➤ Tradeshow promotional items

The possibilities are endless with respect to promotional gifts and giveaways. You can find items that range from inexpensive refrigerator magnets to top-of-the-line crystal vases. You just need to know the purpose of the gift, your budget, and the message you want to send.

Name Badges and Ribbons

One of the most important and noticed items for meetings is the name badge. Most attendees will not know each other, and the name badge provides the initial introduction. When designing your name badge, consider what information goes on the badge. The attendee's name, company or organization, city, and state are the most common. Don't try to list too much. Just the facts, ma'am! The key is to make it easy to read. Also consider the following for your name badges:

Food for Thought

For safety and security reasons, be sure to advise all attendees not to wear their name badges or carry their conference tote bags outside the facility.

➤ **Font size.** Make them readable from a short distance.

➤ **Meeting info.** Add the meeting name and/ or dates.

➤ **Logo.** Use it to represent the meeting or organization.

➤ **Colors.** Use them to highlight the meeting info, logo, and even attendee info.

➤ **Holder style.** Will they be pinned, clipped, or hung around the neck?

Believe it or not, there are considerable options for name badge style, size, and accompaniments. You can purchase preprinted matching stock that includes the name badge, name tents, signage (8.5 × 11 inches), tickets, and jumbo registration envelopes. Or the stock can be blank so you can print your own logo or design to give your meeting a professional, coordinated look. There are even companies that will customize these items with your logo or meeting theme, eliminating the need to print them yourself or outsource to a printer.

Professionally printed name badge with lanyard and ribbons.

When determining the attendee information to print on your name badge, the following printing order works well:

1. Line One: First name with a minimum 36-point font

2. Line Two: First and last names with a minimum 22-point font

3. Line Three: Organization name with a minimum 22-point font

4. Line Four: City and state the attendee is from with a minimum 18-point font

5. Line Five: (Optional) Country or region with a minimum 18-point font

Name badges should have two to four lines. Five gets to be too much but can be done if really necessary. Your name badge can also have your logo, meeting name, and dates printed on the name

The Inside Scoop

Make sure you schedule ample time to print your name badges. Also factor in time to have them preprinted with your meeting information. With attendees registering at the last minute, you might want to print them in batches or consider printing them onsite as people arrive and pick up their materials.

Meeting Speak

A **lanyard** is a necklace or neck-cord that attaches to the name badge so it can hang around a person's neck.

badge stock. You can skip line one above, but having an individual's first name only on the first line makes it easier to read his or her name from a distance.

In addition to the name badges, you will have to select appropriate name badge holders. Many attendees prefer holders with both a pin and clip backing. There also is a growing trend to supply *lanyards* that allow the name badge to hang around the neck. Women especially like these because they don't like pins sticking in their clothes and frequently don't have anywhere to attach a clip.

Consider the categorization of your attendees. Do you want to identify specific groups such as exhibitors, sponsors, committee members, guests, and so on? If you do, then preprinted badge holders or ribbons that attach to your name badge are the way to go. One of the newest advances in ribbon technology is the stackable ribbon. These ribbons (approximately 4 inches wide by 1½ inches tall) stack on top of each other, so you can wear many at once (if you are special, that is). They come in a large variety of colors and preprinted titles. And yes, you can have your logo imprinted and have your own titles custom made. Who knew?

Totes and Carryalls

Another popular item to give your attendees is something in which to carry all their stuff. Totes, carryalls, attaches, bags, and briefcases are great because they can be used again and again and are large enough to put your meeting info or logo on it for the world to see.

Food for Thought

Attach a blank or luggage tag (with your logo, of course) to each bag and ask attendees to put their name on it. All the bags look alike, and some are invariably lost because they cannot be identified. What a useful gift!

If cost is an issue, evaluate your quantity. You can get volume discounts (the more you buy, the less it costs), but also consider getting your bag paid for by a sponsor. You can put your meeting info on one side and sponsor logos on the other. Another thing you can do is ask for "specials." Frequently, promotional product vendors will have sales or specials—ask them.

Awards and Recognition

There are several occasions when special gifts are needed. Recipients of awards, speakers, sponsors, and committee and conference chairs all fall into this category. Again, there is a large selection of special, elegant, and classy gifts:

➤ Awards (plaques, trophies, statues, and so on)

➤ Books (about the venue, topic, and so on)

➤ Bookmarks

➤ Business card holders

➤ Clocks

➤ Crystal (boxes, bowls, vases, and so on)

➤ Desk sets (pens, notepads, calculators)

➤ Donation to a speaker's charity or local organization

➤ Frames

➤ Key chains

➤ Lapel pins

➤ Laser pointers

➤ Letter openers

➤ Paperweights

➤ Pen and pencil sets

➤ Watches

Don't Drop the Ball

Take into consideration how the recipient will get the gift home. Make it small enough to carry in the person's luggage or make arrangements to have it shipped to a home or office. The recipient will appreciate it.

The list is endless, and it's a lot of fun browsing catalogs and Web sites to imagine the possibilities. Since these items are more expensive and are for special recipients, the challenge is to select items that people will like, use, and enjoy. After all, as a recognition piece, you will want the gifts to elicit good memories.

Also consider handing out gift certificates so the recipients can select their own gifts. You can choose a bookstore or a national department store. Another nice gift is a certificate for dinner at a nice restaurant where the recipient lives. This takes more time to arrange, but it makes the gift more special. Doesn't everyone love to eat?

The Inside Scoop

Did you know that many well-known companies have a corporate sales or business gifts department? If you're looking for something extra special, check out Tiffany's (www.tiffanys.com), Nambe (www.nambe.com), and Lands' End (www.landsend.com) for starters.

Giveaways and Amenities

Giveaways and amenities are any "gift-like" items given to attendees at a meeting, usually for promotional purposes. Everyone likes free stuff, and it's a nice touch to be able to provide your attendees with well-selected mementos. In some circumstances, you, the meeting sponsor, will want to provide your attendees with neato treats every day.

So, what do you give and when do you give it? Here are some suggestions.

At the Meeting

The obvious place to give stuff away is in the registration packets, but you may want to spread it out and give your attendees little surprises throughout the meeting. Meals, especially sit-down lunches and dinners, are an opportunity to place your gifts at a table. Remember to keep it small. You also can place your gifts on chairs at the general session, such as a book written by the speaker. This works especially well if the gift ties in with the theme of presentation.

If you have little giveaways that don't have to be given to each attendee, placing them at registration, computer banks, lounges, or breaks works well. Items in this category include pens, pencils, key chains, bottled water with the meeting logo, candies, notepads, rulers, and so on.

In the Room

What a nice surprise. You come back to your room from a long day, you're tired, your mind is mush, and what do you see? A gift, maybe even personally addressed to you, from a meeting sponsor or perhaps the hotel (negotiate VIP amenities into your contract). These types of amenities are placed in your attendees' rooms by the hotel at your request and for a fee. These amenities can be larger (a bottle of wine, a gift basket) because the attendees won't need to carry it all day in their nifty tote bags. Room amenities are usually reserved for keynote speakers, committee members, and other VIPs, but if you have the funds or sponsors, room amenities for all of your attendees are a nice touch.

Since amenities are delivered to the rooms, you can work with the hotel to provide creative deserts, milk and cookies, fruit and cheese, or whatever flips their switch. Whatever you come up with, your attendee will feel special.

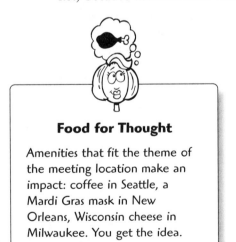

Food for Thought

Amenities that fit the theme of the meeting location make an impact: coffee in Seattle, a Mardi Gras mask in New Orleans, Wisconsin cheese in Milwaukee. You get the idea.

The Selection

It's not possible to list all the choices for gifts and amenities. Start with all the items listed earlier in the "Awards and Recognition" section and add the following:

➤ Apparel (caps, shirts, jackets)

➤ Attaches and briefcases

➤ Backpacks, bags, fanny packs, totes

➤ Binders and portfolios

➤ Calendars and clipboards

➤ Candy and chocolates

➤ Bottled water with meeting or sponsor logo

➤ Clips and pins

➤ Computer accessories (cases, CD/disk holders, mouse pads)

➤ Cups, glasses, mugs, and sports bottles

➤ Electronics (calculators, cameras, radios)

➤ First-aid and travel kits

➤ Food and beverage (the list is endless)

➤ Golf, golf, and more golf stuff

➤ Luggage and travel items

➤ Music (CDs and tapes)

➤ Pocket/purse accessories (key chains, business card holders)

➤ Sports products

➤ Tools and knives

➤ Toys, puzzles, and games

➤ Writing utensils

Yes, there are companies that sell all of this and much, much more—just for your meeting.

At the Tradeshow

Tradeshows are notorious for giving away lots of stuff. They're mostly small, trinket-type items, but you can find some really neat things. In Miami, one resourceful fellow walked out of a tradeshow with a pair of giveaway flip-flops and a pair of swimming trunks—he went right to the beach. You can bet he thought those items were quite useful.

At tradeshows, the exhibitors want to get and keep your attention, so naturally they entice you with

Food for Thought

You can get some great ideas for your own meeting by attending a few tradeshows. Exhibitors are experts at putting logos on just about anything.

cookies, candy, and a variety of interesting freebies—all with their name on it. Here is where you can pick up notepads, refrigerator magnets, letter openers, lip gloss, luggage tags, yo-yos, flashing buttons, bottled water with a logo, and scads of pens (and pins).

"Logo It"

Everything we've talked about can have a logo or other important info imprinted on it. After all, the freebies really aren't free. Someone—a sponsor, the host, or the attendee—pays for it one way or another.

When deciding on what to put on your giveaways, keep it simple. Your logo, phone number, Web site, or a pertinent catch phrase is really all you need. If you have a meeting theme, try to select an item that ties into your theme.

Meeting Speak

An **appliqué** is a small, self-stick, embroidered design used for name badges, lapels, and clothes. These are used for themes and as identifiers.

Don't Drop the Ball

Logos are powerful, especially to sponsors. Pay special attention to their instructions for logo reproduction. Otherwise, you may end up with an upset sponsor or have to redo the job.

Everything Else

There are many items that you need to plan, manage, and produce your meetings. Here is yet another list of meeting-related stuff:

➤ *Appliqués*
➤ Badge carrying cases
➤ Ballot, evaluation and comment boxes
➤ Bells
➤ Buttons
➤ Carts
➤ Certificates
➤ Directional arrows
➤ Display stands
➤ Easels
➤ Gavels
➤ ID bracelets
➤ Laser pointers
➤ Literature holders
➤ Raffle drums
➤ Registration envelopes
➤ Shipping boxes
➤ Shipping cases (hard)

➤ Signage holders and carrying cases

➤ Signage pedestals

➤ Stock roll tickets

➤ Ticket-tag bracelets

➤ Timers

➤ Walkie-talkies and/or radios

Where do you go to find this "stuff"? Check out the following companies—you'll be amazed at what they offer:

➤ 4imprint (www.4imprint.com)

➤ Awards.com (www.awards.com)

➤ Branders (www.branders.com)

➤ Bravanta.com (www.bravanta.com)

➤ Marco (www.marcomeetings.com)

➤ pc/nametag (www.pcnametag.com)

➤ Seton (www.seton.com/events)

These companies provide everything from awards to name badges to meeting supplies such as certificates, tickets, and signage. Just be careful. It's fun to look at all the stuff, and before you know it, your bill can get out of control. It is best to have a shopping list before you shop. That way, you have a better chance of staying within your budget. After all, you wouldn't go grocery shopping without a list, would you?

The Least You Need to Know

➤ Make your name badges stand out. Use large, easy-to-read fonts and themed designs to give them a professional, coordinated look.

➤ Don't give out all your giveaways at registration. Surprise and treat your attendees throughout the meeting.

➤ An enormous selection of items can be printed with a logo and given as give-aways.

➤ Look beyond the office-supply companies. There are companies that specialize in providing meeting-related supplies.

Chapter 17

Yakety Yak

In This Chapter

➤ Find the right speaker for your program

➤ See where to find the right speaker

➤ Find out what to include in speaker contracts

➤ Learn to prepare your speakers for your audience

Selecting the right speaker for your meeting or event is a crucial step in the planning process. We've heard horror stories about keynote speakers who have missed the mark in front of hundreds of people. Can this happen to you? Sure it can. It happens for various reasons, but here are some of the common ones: 1) The speaker and audience were not properly matched, 2) the planner did not prepare the speaker about the organization, meeting goals and objectives, and audience profile, and 3) the planner assumed that "expensive" means high quality.

This chapter explains the ins and outs of speaker selection. Don't assume that, just because you have a signed contract, come Monday morning at 8 A.M. your speaker is in the ballroom ready to go. What happens if his or her flight is cancelled or delayed? What happens if he or she oversleeps? What happens if his or her laptop is not compatible with the projector? Not to worry. We are here to clue you in on how to reduce the potential for a speaker disaster.

Setting the Stage

First, look at your meeting agenda and your goals and objectives. (See, goals and objectives are here again!) Where do you begin? There are five very important steps:

1. Determine potential topics based on agenda, goals, and objectives.

2. Determine how many speakers you need (including keynoters) and whether they will be professional speakers, industry experts, or others.

3. Determine the nature of the presentations and whether they will be motivational, technical, educational, or entertaining.

4. Know your budget and audience.

5. List any recommended speakers.

Food for Thought

The right keynote speaker sets the tone for your entire meeting. Make sure the presentation is tied into your goals and objectives to get the audience on the same page.

By now you should have decided on the number of general sessions, breakouts, and general topics. If any changes are necessary to your agenda, the time to do it is now, before you hire and contract with speakers.

You also need to track your speaker information in your database or meeting-management software. Things such as contact information, audio-visual requirements, session title, and description all should be available in a report format.

For large conferences, breakout session tracks are offered. Tracks can be the level of the audience (beginner, intermediate, or advanced) or be geared to job position such as CEO, middle management, and administrative support roles. In your onsite program, color code or assign a symbol to each. Let your speakers know your designations so they can properly prepare their presentations.

Where Do You Find Them?

Under every rock, around every corner .... They are everywhere including the meetings you attend and in trade magazines and newspapers. They are even the business professionals you meet and work with.

No matter what type of speaker you are looking for, here are the places to look:

➤ Convention and visitors bureaus

➤ National Speakers Association (NSA)

➤ Your state speakers association

➤ Referrals

➤ Speakers bureaus

➤ Industry Web sites

If you know what you want with regard to topics and experience levels, finding a speaker is not too difficult. Frequently, we see planners looking for a result, but they have no clue who can provide it. If you are looking for a professional speaker, we suggest the National Speakers Association. This group can put you in touch with your local state speakers association, which can help you find speakers in your own backyard. The NSA can be reached at www.nsaspeaker.org.

Another easy way to find a professional speaker is through a speakers bureau. *Speakers bureaus* represent hundreds and even thousands of speakers and act as an "agent" for them. The bureau receives a fee from the speaker, not you, so don't hesitate to look into them.

Another organization we told you about in Chapter 1, "What Is a Meeting or Event Anyway?" is the International Association of Speakers Bureaus at www.iasbweb.org. This group also can point you to many speakers bureaus.

Meeting Speak

Speakers bureaus are organizations that represent professional speakers. Speakers pay the bureau a portion of their contracted speaking fee for their services.

Hired Guns

Hired guns are professional speakers who make speaking their full-time career. These days, professional speakers are generalists, specialists, or both and oftentimes (but not always) are represented by a speaker's bureau.

Hired guns also can be celebrities. You often hear about famous athletes who hit the speaking circuit during or after their sports careers. Just by name recognition alone, they can command some pretty high speaking fees. Celebrity speakers come in many flavors: CEOs, commentators, politicians, journalists, writers, sports figures, and of course, entertainers and radio/TV/movie stars.

You also have the "expert" speakers. They usually have influence, are respected in their field, and have developed a niche. They may or may not be

Don't Drop the Ball

Raise your right hand and repeat after us. "I will always preview a potential keynote speaker in person, on videotape, or via a Web demo before signing any contracts."

represented by a speaker's bureau. The price range varies from speaker to speaker. You can cut a good deal on someone just starting out or shell out big bucks for someone in demand.

Hiring the Hired Guns

Contracting with a professional speaker is different than securing other types of speakers. Professional speakers will most likely require you to sign their contract. They also have a list of extra needs. They may ask for the following:

➤ First-class airfare

➤ First-class airfare for an assistant

➤ Limos

➤ Suites

➤ Special amenities in their room (gourmet food, flowers, and so on)

The Inside Scoop

Ask your speakers if there is anything you can do to reduce their fees. Sometimes being flexible on travel schedules or dates allows them to piggyback the trip with another speaking engagement or a personal vacation.

Meeting Speak

Learner outcomes is a fancy name for course objectives.

The Dotted Line ... Getting Together

Here are the most important items to address in speaker contracts:

➤ Day and date and start/stop times of the presentation; location of presentation.

➤ The topic and any customization required.

➤ Q&A time throughout the presentation (if any) and book signings if appropriate.

➤ Breakout sessions and additional costs (if any).

➤ Approval for video- and/or audiotaping of the program. If yes, have the speaker sign a release.

➤ A short bio for introduction purposes and the program.

➤ A presentation outline and *learner outcomes*.

➤ Handouts (if yes, who copies them?) and deadlines for receipt of originals with permission to reproduce them.

➤ A statement that ascertains the material (verbal or written) is the speaker's own work.

➤ Reimbursable expenses and caps on expenses if any.

➤ Travel arrangements.

➤ Travel requirements (first-class airplane ticket?).

➤ Audio-visual requirements and room set requests.

➤ Date the deposit (if applicable) is due.

➤ No-show, cancellation, and termination clauses.

➤ The date final payment is due.

➤ The date expense reimbursement forms and receipts are due.

Speaker fees are based on many things including the date, the length of presentation, the topic, and demand for the speaker. Some speakers will donate their time because your organization is near and dear to their heart or they want the exposure. Some may only present at one or two conferences during their entire career.

Breakout Speakers and One-Shot Deals

There are community, business, industry, and educational leaders who make presentations to groups. These people speak on a variety of topics and can enhance your program.

Not only are these individuals good for breakout sessions, also consider them for facilitating sessions or roundtable discussions on their area of expertise. Attendees love roundtable sessions because there is interaction and it is a more intimate session.

Food for Thought

If possible, let speakers have input on when their sessions are scheduled. Also, when repeating a session, don't put the same speaker on the schedule first and last.

Call for Presentations

Although all presenters are just as important as your keynote speaker, they need to be handled in a slightly different way. Since some of these speakers are not experienced, sometimes they need extra help in submitting their proposal or customizing a presentation for your meeting.

To begin with, large conferences distribute a *call for presentations* or a presenter's application. This document is an opportunity for individuals to apply to speak at your conference. It provides you with information in a consistent format from each potential speaker, which helps you make an informed decision.

Meeting Speak

A **call for presentations** is an application to speak at a meeting or conference. Conference organizers are usually looking for specific topics, and carefully following the application guidelines gives you a better chance of being selected.

A call for presentations or presenter application includes the following:

1. Presenter information (name/organization/address/phone/fax/e-mail)
2. The title of the proposed session
3. The session description and learner outcomes
4. Track information (so they can prepare for the audience)
5. The presenter bio and other credentials
6. Audio-visual requirements
7. A question regarding audio- or videotaping of the session
8. What the speaker will receive for speaking (travel costs, honorarium or fee, complimentary registration or registration discount, name and bio in the program, and so on)
9. Due date and to whom to send it

Once you have received responses to the call for presentations, make your selection(s). Send the speakers you select confirmation letters. Send the people who are not selected a thank-you letter for submitting an application and why their session was not selected, and invite them to the conference.

Most of the speakers who do not charge a fee are people who do not speak professionally for a living. They may not have their own contracts, so you need to send them one. Sometimes just a confirmation letter is enough. See the preceding criteria for professional speaker contracts and simplify it for them.

Instead of an honorarium or a speaking fee, offer a registration discount or a complimentary registration to the conference. Many of these speakers would normally attend anyway, and this saves them money. See Appendix A, "Sample Forms and Checklists," for a sample breakout speaker agreement letter.

Meeting Scoop Sheet

Create a meeting information sheet for all speakers. This document is different from a contract and should provide important information about the meeting. This should be created a few weeks in advance of the meeting or conference when you have registration data. The scoop sheet should contain the following:

➤ Confirmation of the day/date/time of the presentation, and expected time to be at the venue.

➤ Audience statistics, the number of males/females, a sampling of job titles, age range, where attendees are from, and the number of expected attendees for the session.

➤ A review of meeting goals and objectives.

➤ The visual and handout expectations and procedures. (Who copies and brings them to the meeting?)

➤ The guestroom reservation confirmation number, if applicable.

➤ Transportation details, if applicable.

➤ A meeting program if it is available or at least a final agenda with meeting room assignments. Also include a facility floor plan and driving directions.

➤ Information on the speaker-ready (rehearsal) room.

➤ Instructions for expense and speaking-fee reimbursement, if applicable.

Food for Thought

Speakers are very particular about how they are described in brochures, on name badges, and so on. Be sure to double-check all references for accuracy and ask how the speaker wants to be listed on all materials.

Books, Tapes, and Other Sale Items

Address audiotaping, publication of articles, and book and tape sales in advance of the meeting. Don't wait until the speaker shows up with 50 boxes of books and tapes to sell.

Recording speakers on audio- or videotape is a common practice in today's meeting world. This allows attendees to take the sessions home with them, and it also lets people who were unable to attend the meeting see or hear the sessions. You need to get prior permission to tape a speaker. Do it before the meeting.

Taping and Publication Release

There are companies that provide taping services. They tape, reproduce, and sell the tapes and CDs onsite during your meeting! These items are also for sale for a few months after the meeting.

In addition, make sure you ask the facility what charges you will incur as a result of this process. Most will charge a "patch" fee, which allows the taping company to access the facility's sound system. You will also need to provide a microphone for all speakers being taped.

The breakout speaker agreement letter in Appendix A also has a basic speaker taping release. You should consult with an attorney to ensure that your form is properly customized for your organization. This is a sample only and needs approval from your attorney.

The Inside Scoop

If a speaker agrees to be audio- or videotaped, the speaker should sign a tape release form. Have your attorney prepare this document, which should be signed in advance of the conference. Basically, a release ascertains that the material is the speaker's own work, not previously copyrighted by anyone else, and that he or she agrees to be recorded. The speaker also waives the right to any proceeds from sales of the tapes.

In addition, if any of the speaker's material is published in your newsletter, magazine, or other printed format, your speaker should sign an appropriate copyright release form.

Book and Tape Sales

Inevitably, your professional speakers will want to sell their wares. Books, tapes, CDs, T-shirts, you name it. Any reasonable request should be considered, but think about how you can benefit, too.

For example, sell their tapes and/or books after the session and, to increase sales, have the speaker donate a percentage back to the organization or to a charity.

You can also buy the books and/or tapes (negotiate a discount) and give them to every attendee. This reinforces the meeting's message because attendees get to take it home, and it is perceived as a valuable gift.

Getting Them There and Other VIP Issues

Meet your keynote and VIP speakers at the airport. If a limo is picking them up, a company executive, committee member, or other appropriate person should go to meet them personally.

Many times, your breakout speakers are on their own for transportation and other travel arrangements. You should offer them assistance and additional information on the location.

When your speakers arrive at the meeting, give them a map of the meeting facility, an onsite brochure, and the same packet you give to all attendees. Tell them about the monitor, if any, assigned to their session, and what to do if they need assistance with the audio-visual equipment should the monitor not show up.

Always let your speakers know the sequence of events that pertains to them. Introduce your speakers to who is introducing them to the audience and let them know whether they should be seated in the front of the room or enter from backstage.

Speaker Ready Room

Have a room just for your speakers to practice and review their presentations. Stock it with basic audio-visual equipment (you should know what they are using based on their audio-visual requests) and food. Have bottled water, soda, coffee, tea, decaf coffee, and snacks available.

Don't Drop the Ball

Always have water (with no ice) on stage for the speaker. Usually a bottle of water and a glass are sufficient. A glass is a must because it looks unprofessional to have your speaker guzzling from a bottle! If possible, ask your speaker what he or she prefers.

Cancellations and No-Shows

Okay, it is inevitable. Just what do you do if a speaker doesn't show up? The meeting must go on. For keynote speakers and other professionals, there had better be a very good reason. Make sure your contract stipulates what *you* get if they are late or don't show up. Always have a backup plan. If you went through a speakers bureau, call it first.

If you are stuck in this situation, who could pinch hit? A CEO? The association's executive director? If the speaker is running late, is there a way to switch the program around? Can you spend the time wisely with the audience in some other way? Call the key players together, brainstorm, and make the best decision you can.

Another idea (if you have a few hours) is to contact the local CVB. It might know of a local speaker you could call to ask if he or she could fill in. You won't have time to preview this person, but it may be your only option. Be honest with the audience, and they will hopefully understand.

Monitors/Facilitators

Monitors are very helpful when assigned to each breakout. They are also called facilitators, and these individuals make sure that all is progressing as scheduled.

Don't Drop the Ball

For breakout speakers, clarify who is responsible for making copies of their handouts. Ask for an original in advance just in case you need to make copies at the last minute.

Speaker Support

Some speakers will inevitably arrive and need copies, transparencies for an overhead projector, and other miscellaneous items. Most hotels have a business center, but it will cost you some bucks.

First, work directly with speakers in advance to assist them in preparing for the meeting. If you are responsible for supplying the handouts, get their originals in advance (via e-mail) and make copies at the office. If it is a lot of paper and is heavy to ship, consider e-mailing the document to a quick-copy place near the hotel. These places can copy and deliver to your hotel in time for the meeting. By doing a little work on the front side, you can save the last-minute rush onsite.

Larger conferences and seminars provide a binder with handouts from all the sessions in it. In this case, you need all the originals. Outsource this job to a quick-copy place to save time.

Rehearse, Rehearse, Rehearse

Always have your general session speakers come early for a rehearsal. Start from the beginning and run through the entire show if possible. Leave nothing to chance and never "wing" it. One time during a rehearsal, we realized that the second set of stairs to the stage was not there! The speaker had no easy way to access the stage. Luckily, we were in rehearsal and it was no big deal. Conduct a rehearsal as if it were the actual meeting. Leave enough time to make changes if necessary. The actual presentation will be a breeze!

The Least You Need to Know

➤ Prepare your speakers in advance as to the meeting's goals and objectives and the audience profile.

➤ Carefully review your speakers' contracts so there are no misunderstandings.

➤ Industry hot topics and networking provide valuable leads to find speakers.

➤ Take care of your speakers. Focus on their needs so they can focus on imparting valuable information.

Chapter 18

Planes, Trains, and Automobiles

In This Chapter

➤ Discover the benefits of meet and greet

➤ Learn what to ask ground transportation providers

➤ Learn to negotiate discounted fares with the airlines

➤ See what kind of info attendees who drive need to know

➤ Find out what a "city-wide" is

How attendees get to your meeting and how they move around once they get there takes a lot of coordination. In this area, you definitely need to rely on trusted, competent, and efficient transportation providers. In some cases, such as with airlines, their performance is out of your hands, but you can still try to get your attendees airfare deals.

When considering the broad category of transportation, the components include air, sea, private train cars, chartered jets, cruise ships, helicopters, and private automobiles. However, the reality is that, for the majority of meetings, you deal with airlines to get your attendees to the city and then ground transportation providers to move your people locally. That is the focus of this chapter.

Getting There

In many cases, the meeting host is not responsible for getting the attendees to the meeting site, but there are some important things you can do to make it easier for them. Since air travel is the primary mode of transportation, you should research the major airlines servicing the airport nearest your meeting. Convention and visitors bureaus can help with this. Also know from what cities your attendees will originate. Some airlines have meetings programs in which they provide the following:

➤ Special fares or airfare discounts

➤ Promotional support

➤ Free tickets based on volume

➤ Passenger lists with arrival/departure times

➤ Coupons for drinks or movies

Each airline's meetings program has a different level of support. Negotiated discounts will vary depending on the type of fare, when the passenger books a ticket, and how many passengers are expected, in addition to other criteria.

Airlines will ask you where your attendees are coming from, the meeting dates and location, and your passenger estimate. Usually 10 or more tickets will qualify as a group booking. However, this varies by airline.

Many airlines have a group department that handles meeting contracts. Once a contract is signed, you will be assigned a group code for publication in your meeting materials. Your attendees must use this code to identify them as part of your group.

The Inside Scoop

Don't plan on using your free airline tickets for your current meeting. The airlines won't know the total number of tickets sold and thus can't provide your free tickets until after the meeting. You'll have to use them for a future meeting.

Food for Thought

Make sure you let all attendees know the convention identifier code for each airline discount you have negotiated. The only way to take advantage of any discount is to use the code when booking the flight.

Meet and Greet

Say what? *Meet and greet?* Sometimes you will want to have people at the airport "meet" your attendees upon arrival and "greet" them. This is usually done at baggage claim because you can't possibly know when and from which gates your attendees will arrive (unless you have a very small airport or a very small group). People with banners or signs stand around the baggage claim and direct your attendees to your designated ground transportation. Smiling, of course.

In general, when using meet and greet for groups, the attendees pay for the transportation to the hotel. The meet and greet simply helps them locate the ground transportation. You, the meeting host, pay for the meet and greet service.

Meet and greet is also frequently used for VIPs, executives, and speakers. Some companies have services where you can request a representative to greet your attendees or VIPs at the airport gate, carry their baggage, escort them to their car, and assist them at hotel check-in. In these cases, you pay the company directly and cover the transportation cost and gratuities.

Providers of these services are ground transportation, limousine, and destination-management companies. The cost of these services will depend on the city or location, type of vehicle, and services required. Meet and greet makes a strong, professional impression.

Meeting Speak

Meet and greet is commonly used at airports to meet special passengers and either direct them to ground transportation or take them to their final destination.

Ground Transportation

In most cases, the attendees are responsible for getting and paying for their travel to the hotel or venue. At the very least, you should research local transportation options and provide this information in your meeting materials.

Start with the hotel and ask how they transport their guests to and from the property. They may have a dedicated shuttle service. If so, you could negotiate in your original hotel contract to have this service provided free or at a reduced cost. If there is a charge, ask if they can add the cost directly to the individual's hotel bill.

Food for Thought

Flights get delayed and things happen. Whenever possible, get a cell phone number for your VIP, executive, or speaker and give it to the meet and greet company so it can contact the passenger if he or she doesn't connect.

Whatever arrangements you work out with the hotel, make sure you inform the attendees in advance so they know what to expect. Conference centers often provide their own transportation, at no cost or minimal cost.

If the property does not have its own airport transportation, it should have recommendations on local shuttle or limo services. Call these vendors and a few others, if possible, to compare costs and services.

Don't Drop the Ball

Make sure you provide your attendees with the hours of operation of all selected ground transportation companies. You don't want attendees arriving at midnight thinking they can just hop on the shuttle.

The Inside Scoop

Nothing changes more than travel schedules—either by choice or by fate. If you are responsible for coordinating travel for your attendees, be prepared for a lot of changes and wrong information. Really good transportation companies know this, too. Find one that is flexible and that works with you when things don't go as planned.

Here are some of the questions you need to ask:

➤ How long have you been in business?

➤ How many vehicles do you own?

➤ What kind of vehicles are they?

➤ What is their condition? Their age? When did they last pass inspection?

➤ What is the cost? Are there discounts for groups?

➤ Do children ride free? Are they discounted? Are child-safety seats required in vans or cars? What is the cost?

➤ What are your hours of operation?

➤ Can the drivers be contacted at all times? Are they full or part time? Do they wear uniforms?

➤ What is the company's safety record?

➤ What are your emergency procedures, and how are drivers trained?

➤ Are the drivers trained in CPR? Are they required to take drug and alcohol tests?

➤ Is there a contact available to us 24 hours a day? At what number?

➤ How far is it to the airport? How long does it take in rush and nonrush hour?

➤ Do you make other stops or is this door-to-door service?

➤ Are reservations required? Is the service paid for in advance?

➤ When do return reservations need to be made?

➤ What is your insurance coverage?

➤ Are backup vehicles available for overflow or breakdowns?

➤ How does an individual locate the transportation?

Also, it's a good idea to provide alternate transportation, including taxicab information (phone numbers and estimated costs), for people who will arrive late or may get delayed.

If your meeting is one in which the meeting host pays for all of the attendees' travel costs, such as for a corporate or incentive meeting, you still need to do the same research and ask the same questions. The difference is that you are contracting directly with transportation providers, so you can expect dedicated, even customized service to meet your needs.

Also influencing transportation decisions are some circumstances beyond your control such as labor strikes, weather, traffic jams, road construction, and traffic accidents. Therefore, when making decisions about transportation, prepare for these occurrences. They impact your choices of transportation and the providers.

Remember that you are researching ground transportation companies on behalf of your attendees, and it's important to check out the company's reputation. You don't want your attendees riding in dirty, run-down vehicles or being driven by rude drivers—what a horrible first impression of your meeting. Ask around or use the companies yourself so you know.

Driving Directions

Some attendees will decide to rent a car at the airport or drive from their home. You will need to obtain and provide complete, accurate driving directions to the property.

You need to consider from which direction people will be coming and also provide directions from the airport. You can easily get this information from the property. They will most likely have prewritten directions and maps available. Some properties will have this information on their Web site. Simply provide a link from your meeting Web site to theirs!

If possible, make sure the directions have road numbers/names and ramp exit numbers. Add how many miles from point A to point B and estimate driving times. This is very helpful, especially to people who are unfamiliar with the area.

As your meeting date approaches, research potential driving obstacles such as road closures, construction, or weather-related problems like snow or ice. The concierge, bell captain, or CVB will know about these obstacles. You can inform attendees via your Web site or do an e-mail blast. It can save them considerable time and prevent frustration.

Food for Thought

Remember to give attendees info on parking costs. It can be expensive, especially in big cities. They may decide to take alternative transportation or share a ride instead.

Food for Thought

Provide distance information in both English and metric units for the benefit of your foreign attendees. Go to www.worldwidemetric.com/metcal.htm for online calculators!

Moving the Masses

Okay, everyone has arrived. They are happily attending sessions, eating great food, and networking away, but now you want to take them to an offsite location for a big shindig. You need to hire motor coaches. Where do you start?

Know the answers to the following questions because any motor coach or ground transportation company will ask:

1. How far away (and where) is the offsite location?

2. When do they need to arrive/depart that venue?

3. How many people are being transported?

4. Is it a single trip or a continuous loop?

5. Is there nearby parking for the vehicle? Where can buses be staged?

6. When should the vehicles arrive for pickup?

7. Where (specific location) will the vehicles pick up and drop off passengers at both ends?

8. Do they all need to arrive/depart at the same time?

You will also need to ask the same questions about operations procedures and drivers that you asked the ground transportation companies earlier in this chapter.

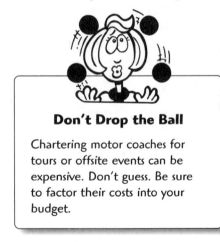

Don't Drop the Ball

Chartering motor coaches for tours or offsite events can be expensive. Don't guess. Be sure to factor their costs into your budget.

Motor coaches and buses come in a variety of sizes (number of passenger seats). Most have luggage storage and restrooms, public address systems and air-conditioning; many have TVs and VCRs. Because demand is high and gas and maintenance costs continue to increase, don't be surprised to find a four- or five-hour minimum rental or fuel surcharge. They will ask you to sign a contract and make a deposit. Read it carefully and make sure you understand it, especially the liability issues.

You can also rent school buses for some events. These are cheaper but are limited in availability during school hours. Sometimes a school bus is the perfect way to transport your attendees!

Here are some other things to consider:

➤ Can attendees leave belongings on the motor coach?

➤ Will the motor coaches be accessible but secured during the event?

➤ Will you feed the drivers or are they on their own?

➤ Will you or the company provide signage for the front of the vehicle?

➤ Will you or the company provide detailed driving directions?

➤ Will you need a guide? Will you or the company provide the guide?

You may have a situation in which you need to transport attendees to different locations simultaneously, such as for site tours. Pay special attention to direct people to the right motor coach (consider using tickets and/or tour hosts), and once people are on the bus, reconfirm the destination. Also give the drivers accurate directions and depart promptly.

It is a good idea to verify that the driver knows the right directions. Be prepared to provide another copy of the map and directions, and review any detours or route changes.

Food for Thought

Try to provide your own signage for each motor coach. You then have control over size, color, spelling, and readability.

City-Wides

A *city-wide* refers to a meeting that is sooooooooo large that it cannot be contained in one hotel. City-wides usually use convention centers, and attendees stay at two or more hotels throughout the city. The challenge is to provide transportation for your attendees throughout the meeting so that they can get from their hotels to the convention center or other venues and back, quickly and easily.

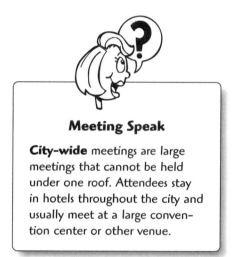

Meeting Speak

City-wide meetings are large meetings that cannot be held under one roof. Attendees stay in hotels throughout the city and usually meet at a large convention center or other venue.

For city-wides, motor coaches will need to run on a continuous loop schedule. Usage will be heavier in the morning before your meeting begins and when your meeting is over each day. You may even decide not to run them in the middle of the meeting when you expect passenger counts to be low.

Another way to provide continuous service is to provide it on-demand. That is, instead of running buses on a fixed schedule, always have a bus at each hotel and at the convention center or other venues. As it gets reasonably full, it can depart and another bus will take its place. This may not save you any money, but it will decrease the number of almost-empty buses traveling the city streets. Ask the company providing the motor coaches to help you with a schedule and to assist in determining how may coaches you need. They know their business best!

The Least You Need to Know

➤ Meet and greet makes a nice first impression and makes it easier for attendees and VIPs to get to their hotels.

➤ Prior to the meeting, provide attendees with accurate information for all ground transportation options.

➤ Work with the airlines to negotiate discounted fares for your attendees.

➤ In your ground transportation plans, factor in alternative solutions in case of bad weather, traffic jams, road construction, or traffic accidents.

Chapter 19

You Gotta Feed 'Em, Too

In This Chapter

➤ Test your food-and-beverage-planning knowledge

➤ Learn some basic rules to apply to any meal-planning process

➤ Discover food and beverage tricks of the trade

➤ Understand banquet event orders (BEOs)

There are a lot of things to know about food-and-beverage (F&B) planning. Of course, the catering manager at the meeting facility will assist you in this process. However, it helps to have a basic understanding so you know what questions to ask and how to get the biggest bang for your buck.

In this chapter, we will tell you about planning breakfasts, lunches, dinners, breaks, and receptions. You will also learn some neat tricks of the trade and a bit about negotiating. Finally, it's down to the paperwork, finalizing your meal plans and determining how many to guarantee. Get ready, get set, go!

Pop Quiz

Do you like to entertain? Do you think it is easy to plan meals for hundreds of people? What exactly do you need to know? Before we get started, let's take a short quiz on the subject of food-and-beverage planning.

1. How many cups of coffee are in a gallon?

   a. 20

   b. 8

   c. 13

   d. 25

2. Who pays for the beverages at a cash bar?

   a. Attendees

   b. Meeting host

   c. Meeting facility

   d. Bartender

3. Who pays for the beverages at a host bar?

   a. Meeting facility

   b. Meeting host

   c. Attendees

   d. Bartender

4. A guarantee is …

   a. The number of people the meeting sponsor tells the meeting facility to prepare for.

   b. The service promise from a meeting facility.

   c. The total number of people registered for your meeting.

   d. A promise from the chef that the food will be good.

5. At most facilities, how many additional people will the facility prepare to serve over your guarantee?

   a. 10 to 15 percent more than the guarantee

   b. 0 to 5 percent more than the guarantee

   c. 8 percent more then the guarantee

   d. 15 to 20 percent more than the guarantee

6. How are you billed for a meal function?

   a. The number you guaranteed

   b. Your guarantee or actual served—whatever is greater

   c. Your guarantee or actual served—whatever is less

   d. The total registered for your meeting

7. A buffet is usually more expensive on a per-person basis than a plated meal.

   a. True

   b. False

8. On average, how many bartenders should be scheduled for a reception?

    a. 1 bartender for every 75 to 100 people

    b. 1 bartender for every 25 to 50 people

    c. 1 bartender for every 150 to 175 people

    d. 1 bartender for every 125 to 150 people

9. On consumption for bottled beverages or packaged foods means …

    a. You pay for only what you open.

    b. You pay for what you order.

    c. You pay for what was opened plus 10 percent.

    d. You must consume all the food and beverage you order.

10. On average, how many servers should be scheduled for a plated meal function?

    a. 1 server for every 20 to 25 people

    b. 1 server for every 15 to 20 people

    c. 1 server for every 25 to 30 people

    d. 1 server for every 10 to 15 people

Answers:

    1. a, **2.** a, **3.** b, **4.** a, **5.** b, **6.** b, **7.** a, **8.** a, **9.** a, **10.** a

If you answered …

8 to 10 correct	Congratulations! You are ahead of the game!
5 to 7 correct	Read this chapter twice.
4 or fewer correct	Read this chapter three times.
0 correct	Hire a professional meeting planner.

A Few Rules to Get You Started

See what we mean? Planning, serving, and managing meals for the multitudes can be a real eye-opening experience. It is very different from large or small, personal gatherings. Let's start with a few guidelines about this process.

1. **You don't have to order off the menu.** Ask the catering manager to ask the chef for other ideas and make special requests when needed.

2. **Plan for the taste of the majority, not yourself.** Consider your audience. Age, nationality, religion, and special meal circumstances are considerations in your F&B selections. Just because *you* don't like mushroom-stuffed chicken breasts and tiramisu doesn't mean you shouldn't serve it.

Don't Drop the Ball

Evaluate whether to order quantity or per person. Quantity means specifying exact quantities of food versus per-person packages. Sometimes it is less expensive to order your morning coffee and continental breakfast foods by the gallon and dozen.

3. **Always order "on consumption" when possible.** If you order 350 sodas for the morning break and only use (consume) 325, then you only pay for 325. If you don't do this, some facilities will charge you for 350. They will then resell the other 25 cans to another group or maybe back to you! This applies to bottled beverages and prepackaged food items such as granola bars and bags of chips.

4. **Commit to high-quality, healthy food.** Ask the facility what food items are in season and how to keep the menus healthy.

5. **For large, important meal functions, do a tasting.** Most facilities will allow you to taste the potential meal selections in advance. If you can't decide between two or three dishes, ask for a tasting.

6. **Understand the food and beverage policies.** Most facilities will charge you a fee to bring in your own food and beverage or will flat out disallow it. Obviously, they are in business to sell you the items, but is there anything you are allowed to bring in? Sometimes organizations will put their logo on prepackaged food and beverages and will want to distribute these items to attendees. Try to negotiate this if possible. It can amount to considerable savings.

7. **Use leftover food not purchased on consumption for the next break.** Items like breakfast breads can be retrayed and put out at the mid-morning break. You also could have them delivered to the staff office or donated to a local shelter or food kitchen.

8. **Ask how many servers and bartenders will be assigned to your functions.** Service levels vary at every facility and knowing how many dedicated servers and bartenders you have will give you an indication of what to expect from the facility.

9. **Carefully consider the appropriate type of service for a meal.** Need a quick lunch? Maybe a box lunch is the answer. Need people to mingle? Try a buffet. Use a variety of service methods. If you have a buffet, use double-sided buffets whenever possible and have at least one double-sided buffet line for every 75 to 100 people.

10. **Use decorative props and themes for breaks and meals.** Ask the hotel what props and decorations it has in inventory. Try to negotiate them into your facility contract at no charge. You can also rent props from companies specializing in themed events. Local DMCs, CVBs, and your facility contact can provide the resources.

Before we take a look at all the various meal functions, you need to know that all meeting facilities have banquet menus available to you for planning purposes. You will have the option of selecting plated meals, buffets, break packages, and à la carte items. These are either sold at a per person price, by the dozen, gallon, or piece. All prices are then subject to applicable service charge/gratuity and taxes. Find out the tax and service charge or gratuity percentages and factor them into your budget. On average, they are 20 to 30 percent of the total food and beverage bill.

At conference centers, you pay a per person price called a complete meeting package or CMP. This price includes three meals a day, refreshment breaks, basic A/V equipment, and other items associated with a meeting. Having a meeting at a conference center takes the guess work out of food and beverage planning! Check out www.iacconline.com to learn about other benefits of using conference centers.

You should always obtain a copy of the menus at the beginning of the booking process so you can take a look at the prices, creativity, and food options. Along with the menus, many facilities have catering policies and a general information sheet. These will explain the specific food and beverage policies at that facility. These might include when your menu selections and guarantees are due, table linen choices, floral arrangements, ice carvings, coat checks, extra labor charges, liquor liability issues, liability statements, and so on.

Finally, when you book a meeting at a facility, try to negotiate firm menu prices. Most facilities will guarantee food and beverage prices six to nine months in advance of the functions. You can ask them to guarantee current menu prices at the time of booking or at least get a firm date on when your prices are guaranteed.

Breakfast

Breakfast is important. Your attendees are hungry in the morning and, at the very least, will be looking for coffee, tea, or soda. It depends on the location and attendee profile, but as a general rule, order 65 percent hot and 35 percent cold beverages in the morning. The reverse is true in the afternoon. For coffee, the rule of thumb is 70 percent regular and 30 percent decaffeinated. Offer hot tea, too. And be sure to have regular, diet, and caffeine-free sodas.

For breakfast, you have several choices. From the catering menu, you can order a sit-down, plated meal; a full breakfast buffet; or a continental breakfast. Your agenda and your audience determine which you select. An awards breakfast is the perfect candidate for a sit-down, plated breakfast. A full breakfast buffet presents more food options and covers a wide variety

Food for Thought

Offer fruit for breakfast. A lot of less expensive continental breakfasts do not include it. Usually there is an additional per-person charge to add it, but most people will appreciate it.

of tastes. A continental breakfast is good when you are not presenting a program, and the attendees will be arriving at various times.

Another option is to create your own breakfast buffet. Take a look at the *à la carte* prices. Does it make sense to start with the less expensive continental breakfast and add yogurt, fruit, and French toast? Or, would it be more economical to order in quantity: breakfast breads by the dozen, fruit by the platter or person, whole fruit by the piece, and beverages by the gallon? Then you could add an omelet bar (fresh omelets cooked to order). Determine what you want and play with the menus. Ask the catering manager for recommendations on how to package your desired result.

Meeting Speak

The term **à la carte** means each item is priced and sold individually on the menu.

The Inside Scoop

If you order on a per-person basis, the facility is responsible for providing enough food to feed your guaranteed number. If you order in quantity (by the gallon, dozen, or piece), the facility is only responsible for the amount you order. The pressure is on you to order the right amount of food.

Breaks

Have fun with your breaks. The breaks can be a source of motivation and fun for your attendees. Some meeting facilities have created some really creative and cool breaks. Obviously, it depends on your budget (breaks can get pricey!), but no matter how much you can spend, be creative. Tie in your meeting theme or a theme that relates to the location, the season, or a regional sports team. Offer a combination of sweet, salty, and nutritious to please everyone. Or, mix your offerings up over several days. Here are some ideas to ponder:

➤ Ice cream bars (if the facility has the capability to keep them frozen during the break)

➤ Popcorn served from a popcorn cart

➤ Fruit smoothies (yummy!)

➤ Small bags of trail mix/sunflower seeds

➤ Candy bars

➤ Whole fruit

➤ Granola bars

➤ Pizza

➤ A sports theme (popcorn, peanuts, and caramel corn)

You'll want to offer beverages in addition to food items. The standard coffee, tea, and soda are fine, but also consider fresh lemonade, fruit punch, or other specialty beverages. Offering items other than the standard fare adds variety and is a refreshing change for attendees.

Don't be afraid to ask the hotel to create special breaks just for your group, or to alter the location to liven things up. Can you have the break outside on a terrace or poolside?

Lunch

No matter what meals you are planning, take a look at all of them together to make sure you are using a variety of serving methods and the same food is not served twice. Lunch is a great opportunity to take a trip off the beaten path.

Offer a box lunch, serve pizza, give them an hour off on their own, or serve lunch in a section of the restaurant or another nonmeeting room location. If you give them lunch on their own, offer suggestions for where to get lunch. See if the hotel will offer your attendees a discount if they eat in one of the onsite restaurants. Most hotels will comply and appreciate your effort to keep them in the facility.

Dinner

Dinner can be very extravagant or very simple. The goals, objectives, theme, timeframe, and purpose for the dinner will set the tone. It can be as simple as a backyard, poolside BBQ or as elaborate as a steak and lobster plated dinner with wine service. Before you decide, look at the menus. If there is something you want but don't see, talk to the chef.

For special dinners, consider decorating the room. Centerpieces, chair covers, special table linens, and props can make the difference between a plain setting and an experience.

Don't Drop the Ball

Whenever possible, have food such as donuts, Danishes, breakfast breads, and brownies cut into bite-size pieces or ask for mini versions of each. There is less waste, and attendees can try a variety of items.

The Inside Scoop

A conference we help plan for 1,000 people offers two options for lunch: a box lunch in the exhibit hall or a deli buffet in a roundtable discussion format. Attendees can purchase tickets for either, and both options are very popular!

End your dinners with a gourmet coffee station. This is a great way to end the evening, and it fosters networking. Along with this, instead of serving dessert at the table after dinner, offer a sweets table near the coffee station. Have a small assortment of sweets and chocolates available to satisfy people's sweet tooth. Attendees love this one! (Don't forget noncoffee drinkers!)

Receptions

Receptions are great because attendees can relax and get to know people better, or receptions can *be* the dinner. If you hold a reception in a famous museum, you may want the attendees to mingle and network the entire evening.

Don't Drop the Ball

Work with the catering manager to make sure you have enough food. The start time, length of reception, and number of people all need to be taken into consideration to order the right amount.

Your menu is determined by the length and timing of the reception, your budget, and whether it is followed by dinner. When the reception is the dinner, serve heavy hors d'oeuvres. Items to consider: pasta bars, mashed potato bars with all the toppings, and carving stations. A carving station features a chef slicing some sort of meat such as beef, ham, or turkey with rolls and condiments available. These types of items fill people up, and you look like you're going all out. Then you can add a variety of hors d'oeuvres including fruit and cheese.

Receptions held right before dinner should have a lighter menu. As a general rule of thumb, six to eight pieces of food (hors d'oeuvres) per person per hour are adequate. If you offer a heartier option such as a carving station or a pasta bar, you can get by with fewer pieces per person.

If you order on a per-person basis, your guarantee will dictate the amount of food prepared. The facility is then responsible for making sure there is enough food. A per-person price will be for an agreed upon timeframe (for example, 1, 2, or 3 hours). If you order by quantity, the facility prepares only the specific amount of food you requested, so order carefully or you may run out.

You will have several options for the bar setup. The number one question is who pays for the drinks? The options are as follows:

➤ **Host bar.** The meeting sponsor pays for the drinks, either by the drink, per person per hour, or per bottle.

➤ **Cash bar.** Attendees pay for their own drinks.

➤ **Cash bar with tickets.** Attendees get a specified number of free drink tickets (paid for by the meeting host), and then pay cash for additional drinks. You determine how many free tickets.

The most common way to pay for beverages at a host bar is per person per hour or by the drink. You will designate either house, name, or premium brands and the attendees can order from that selection. Have sodas, water, and juices available too. For bottle sales, make sure you obtain the beginning and ending inventory, which will tell you the precise brands and amount consumed.

Ask for a complete report on bar sales for your food and beverage pick-up report. This is great information to have when planning future functions.

Keep in mind each state has different laws regarding the sale and distribution of alcohol. Ask about local laws and facility policies and regulations that could affect your functions.

For a cash bar, the attendee either pays the bartender directly or buys tickets from the cashier to give to the bartender. Ask about the additional cost of the bartenders and cashiers. It is standard to be quoted a flat or hourly fee for each bartender unless each bar achieves a predetermined amount of sales. This is negotiable, so ask about it. You need one bartender for every 75 to 100 people, so it is important to know what you are paying for. Cashiers are also charged on a flat or hourly fee basis. These charges often add up and can be a surprise on the master bill!

Food for Thought

When you have a cash bar, you should also provide complimentary soft drinks, juices, and bottled water. It is a nice gesture, and it limits your organization's liability.

Tricks of the Trade

Planning food and beverage gets easier as you learn the ropes. Here are some tricks of the trade to give you a boost:

➤ **What's best—buffet or a plated meal?** A buffet is great for networking and for offering multiple entrée options. Attendees also do not get stuck at one table the entire night with the same people. Buffets are usually more expensive because more food needs to be put out and more options are offered.

➤ **Carefully watch your food functions.** What do the attendees like? What don't they like? Do you have enough food? What works well with other groups? Ask the waitstaff, bartenders, and catering manager. Write this information down for your next meeting.

Food for Thought

Have the facility preset salad and dessert on the table if you are on a tight schedule. Select items that hold well until they are eaten. Desserts can be used as centerpieces.

➤ **Is a minimum number of people required for a specific meal?** If you don't qualify, ask if you can combine with another in-house group to meet the requirement.

➤ **Ask the catering manager to have all the food on a buffet labeled.** If it fits into the theme, create unique names that still describe the food.

193

➤ **Have a special dinner or reception offsite.** Select a museum or other unique venue, and work with either the facility catering office or another catering company.

➤ **Find out if the facility has standard centerpieces available to use.** Add votive candles or some flowers to embellish them. If you use floral centerpieces, ask the florist to create them to be reused for another function. Some florists will even come back the next day to make them look different. Don't forget to ask the facility to store them overnight in the cooler. And never have them so tall that you can't see across the table.

➤ **Always use double-sided buffets when possible.** Ask and double-check—do not assume the facility will do this.

➤ **Guarantees are due to the facility 48 to 72 hours prior to each meal function.** If you aren't sure how many to guarantee, err on the low end. You can sometimes raise them and often the overset will be increase enough.

➤ **Ask the facility to place reserved table signs if needed.** Specify which tables on your diagram. (See how handy a diagram is?)

➤ **If you are using a ticket system for meals, don't assume the hotel will collect them for you.** This detail, like all others, needs to be discussed in advance. Don't wait until the hungry herd is stampeding your event!

➤ **Ask for a fancy napkin fold.** This can jazz up your table setting.

➤ **If you do not have entertainment, ask if music can be piped into the room.** Sometimes you may have to pay for a CD player, but this is much cheaper than live entertainment!

Banquet Event Orders

Now it is time to create the *banquet event orders* (BEOs) or *banquet prospectuses* (BPs). A BEO or BP outlines the details of all the food and beverage functions. It includes start/stop times, the number of people, the menu, audio-visual equipment, bar setups, and other things pertinent to the meals. This is the document the catering department uses to prepare and serve the meals. The catering manager prepares this document.

You may also be asked to spend a *food and beverage minimum*. Based on your total meeting specifications, you may have to agree to pay for a minimum amount of food and beverage. This is negotiable and agreed to during the contract phase; pay attention to the fine print!

Banquet event orders are not just for meal functions. Many hotels use BEOs as documents to outline all of a group's meeting functions. These are also called function sheets. They list the times, the number of people expected, room set, audio-visual equipment, and any special information. The reason for doing this is that each facility must have a single format that all staff members understand. Usually, a BEO will be prepared for each unique event, even if nothing changes except the date. That means you could easily have dozens upon dozens of BEOs or function sheets for your meeting.

Review each BEO carefully because this is the document or work order from which the facility gets its instructions. With so many different eyes looking at them, you must be sure your instructions are clearly stated. It's very important to double-check each BEO, especially as it is updated.

Guarantees

Here is where knowing your group, and paying attention to other factors such as outside activities and timing really come in handy. A *guarantee* is the number of people you tell the meeting facility to prepare for. You will need to provide a guarantee for every meal function as well as how many people to set for in each meeting room.

Let's say you have 200 people registered for your meeting. It is highly unlikely that all 200 people will show up for each meal. As a general rule, you never guarantee the exact number of registrants. This is one of the reasons you need to track your history and know the facility's overset percentage. Your meeting history sheet should include the number of registrants, guarantees, and the actual served for each meal. Continental breakfasts are definitely a prime candidate for subtracting some people from your attendee count. Some people will come down at the posted time, and others will skip it entirely.

Meeting Speak

A **food and beverage minimum** is an amount you must spend for food and beverage, not including taxes, gratuities, or service charges. If you spend below the amount, you pay the difference between the minimum and the actual amount spent.

Meeting Speak

A **guarantee** is the final number of people you expect for a meal function. You either pay for the guaranteed number or the number of people served, whichever is greater.

Giving the facility an accurate count is necessary to make sure enough food is prepared. Many facilities will prepare some percentage over your guarantee. In other words, if you guarantee 100 people, and the overset is 5 percent, they will set for and be prepared to serve 105. If 120 show up, most likely there will not be enough seats or food. What happens in this case? The facility scrambles to bring in tables and chairs, and the chef prepares more food. Everyone looks disorganized and unprepared—including you. And these people will have to eat late.

If you order by quantity, then the guarantee is the quantity you ordered. How do you order in quantity? You need to consider three things when ordering this way: the attendees' appetites, the weather, and the food items. Make sure you have enough beverages and food items for all attendees and know what the facility can quickly replenish if you are running low. Make sure the BEO gives specific instructions about replenishing. Does the facility need to get your approval? Make sure to ask for the catering manager's input if you order by quantity.

Service and Presentation

One detail you shouldn't overlook is the timing of a meal. Always have the facility ready to go at least 15 minutes prior to the start of a food function. If there is a program, create a script with the start and stop times of every speaker.

Don't Drop the Ball

Don't forget to make sure the BEOs state when the doors can open for seating. You do not want your attendees entering a room where a speaker is rehearsing and the waitstaff is setting tables.

Include the time when the servers should leave the room and when it is okay for them to clear tables. Include the catering manager in this part of the scripting—he or she will know how much time is needed for serving and clearing.

Have the facility prepare floor diagrams of all your meal functions. This makes it easier for the meeting facility's staff to set the room to your specifications.

Also make sure your BEO states the number of bartenders and servers assigned to your function. As a general rule, you should have one server for every 20 to 25 people for a sit-down meal, one bartender for every 75 to 100 people, one cocktail server for every 50 people, and one double-sided buffet line for every 75 to 100 people. If your sit-down meal includes wine service, 16 to 20 people per server is the norm.

Special Needs

Make sure your registration forms include a place to state specific food requirements. Some people have dietary restrictions, some want vegetarian meals, and some are just plain picky! Make sure to include these meals in your guarantee. Have food labeled when you can to alleviate any problems. Be flexible and accommodating, and everyone will walk away happy.

The Least You Need to Know

➤ Don't automatically select the per-person meal packages. Evaluate your food and beverage order based on à la carte prices for comparison.

➤ You don't always have to order off the menus. Talk to the catering manager and chef.

➤ Consider having heavy hors d'oeuvre receptions instead of sit-down dinners. This creates a better networking atmosphere.

➤ Check and double-check your BEOs for accuracy.

➤ Carefully track your meeting history so you can fine-tune your meal guarantees.

Seeing Is Believing

In This Chapter

➤ See what audio-visual is really about

➤ Discover overlooked audio-visual costs

➤ Learn what to ask the in-house audio-visual provider

➤ Learn when to hire outside audio-visual and/or production companies

---

In the old days of meeting planning (just a few years ago), audio-visual (known as A/V) consisted mostly of a microphone or two, an overhead projector and screen, and maybe a 35mm slide projector. But as with everything, technology advances are changing A/V and thus are changing the way we communicate with our attendees. Today, computer-generated slide shows are standard, and attendees are wowed with giant screens, live video feeds, and high-tech laser light extravaganzas. It can be quite a show with quite a budget!

Because A/V is complex, this chapter is not an A/V technical primer. We do not discuss all the different types of equipment, formulas, or laws of physics; that's for trained A/V professionals. Instead, we provide a basic overview of A/V rental considerations and support issues. You will soon have enough knowledge to speak intelligently with A/V professionals to make your next meeting's A/V rental order a breeze.

What Is A/V Anyway?

Did you know that A/V is more than just equipment? It's labor, power, and a plethora of items. When preparing your budget, factor in the following costs as they apply to your meeting:

➤ Audience response systems

➤ Audio, CD, and video duplication

➤ Bulletin boards

➤ Carts and projection stands

➤ Computers, monitors, and printers

➤ Easels for signs or flipcharts

➤ Extension cords

➤ Fax machines

➤ Flip charts

➤ Labor (technical support, setup, riggers)

➤ Lasers

➤ Laser pointers

➤ Lighting

➤ Microphones (and associated equipment)

➤ Power

➤ Power strips

➤ Radios and walkie-talkies

➤ Recording equipment

➤ Screens

➤ Staging (pipe and drape, risers, stages, and so on)

➤ Video equipment (TVs, VCRs, projectors, cameras, and so on)

Most meeting facilities either own their own equipment or have a separate A/V equipment rental company onsite. Before finalizing a facility contract, you should obtain an A/V price list (including labor) and find answers to the following questions:

➤ Who provides the A/V equipment? The meeting facility or an onsite company?

➤ If it is an onsite company, are you required to use that company? If you don't, are there any additional "usage" fees?

➤ Can the onsite company provide the level of service and skilled labor to manage your general sessions?

➤ Can you bring in your own equipment regardless of who provides the A/V?

➤ What is added to each rental item? Percentages for labor, service charges, gratuity, taxes? Ask how to calculate the total.

➤ For larger stage productions, what are the labor fees? Is union labor required?

For most small meetings, you will only need limited A/V equipment such as overhead, data, or video projectors, screens, microphones, and flip charts. A large show or general session might include, for example, computerized game shows, big-screen video teleconferences over satellite links, entertainers flying on the stage from above, fireworks, smoke, mirrors, you name it. If your budget allows for some big-time fun, you'll need to work with a full-service A/V production company. We'll discuss this in a bit.

The Inside Scoop

If you need labor at odd hours, weekends, or holidays, prepare to pay higher hourly rates. If possible, plan to have your setup and teardown during regular hours.

A/V equipment is usually rented by the day for a flat rental fee for each piece of equipment. The rental fee includes setup and testing. As your meeting gets bigger and more involved, however, you should hire dedicated technical support to monitor your A/V in one or more rooms. The A/V provider charges an hourly rate for this and will give you an estimate of the amount of time necessary. In addition to the hourly fee, there is usually a service charge and tax. For meetings with a lot of A/V, labor can be a significant expense. You may also need to hire labor to set up and tear down your staging. This labor includes carpenters, electricians, and riggers. Also check into union rules and regulations at the venue. Be sure to ask if union labor is included or is in addition to your A/V quotes.

Know What You Need

Every meeting has a message to communicate. Meetings are an excellent educational tool, but only if they are designed and produced with the organization's goals and objectives in mind.

When you work with an A/V provider early in the planning stage, you will accomplish two things: You increase your A/V knowledge, and you identify and include all of the A/V costs in your budget. By now, you probably realize that A/V can be a considerable chunk of change.

If at all possible, walk through your meeting venue with the A/V provider and a representative from the venue well in advance of your meeting. Look

Food for Thought

If you have a general session and breakouts, consider using your general session room as one of your breakout rooms. This will save you money on A/V costs for one breakout!

at ceiling height and the location of pillars, doors, chandeliers, windows, and mirrors. Look at the in-house lighting and listen to the sound system. Discuss the room set, both style and number of people. Make sure any room diagrams include your stage and other A/V equipment that uses space.

One thing you should do to determine your A/V needs is ask your speakers what they need. The breakout speaker form in Appendix A, "Sample Forms and Checklists," includes a place to indicate A/V needs. For speakers, A/V needs should be part of the contract agreed to by both parties in advance.

Determine which speakers have similar A/V needs. Try to schedule them so they speak on the same day and/or in the same room. Your goal is to reduce the volume of A/V equipment by consolidating speakers with like needs in one location. Be sure to reconfirm all A/V with each speaker in writing a few weeks prior to his or her presentation.

Don't Drop the Ball

If you own some A/V equipment, consider bringing it with you. You will save money. The disadvantage is you do not get technical support if something doesn't work. Make sure the facility can supply you with a backup if something goes wrong; otherwise, don't do it. You are responsible for keeping tabs on your own equipment.

You can also determine a "standard set" for your breakout rooms. For example, on your speaker contract or form, tell your speakers that each room will have a standard set including an overhead projector, screen, laser pointer, wired lavaliere microphone, and flip chart. Your form can then ask the speakers for additional equipment needs such as LCD projectors, VCRs, 35mm slide projectors, telephone lines, and so on.

Once you have decided on your A/V needs, make sure you get a written quote for every item. Don't assume that easels, carts, extension cords, and so on, are free. If you have a lot of A/V, you should get competitive bids from outside A/V companies. You might find better rates elsewhere, and the competition might motivate the in-house A/V provider to reduce its rates.

In most cases, your best bet is to use the onsite provider because it has the inventory onsite and knows the facility well.

The Visual Basics

Most people are visual learners, so most speakers use visual tools. These are the most common (visual) items that most meeting rooms use:

➤ Flip chart
➤ LCD or data projector

➤ Overhead projector

➤ Screen

➤ VCR and monitor

More and more speakers are moving from the overhead projector to the LCD (liquid crystal display) projector. The LCD projector is used to display computer presentations on a screen. The major consideration here is cost. They are very expensive. The higher the projector's resolution and *lumens,* the higher the cost.

Naturally, most speakers will want the best projection system, but depending on the meeting room's size and the number of attendees, you may be able to use projectors with lower resolution and intensity and spend less. When deciding on the type of LCD projector to use, consult your A/V provider. Make sure to inquire about the various projectors and what is best for your specific needs.

Screen type and size are always considerations. You want to make sure that all attendees can see the screen(s), especially from the far sides and the very back. Also consider projection image quality. It may impact the type of screen(s) you use. In some cases, meeting rooms have screens that pull down from the ceiling. If so, set the room so they can be used instead of renting another one.

Meeting Speak

Merriam-Webster's Collegiate Dictionary defines **lumen** as "a unit of luminous flux equal to the light emitted in a unit of solid angle by a uniform point source of one candle intensity." Yeah, we knew that ....

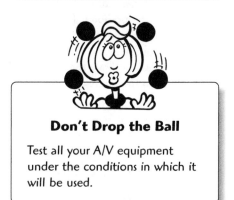

Don't Drop the Ball

Test all your A/V equipment under the conditions in which it will be used.

For large general sessions, you need to decide whether you are using front- or rear-screen projection. Front-screen projection means the image is projected onto a screen from the front of the room, usually within or behind the audience. The screens can be placed in front close to the wall. This is less expensive and takes less space.

Rear-screen projection means the image is projected from behind the screen. The advantage of rear over front projection is that, with rear projection, there are no visible projectors, cords, wires, and so on. They are all behind the screens and stage. Rear projection also tolerates a wider range of light reduction in the room. The downside is that it takes up significant space behind the stage/screen. In most cases, the screens will be placed 25 to 30 feet from the wall. You need to drape the stage/screen, and you may require special equipment.

The bottom line is this: Rear projection looks very professional, but is usually a costlier way to go and can be a "space-hog." The decision to use front- or rear-screen projection should be made when booking the meeting because space is an important consideration. With both front- and rear-screen projection, you will incur labor fees to run the projectors, keep the speakers on track, and in general, manage the flow of the show.

Food for Thought

Have a sign made with your conference or organization logo to attach to the podiums. This covers the facility's logo and customizes your meeting. For large general sessions, have the same logo up on the screen(s) before and after the sessions.

Meeting Speak

A **lavaliere** microphone is a small microphone that can be attached to clothing, allowing the speaker's hands to be free.

Other visual devices typically used in meeting rooms are VCRs and, to a lesser extent, 35mm projectors. Considerations here are the size of the room and the number of attendees. Consult with your A/V provider to determine whether you need additional screens or monitors. Remember that every itty-bitty piece of equipment costs money.

The Audio Basics

Your venue will most likely have its own in-house sound system. What you want to do is patch into that system. Although this is relatively easy to do, be aware that there are a host of sound problems that can surface. Humming, feedback, squeaking, or just plain bad sound can happen. The A/V technical staff can solve these problems, and this is a good reason to have dedicated A/V personnel.

If you have a very important session or sessions, you should consider adding an additional sound system to either supplement or replace the in-house system. Naturally, this adds to the cost, but you have more control over the quality.

Every speaker needs a microphone (mic) unless it is a very small meeting. Here are your options:

➤ Handheld mic (wired or wireless)

➤ *Lavaliere* mic (wired or wireless)

➤ Lectern or podium mic

➤ Multidirectional mic

➤ Standing or floor mic

➤ Table mic

Your selection of microphones will depend on the type of presentation, your budget, and the speakers' preference. A formal presentation on a stage to a large audience usually dictates a microphone on a podium or a wireless lavaliere. An emcee may use a wireless, handheld mic. Speakers for smaller presentations and breakouts may prefer wireless or hardwired (with long cords) lavaliere mics, especially if they need to handle slides, transparencies, or other materials. You should ask speakers for their preferences, especially for general sessions and keynotes. For panel discussions in which the presenters are seated at a head table, consider using one table mic for every two people.

Don't Drop the Ball

As you increase the number of mics in a room, you will need to have sound mixers. Be sure to budget for this.

When selecting handheld or lavaliere mics, it is preferable to use wireless. The wired types (a cable leads from the mic to the sound system) are cumbersome and have a limited range due to the cable length. Naturally, the wireless mics cost more. If you don't have the budget for wireless mics for each speaker, at least provide wireless for your main speaker(s) if appropriate.

Audiotaping

An option for your meeting is to provide an audiotape or CD of each session for purchase. There are companies that specialize in onsite recording and duplication. The process goes like this: The recording company, contracted by the meeting host, provides the labor, equipment, and supplies needed to record the desired sessions. The company then duplicates and sells the tapes or CDs to your attendees during the meeting. These companies usually rebate the client (meeting host) a percentage of each tape or CD sold after a certain sales figure has been reached. If that sales figure is not reached, the client pays the difference between the amount sold and the minimum sales figure required by contract.

As the meeting host, you should get or ask for a complimentary copy of each session recording from the taping company. In addition, each speaker should receive a free tape or CD of his or her session. It is important to market these items during the meeting. Make frequent announcements and make it easy for attendees to find the vendor. Tapes and CDs are available for at least a few weeks after the meeting.

Food for Thought

Sometimes speakers choose not to use a microphone. If you are recording their sessions, you must remind them to use one and to repeat all audience questions and comments.

Professional A/V Production

One of the biggest challenges when planning a meeting is how to present the material for maximum impact. There are two options: Produce it in-house or hire a professional production company. How do you conceptualize your message, package it, and deliver it? Do you have the internal resources? Do you have the time? Most organizations only hold a few meetings per year and probably do not have dedicated staff members who are experts in presentation production. If you need to make a strong, professional impression, consider hiring a professional production company.

The Inside Scoop

Have your A/V production company produce a happy video onsite. Throughout the conference, under your direction, the company takes pictures of people meeting, eating, having fun, and so on. Then the photos are set to music and are shown at your last general session. People love to see themselves on the big screen. Then, once back at the office, put some of these photos on your Web site, too!

Within the meetings industry, there are many A/V companies. For some, their primary focus is equipment rental, setup, and technical support. Others provide state-of-the-art presentations, slides, and videos. Still others custom design a variety of presentation technologies that incorporate projection systems, audio systems, lighting, and remote controls. Others focus on technology based on ISDN, T-1, Internet, and networking systems. Some production companies prefer to concentrate on the logistics of staging and production; others will offer more. Sorting out which type of company will meet your needs is a challenge, and you will need to do some research.

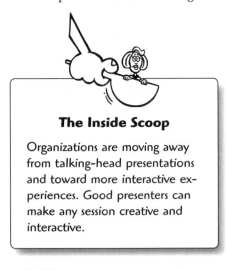

The Inside Scoop

Organizations are moving away from talking-head presentations and toward more interactive experiences. Good presenters can make any session creative and interactive.

In addition to content development, A/V production companies also provide video presentations, animation, interactive multimedia, staging, production design, and execution. They provide speaker support and message enhancement. They are often involved in new product launches, annual stockholder meetings, and national or regional sales meetings. They bring new, fresh, cutting-edge ideas on how to maximize the impact of your message.

The Least You Need to Know

➤ Communicating your message using A/V technology is getting fancier, more fun, and more expensive.

➤ Review all A/V needs with an A/V provider early in the planning process.

➤ A/V rental is expensive and covers more than just equipment. Labor, power, and supplies quickly add up.

➤ Big shows require a lot of production. Talk to experienced, qualified, full-service production companies at the onset.

Chapter 21

Registration and Housing

In This Chapter

➤ Learn what a meeting registration form should include

➤ Learn some important tips for your attendee database

➤ Distinguish between a registration list and a reservation list

➤ Discover online registration and where it's going

➤ Find out why a cancellation policy is a must

One of the most important aspects of meeting planning is collecting data on who is attending. Why? To communicate with them. You also want to market future meetings to them. You need to know when they are arriving and departing, where they are staying, if they are bringing guests, what sessions they have signed up for, if they have any special needs, and more. Knowing this type of information is critical when you have to make decisions regarding space, capacity, amounts of food, transportation, and so on.

Another key area is housing management. If you have hotel room block commitments, you must be proactive in getting your attendees to fill those rooms because it will impact your bottom line and maybe the success of your meeting.

In this chapter, we delve into the world of meeting registration, housing registration, and related issues.

Designing Your Registration Form

The design of your attendee database is synonymous with the design of your registration form. What comes from one (the form) goes into the other (the database). Because they go hand in hand, we suggest you begin by drafting your registration form in gory detail. To do that, you need to identify what information you want to track. Here is a big list; you may need all or just some of this info:

Registration Information	Designations
Last name	Board of directors
First name	Committee member
Middle initial	Conference committee
Title	Exhibitor
Company/organization	Facilitator
Address (line 1)	Faculty
Address (line 2)	Guest
Address (line 3)	Host
City	Press
State/Territory/Province	Speaker
ZIP code/postal code	Sponsor
Country	Staff
Phone/TDD number	Student
Fax number	Volunteer
E-mail address	Customize your own
Web site	

Badge Information	Guest Badge Information
First name	First name
Attendee organization	Guest city/state
Attendee city/state/territory/province	Guest country
Attendee country	Guest of

In Case of Emergency	Special Needs
First name	Diabetic
Last name	Vegetarian
Daytime phone	Vegan
Evening phone	Low salt
Cell phone	Low salt
Relationship	Kosher
	Food allergies

Session Selections

Customize to your meeting

Conference Events	Registration Fees
(Will they be attending ...)	(Early bird/regular/onsite)
Breakfasts	Member
Lunches	Nonmember
Receptions	Student
Banquets	Guest
Workplace tours	One day
Customize to your meeting	Banquet only

Additional Events/Fees	Payment Information
Conference outings	Check
Preconference tours	Money order
Postconference tours	Purchase order #
Preconference workshops	Credit card #/expiration date
	Signature line

Let's elaborate on a few categories. Let's start with the designation category. With large conferences, you may want to call attention to some of the different classifications your attendees fall into. This is where name badge ribbons come in. You can identify people by broad classification such as speaker or exhibitor, or you can customize titles for your attendees such as butcher, baker, or candlestick maker. For a geographically diverse crowd, you can give them a ribbon identifying their state, territory, province, or country!

With respect to the special-needs category, a registration form cannot possibly list all the questions that pertain to someone's special needs. Therefore, the best thing to do is make a statement similar to the following on the form: "Accommodations for persons with special needs will be made if requested in writing and if possible. Fax or e-mail your request to ...." Once you have a request in writing, you can follow up. Payment information is another category people frequently have questions about. This is where you must incorporate your policies about who pays, how they pay, what happens if they cancel, and so on.

The Inside Scoop

There are tons of registration forms to use as examples, especially on the Web. Fill them out yourself but don't hit the submit button! You can get some good ideas of what to do and what not to do by looking at other registration forms.

Don't Drop the Ball

In some cases, you may waive or reduce a registration fee. Don't put this information on the standard registration form. Either create a separate form (called fee waived) for these unique cases or send a cover letter with the standard form explaining that the fee is waived or reduced.

You will have major headaches if you don't get the payment information right from the start. If your instructions are not clear, attendees will pay the wrong amount, and you will either have to bill them for the amount owed or refund an overpayment. On your form, be sure to address the following payment criteria:

➤ Is payment required at the time of registration?

➤ Make the check payable to what organization?

➤ Must check be in U.S. dollars only?

➤ If funds are in a different currency, will they be rejected or will a conversion fee be assessed?

➤ Ask that the attendee's name be put on the check, especially if it is an organizational check.

➤ Is there a cancellation or substitution fee? Under what conditions? Are substitutions allowed?

➤ After what date will there be no refunds?

➤ Identify what the registration fee includes (refreshment breaks, reception, registration materials, and so on).

➤ Spell out all additional fees (meals, outings, and so on).

➤ Add complete contact info (phone, fax, e-mail) for questions.

Don't forget to include complete instructions for how to register. If you have online registration, also provide options for fax and mail. It is a good idea to state that a confirmation will be sent within X number of days and that, if no confirmation is received, the attendee should contact the registration office, and how. Be sure confirmations include a confirmation number. Remember that it's an extra verification to help you identify your attendees, and it does come in handy.

Developing Your Database

The kind of database software you choose depends on what you may already be using for other applications or what kind of meeting software package you decide to invest in.

The next step after registration-form design is to set up your database. One very important consideration is to create a unique identification number for each entry or *data record.* What if you have two Bob Smiths in your database? Bob Smith from New York may call and say he thinks he has registered twice and wants to correct the situation. Do you have two records for the same Bob Smith, or are there actually two different Bob Smiths both from New York City? A unique data record number (which can serve as your confirmation number) helps you sort it out.

This leads us to another tip. Design your database so it can distinguish possible duplicate entries. Sometimes an individual will register and then his or her assistant will also send in the registration form. If you test for duplicate names at the input process, you might avoid duplicate entries. Going through your database to cull out duplicates is a time-consuming, but necessary, process.

Create a unique field for each piece of information. You may not need it all, but you never know when you will want to print a report or sort on a specific field. The more unique fields you have, the better you can manipulate your data. For example, don't combine the first and last names into a field called Full Name. Separate them into two fields called First Name and Last Name. That way, you can sort and alphabetize on just the last name. It's much easier to input the data into many different fields from the beginning than it is to go back and separate this information after the fact.

Signup Made Easy

Now that you have created your registration form and your database is ready to go, you must make it easy for potential attendees to receive and submit their registration.

The Old-Fashioned Way

Many people still like the old-fashioned way of filling out a paper copy and mailing or faxing it in. Even if you want most of your attendees to submit their registrations electronically, you should still have a paper version.

Try to keep your registration form to a single page, but if that's not possible, at least have a version that is printable in 8½ × 11-inch format. If someone requests a copy of the registration form, having one in an 8½ × 11-inch format makes it easier for the attendee to complete and for the registration staff to read.

Meeting Speak

A **data record** is the unique collection of information about a specific object (in this case, an individual).

Don't Drop the Ball

After you have designed your registration form and database, do several trial runs. Get people unfamiliar with your project to register. Listen to their feedback and improve the process.

Food for Thought

For hard-copy registrations, write the attendee's last name in big, bright letters in the upper-right corner. You'll be able to find forms much faster that way.

Some planners like to have a hard copy of each registration in a binder, alphabetized. That way, they can access registration info quickly. They also have the registration information as supplied by the attendee if there are any questions.

Do It Online

The technology to register people online is here and is progressing beautifully, to everyone's advantage. If you are thinking about online registration, consider these points:

1. People access the Internet in droves, and just about everyone has at least limited access. Computer prices continue to decline, and so does the cost of high-speed Internet access. Expect the number of Internet users to increase.

2. Payment information via credit card is secure, and this technology will only get better.

3. The new online-registration Web sites are template driven, so you don't have to know or even understand Web site design. They make it super easy for you to enter your information and manage your data.

4. These days, people expect to go to the Web to find current, accurate meeting information, to register, and to make housing and travel arrangements.

The Inside Scoop

There are comprehensive online attendee-management programs that do much more than just meeting registration. These programs take care of meeting/event registration (including signup for sessions and social events), housing reservations, flights, ground transportation, tours, printing name badges, confirmations, tickets, and other data management. They allow basic customization to your meeting specifications; generate up-to-date, accurate reports; offer password protection; and allow attendees to register 24/7.

To decide which online-registration service would work best for you, think about your needs. How many meetings do you plan? How big are the meetings? Do you want just meeting-registration capability, or do you want your participants to be able to make a room reservation and book an airline ticket?

Then consult Chapter 5, "Technology Soft-Where?" and also do a little research of your own. Go to each of the online registration companies' Web sites and check them out. Most provide online demos. Pay attention to what they provide versus what you really need. Rank the top three potential companies and get more information. Investigate how your data management fits into their system. Then make a decision based on your budget and what will work best for you.

Heads in Beds

Actually, "heads in beds" is lingo from the supplier side, meaning they want occupied rooms. For meeting planners, keeping track of heads in beds is important, challenging, and time consuming. Why? Read on.

You need to make sure you are filling your contracted room block at your hotel(s). However, making housing reservations on behalf of each attendee is daunting, especially if individuals are paying their own charges. It's best to have each attendee make his or her own arrangements. You rely on the hotel to periodically give you a *reservation list*. Here comes the time-consuming part. You must now compare the hotel's reservation list to your registration list. That way, you can identify who has not made a reservation. Since your registration system is different than the hotel's, you must compare a hard-copy hotel reservation list with your registration list every time.

Food for Thought

Always have a downloadable or printable registration form on your Web site for people who are not comfortable with online submissions.

Meeting Speak

A **reservation list** is the list of reservations under a specific group's room block.

It is very important to track your attendees' housing status. If you are below your contracted room block, it may be that fewer people than expected are registering for your conference. However, if your meeting attendance is good but your room block is low, possibly two things are happening: either your attendees just haven't yet gotten around to making their housing reservations, they are staying elsewhere, or maybe both. Either way, you need to get the heads in the (contracted) beds. Otherwise, you could miss your room-block commitments and then attrition kicks in. Not good.

If you have designed your database to capture attendees' housing status, you can easily identify which attendees do not have housing. At this point, you should generate an e-mail reminding them, gently, that they are not listed on the hotel's reservation

The Inside Scoop

It is getting harder to fill room blocks. Everyone has instant access to information online, including special rates at hotels near your meeting hotel. Attendees can find a bargain with a simple click of the mouse. You can't make them stay in your room block!

Food for Thought

Always provide toll numbers in addition to toll-free telephone numbers.

list and should promptly make a reservation. You may also want to ask them if they have alternate housing (so you won't bother them again). This will generate some action, but be prepared to send out a second reminder, too.

Housing Reservation Forms

Regardless of who is making the housing reservations, you or the attendee, you will need to provide detailed housing-reservation information in your registration materials. What do your attendees need to know? Here's a list:

➤ Hotel reservation phone numbers; local and toll-free, TDD (telecommunications devices for the deaf), and fax

➤ Hotel reservation e-mail and Web site, if applicable

➤ Reservation cutoff date

➤ Room rate(s) (single, double, or multiple occupancy) and room types

➤ State and local taxes

➤ Group identifier code

➤ Timeframe rates are valid

➤ Cancellation and substitution policies

➤ Early departure or extended stay fees, if any

➤ No-show charge, if any

➤ Reservation/payment information

➤ Description of rooms, décor, and amenities

➤ Description of the hotel (pools, health clubs, grounds, nearby attractions, restaurants, room service, and so on)

➤ Check in/out times

➤ Extra person charge, if any

➤ Maximum occupancy per room

➤ Children (at what age) stay free

➤ Choice of hotel (1st, 2nd, 3rd) where applicable

➤ How the reservation will be acknowledged

Earlier we discussed the attendee registration database as it pertains to capturing attendee registration information, and we described a scenario in which we needed to identify attendee housing information. Here is a list of the housing information you should collect for each attendee and add to his or her registration data record:

➤ Arrival day, date, and estimated time

➤ Departure day, date, and estimated time

➤ Number of guests/children (names optional)

➤ Sharing with (other attendee or guest)

➤ Name reservation is in

➤ Hotel name (if several to choose from)

➤ Hotel confirmation number

Don't Drop the Ball

The arrival, departure, and guest information from the hotel's reservation list is almost always more accurate than what is on the registration form submitted by the attendee. Update your database with the hotel's data.

You will get some of this information from the attendee registration form. You will get other info, such as a hotel confirmation number, from the hotel's reservation list. Update your registration database as frequently as you can with any and all pertinent information.

Housing Bureau

For city-wide meetings or conventions, a housing bureau is recommended. Either a CVB or an outside company can provide a registration service. CVBs are now partnering with some of the online housing companies. Individuals rank their hotel preference and are assigned a hotel on a first-come, first-served basis. This is done either via a registration form or online.

Rooming List

You will submit staff and VIP room reservations to the hotel on a rooming list. Notify everyone for whom you are making a reservation and get a confirmation number from the hotel to give to each person. Make sure you keep your staff/VIP block separate from your regular block of rooms. You can even do this during the contracting stage, but the sooner the better! Ask the hotel to create two separate room blocks.

You may decide to collect attendee housing requests yourself and submit them to the hotel using a rooming list. For companies who are having a mandatory meeting, this is particularly helpful. Attendees' special needs, roommate information, cancellations, and additions are communicated to the meeting planner who works directly with a hotel reservation agent. The housing charges are added to the meeting's master bill.

Call-In or Online

Attendees can also be instructed to call the hotel directly. In this case, they should identify themselves as part of your group or organization and, in return, will receive the negotiated rate. Make sure you provide both toll and toll-free numbers for the hotel as well as a fax number. Some hotels also offer online registrations.

Food for Thought

An example of a meeting cancellation policy is as follows: "All cancellations are subject to a $25 cancellation fee. Cancellations after March 21 will be assessed a $150 cancellation fee."

Cancellations

Meeting registration cancellation fees are growing in popularity. Clearly outline your cancellation policy on your registration form. A cancellation fee makes an attendee's commitment stronger and eliminates people who would sign up knowing they can cancel at the last minute with no financial penalty.

For example, if someone cancels the day before the meeting, but you have provided the meal guarantee to the facility two days before, you still pay for the meals. Of course, your guarantees have a fudge factor and you will have walk-ins onsite, but still be firm. You can always make exceptions for a family emergency or other major obstacle that prevented someone from attending. After all, we are all human.

The Least You Need to Know

➤ Name badge ribbons are a great way to identify VIPs, speakers, committee members, officers, and other people who need to stand out.

➤ Always compare your registration list with the hotel reservation list to identify people who have not made a hotel reservation.

➤ Research the online attendee-registration and -management programs.

➤ A cancellation policy protects your budget and reduces the number of casual cancellations.

Part 4

Center Stage and Beyond

Lights! Camera! Action! You are on stage, and this is your production. You are in charge, and this part tells you what to do once you arrive at the meeting facility for your meeting. We'll walk you through the process, from checking in to organizing your meeting office to getting acquainted with the facility staff. You'll also learn about paying the bills, tipping, tabulating the evaluations, and obtaining final facility reports. We'll also show you how advance planning can prepare you for crisis management, so you'll be ready if disaster calls on your next meeting.

There is also a chapter for suppliers only (although planners can take a peek) that will provide the inside scoop on what planners really look for and need when booking a meeting. We'll also look at industry certifications and evaluate whether letters after your name are worth the time and money. Then, we'll leave you with a few tips for maintaining control in this crazy profession. After that, you are on your own. Good luck!

Chapter 22

The Final Stretch

In This Chapter

➤ Learn what to do once you arrive at the meeting facility

➤ Identify the meeting facility players

➤ Understand the value of managing your rooming lists

➤ Understand your role and responsibilities onsite

➤ Distinguish between pre- and post-convention meetings

The day has finally arrived—you are going onsite. What exactly should you expect? What can you do to make things run smoothly? What exactly is your job onsite? In this chapter, we explore these issues to give you a good idea what happens from the minute you check in to the moment you leave.

We will also look at the convention resumé, meetings with the facility's staff, how to set up your conference office, and the lines of communication onsite. Going onsite can be one of the most fun parts of your job, but it is intimidating if you are not familiar with your role and the hotel staff's role in managing your meeting.

You're Here

Upon your arrival, have your meeting boxes delivered to your office. You also should check in to your hotel room and get settled. Ask for a room on a lower floor and if applicable, an early check-in. If the elevators are busy, you can take the stairs. Everyone has his or her own ritual, so getting comfortable first is a way of making your hotel room "home" for a while.

Setting Up Your Office

Once you are settled in, you should let your meeting facility contact know you've arrived safely. If it is after hours, you may have to wait until morning, but at least leave a voicemail. When possible, go to the room designated as your office. By now, your boxes have arrived and you can start unpacking. If you shipped any boxes in advance, call and find out where they are and whether they can be brought to your office.

For one of our big meetings, we had flags from six countries shipped to the meeting site. Once onsite, they were nowhere to be found. It was a Sunday, and the flag company was closed. We ended up getting someone from the flag company (it's a good thing they were local) to bring us an extra set. Later, we found out they were shipped under a different name, and we were not looking for the right "ship from" information. We found the flags upon conclusion of the conference. The moral of the story is to make sure all items shipped to you are accounted for before you arrive onsite. Call vendors to confirm that they have shipped and get all shipping info. Looking for missing items onsite is a huge time drain and can impact your meeting.

Unpack, set up the office, and get organized. If you still have packets to stuff, now is the time to get started.

Exactly what do you need for your onsite office? Here's a checklist so you don't miss anything:

➤ **Registration materials.** Attendee packets, monitor packets, speaker packets, onsite registration forms, brochures.

➤ **Office supplies.** Pack a complete assortment of paper, paper clips, note pads, a stapler, extra staples, transparent tape, masking tape, electrical tape, packing tape, overnight shipping envelopes/boxes, blades for opening boxes, pens, pencils, clipboards, flashlight, tools (such as a screwdriver and hammer), transparencies and pens, aspirin (seriously), and a first-aid kit.

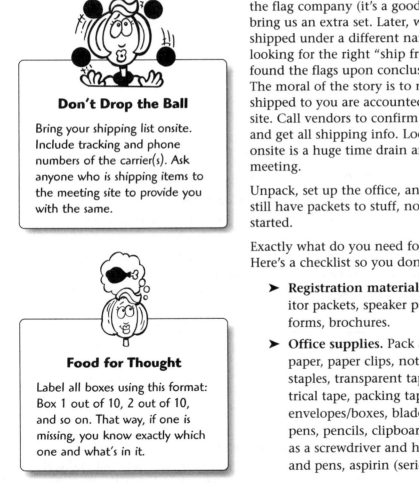

Don't Drop the Ball

Bring your shipping list onsite. Include tracking and phone numbers of the carrier(s). Ask anyone who is shipping items to the meeting site to provide you with the same.

Food for Thought

Label all boxes using this format: Box 1 out of 10, 2 out of 10, and so on. That way, if one is missing, you know exactly which one and what's in it.

➤ **Office equipment as needed.** A computer, printer, copy machine, fax machine, and associated supplies.

➤ **A few extension cords.** You may need them in the office, or a speaker may need one for a laptop. These can be expensive to rent onsite.

➤ **Snacks for the staff.** It's a nice touch, especially when things get busy and time gets short.

➤ **School bell.** You may need it for getting people's attention.

It's a good idea to keep an onsite meeting equipment and supplies checklist. Update it after (or during) each meeting for the next time.

Prior to arrival, prepare a staff assignment list including work schedules, times, and rules (such as no eating at the registration desk). You will need staff for a variety of tasks including working the registration desk, checking meeting rooms for setup accuracy, taking tickets at meal functions, and so on. Review staff assignments before you go onsite.

Another handy thing to have is a list of frequently asked questions (FAQs) by attendees. Brainstorm with staff and key volunteers in advance the questions you think attendees will ask your registration desk personnel. Here are some sample questions:

➤ Where are the bathrooms?

➤ How can I pay for the conference? Can I pay by check or credit card? Which ones do you accept?

➤ Where is the nearest bank or ATM?

➤ Where are the meeting rooms? (Have your staff become familiar with the floor plan.)

➤ I need to cancel the last day. Can I get a refund?

➤ I have a special meal request. Whom do I tell?

➤ Is Suzie Q. registered for the conference? Has she checked in yet? Can I leave a message for her?

➤ Where can I get breakfast, lunch, or dinner?

Food for Thought

Bring preprinted overnight shipping labels to the meeting. These are very handy when you need to ship your leftover materials back to the office.

Also train your staff on the emergency procedures in the hotel. When do you call 911? They all should know what to do in the event of any crisis. Make sure you know the facility's emergency procedures and communicate them to your entire staff.

A Quick Tour

Once you have settled in, take a tour of the facilities. Bring your staff along because they need to see it, too. Reacquaint yourself with the property. Have a bite to eat in the restaurant. Get a feel for the property and what is going on there. Check out the meeting rooms and get a listing of other meetings onsite.

Your Master List

Before the meeting, create a master to-do list that includes your detailed agenda (with times). The master list is different from your timeline and includes everything that you and your staff need to do throughout the meeting such as put signs out, speaker checks, meal and session counts, and so on. It also includes meetings you have scheduled with the hotel staff, when your speakers/entertainers are scheduled to arrive, rehearsal times, vendor setup times, staff training, and so on.

Convention or Meeting Resumé

Put your meeting details in writing. Too many times, verbal instructions are given to the hotel, and important details slip through the cracks. It is the meeting planner's responsibility to provide the hotel with clear directions as to what is needed for the meeting. Create a document including the agenda, audio-visual needs, food and beverage requirements, and other meeting details and give it to the hotel. This is done approximately 30 to 45 days prior to the meeting. The timeframe varies depending on the meeting's size, and how far out it is booked.

Here is some information you need to give the hotel:

➤ A final rooming list indicating who pays for the room, tax, and incidentals for each individual

➤ Billing information—list what should be posted to the master account

➤ VIPs including arrival/departure days, dates, and times

➤ Who gets the comp rooms

➤ Authorized decision-makers and whether they can sign to the master account

➤ Security needs

➤ Registration desk hours of operation

➤ Expected attendee arrival/departure days, dates, times

The Inside Scoop

It is well-known in meetings-industry circles that some kind of form standardization is needed. Well, help is on the way but not for a while. The Accepted Practices Exchange Program (APEX) will eventually include standardization efforts for RFPs, contracts, convention resumés, and more. Much of the funding will come from CIC members and many CVBs from around the country.

➤ Details for each meal including setup and serving times

➤ Accounting requirements—ask to review and sign bills daily

➤ Amenity deliveries, if applicable

➤ Audio-visual requirements

➤ Computing, other technical requirements, if any

➤ Electrical needs

➤ Banners, signs that need to be hung (get prior approval)

➤ Shipping and receiving—provide number of boxes, shipper info, and airbill number if known

➤ Airport transportation needs

➤ Parking—ask about special valet passes

➤ Hospitality suites, including who is hosting and the hours

Meeting Speak

A **convention resumé** is a document produced by the meeting facility that includes the details for your entire meeting. Any memos to the hotel staff, special instructions, BEOs, function sheets, and VIPs are part of this report.

The hotel takes all of this information and creates the meeting or *convention resumé,* which includes the details of the entire meeting. The hotel uses this document to follow the needs of the group and to make sure everything the client ordered is provided.

Since the resumé also contains your agenda, make sure all the agenda information is correct. It will be posted on the in-house monitors and on internal documents used by the hotel staff. If you do not want something posted, such as a staff meeting, indicate that it is a "do not post" function. For example, your office is a "do not post" item. You do not necessarily want meeting attendees to know where it is. The registration desk is where they should go for answers to their questions.

The hotel will also carefully monitor when you do not have group meal functions. If you do not have a scheduled lunch planned on a certain day, then people are "on the loose" and may eat in the restaurants. An accurate agenda is important.

Rooming List—Keep on Top of It!

Your rooming list is a document that outlines individuals for whom you want to make housing reservations directly. It includes the individuals' names, their check-in and check-out dates, room type, billing information, and any special needs. At a minimum, your rooming list should contain your staff, VIPs, and speakers. If your organization is paying for the housing of all your attendees, then your rooming list could contain all attendees.

There are three ways to pay for an attendee's room. Take a look at the following table and pay attention to the billing information.

Name	Number of People	Check-In Date	Check-Out Date	Billing Information	Smoking/Room Type/Comments
John Q. Speaker	1	9-18-09	9-20-09	Room/tax to master, incidentals to individual	Nonsmoking King VIP/keynote speaker
Suzie Q. Banquet	2	9-18-09	9-20-09	All charges to individual	Smoking Two beds
Jane L. Meeting	1	9-18-09	9-21-09	All charges to master	Nonsmoking King

The rooming list should be finalized prior to the cutoff date. However, changes are inevitable, and even onsite you will have some revisions. Have on hand the file documenting every change you sent to the hotel and also a final list just in case there are some questions once onsite.

Every morning, meet with the front office staff to review your room pickup from the night before, any no-shows, and cancellations. This is especially important in case a VIP or speaker was a no-show. Tell the hotel if you want any of these reservations reinstated for that evening. Otherwise, these people could show up and not have a reservation. You should also keep tabs on the current house count so you know if the hotel is oversold during your stay.

Another important reason to review this information on a daily basis is to keep track of any no-shows guaranteed by your organization that will be billed to your master account. Find out what the hotel occupancy was that evening; if it sold out, you shouldn't be charged. The front office staff will also appreciate your interest in helping them manage your group. It makes for a smoother meeting. Then, when you get the master bill, you know exactly what happened.

Your Role

Your role onsite should be like the conductor of the orchestra. Everyone knows his or her job, but someone is there to keep everyone in sync and moving forward.

You are also there to troubleshoot, make last-minute decisions, and act appropriately if there is an emergency.

Too Many Chiefs

Too many people directing the crew (both your staff and the hotel) is not a good thing. Establish a chain of command and communicate it to your staff and the hotel. Before you go onsite, establish who the decision-makers are. At the very least, they should include you, an assistant who knows the meeting well, and possibly your boss or another individual authorized to make financial decisions on behalf of your organization.

This core group of people will be authorized to sign checks to the master bill and make operational decisions on the spot when a hotel staff person asks questions.

The number of authorized decision-makers also depends on the size of the meeting. For very small meetings, it may be only one or two people. For larger 1,000+ person conferences, you may have four to five or more people who need that capability.

If you don't establish this chain of command, be prepared to deal with issues such as who changed the room set? Who ordered more cookies? Who made 1,000 copies and charged them to the master bill? Keep control. A good rule of thumb is the fewer decision-makers there are, the better.

You're Responsible

Even if the president of the company or association is in attendance at the meeting, you, the lead planner, are in charge. Be prepared for people who come onsite and take the credit. When it is all said and done, you should be proud of your accomplishment.

Along with the accolades, you must also deal with the problems. You will have cranky attendees, broken audio-visual equipment, monitors who do not show up, hot meeting rooms, cold meeting rooms, noise from the other meetings invading your space, late speakers, lost boxes, sick attendees, cold food, you name it—it happens. Do the best you can and use your best judgment.

Food for Thought

Ask for an alphabetized printout of all room reservations made under your group code. Compare your registration list against it to make sure everything was entered correctly. Sometimes one person could have a reservation under two different names, or one name might be spelled wrong in the system.

Don't Drop the Ball

Communicate to the hotel staff who is authorized to make decisions and introduce those people. Make sure only people who can make informed decisions have this capability. In other words, do not assign someone who has had no involvement in the planning up to this point.

Meetings About Your Meeting

Before you get onsite, you may meet with the convention services or catering manager or both. You may meet with them one time or a dozen times depending on the size, location, and scope of your meeting. You may also meet with the audio-visual personnel and the chef. This is when you finalize the details.

Once you are onsite, you are introduced to the rest of the staff responsible for the execution of your meeting. Each facility is run according to its own guidelines, but basically, there are seven departments you will work with onsite:

1. **Audio-visual.** Responsible for the sound, lighting, and equipment.

2. **Banquets.** Serves the food and beverages to the attendees.

3. **Bell stand.** Helps the guests carry their belongings to their rooms; it is also a resource for directions and other general questions.

4. **Convention services.** Sets up the meeting and banquet rooms.

5. **Front office.** Checks the guests in and out of the hotel; also oversees concierge.

6. **Housekeeping.** Cleans the guestrooms and public areas.

7. **Reservations.** Makes the reservations and helps you onsite with changes.

Don't Drop the Ball

No matter what happens, stay calm. If you are not sure how to handle an issue, explain to the person that you will get right back to him or her (unless it is an emergency, which you'll handle immediately!). Understand the meeting inside and out and get to know the hotel staff in charge of every area.

Pre-Convention Meeting

A *pre-convention* meeting (also known as a *pre-con*) is a meeting with the hotel staff about your meeting, usually a day or two before the start of the meeting. In this meeting, you meet most of the department heads; review the convention resumé, rooming list, and BEOs; and both sides ask questions. You should also get a complete reservation report for your group.

The meeting begins with each hotel representative introducing him- or herself and giving an explanation of the department's role in your meeting. Then you give a brief overview of your organization and the purpose of the meeting and address any last-minute

Meeting Speak

A **pre-convention (pre-con)** meeting is a meeting with the host facility's staff just prior to the start of the conference or meeting.

changes. Once that is done, everyone briefly reviews the resumé and then the chef and the convention services and/or catering manager, and A/V manager stay to review the BEOs in greater detail. This is also the time to provide guarantees if you haven't done so for the last few days of your meeting.

Daily Chats

Daily chats are something you should institute with most facility managers. It is good to touch base with the catering and/or convention services manager, front office, banquet manager, audiovisual manager, sales manager, and others who are handling your meeting. These are informal conversations to catch up on what has happened, what is going to happen, and any potential problems facing your meeting.

Post-Convention Meeting

A *post-convention* meeting (also known as a *post-con*) is also held with the hotel staff to review the meeting. This is your opportunity to hear from the hotel staff's point of view how things went behind the scene. This can be with all department heads or just the ones you select. You also can review the bill in detail one more time before you leave the hotel.

At this meeting, you should get your actual room pickup, number of no-shows, cancellations, and number of people served at each meal function. In some cases you will already have this information, but here is when you learn that you need to order more vegetarian entrees, that your signage wasn't the best it could have been, and other useful things for next time.

The Three R's—Review, Review, Review

Keep a copy of the convention resumé, rooming list, BEOs, and function sheets on a clipboard that you can carry around with you throughout the meeting. You can reduce these on the copy machine for smaller copies, and then you don't even need a clipboard. At your

The Inside Scoop

Even though your main contact is the convention services or catering manager, once you are onsite, you need to develop a good working relationship with the other staff members. The more proactive you are in learning their names, jobs, and a little bit about them, the better service you will receive. It really works!

Meeting Speak

A **post-convention (post-con)** meeting is a meeting with the hotel staff just after the conclusion of the conference or meeting to review the meeting.

fingertips, you can check room sets, meal information, start times, or whatever you need to know on the spot.

Give your key staff members copies of these documents and leave a copy in the home and onsite offices and at the registration desk.

Before each meeting, you should walk through every meeting room to verify that everything is set according to the BEO. If there are any discrepancies, immediately let the convention services and A/V managers know.

Food for Thought

Consider using a fanny pack on-site to carry paper, pens, radio or walkie-talkie, and other needed items.

The Master Bill Before You Go

At the pre-convention meeting, set a daily appointment with someone from the accounting office. We can't stress this enough. Every day, review your master bill. Make sure you have signed every banquet check. Get copies of everything from the day before.

After the meeting when you get the master bill, you have already approved most of the charges. It is a lot easier than trying to remember or reconstruct what exactly happened and why you are being charged weeks after your meeting.

The Least You Need to Know

➤ Bring plenty of office supplies for your conference office.

➤ Know what boxes you expect to be shipped to the meeting site, including their airbill numbers.

➤ Provide the meeting facility with your meeting details in a very thorough, dated, written document.

➤ Stay on top of your rooming list and room pickup situation by meeting with the front office every morning.

➤ Review the master bill before you leave the property at the conclusion of the meeting.

Chapter 23

Ready, Set, Go Onsite!

In This Chapter

➤ See how to set up your registration area

➤ Learn the importance of training your onsite staff

➤ Understand how the facility gets things done

➤ Identify common onsite problems and how to rectify them

You've unpacked, gotten settled, and it's show time. What do you do? All of the "work" is done. Now it's time to sit back and relax because your meeting will run it-self, right? We wish. Actually you still have lots of work to do. You have registration to manage; attendee, speaker, and VIP questions and needs to address; problems to solve; and decisions to make.

Even though you turn over the implementation of your event to the hotel or venue, what actually goes on behind the scenes to make sure your meeting is a success? Who is responsible to make sure every single detail is taken care of? You still need to stay on top of the details and make sure the facility does not drop the ball.

This chapter prepares you for what goes on onsite including what takes place back of the house in a meeting facility. It isn't magic (although sometimes it looks like it is).

Registration Setup Considerations

One of the most important things you need to attend to is setting up and managing your registration area. If you have a large registration area with booths, hundreds of registration packets, and so on, you should have everything set up and ready to go the day before registration opens. If your registration area is smaller, you can usually set up a few hours before the posted registration time. In any case, once you are set up, don't leave your registration area unattended. If you must, you should lock the room if possible. If your registration is in an open area, take down or cover up your registration signage and place tablecloths over your registration desks. People will understand that you're not open, plus it keeps their paws off of your registration materials.

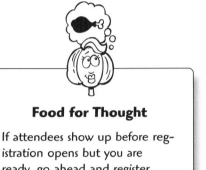

Food for Thought

If attendees show up before registration opens but you are ready, go ahead and register them. It helps reduce lines during registration hours, and is good for PR!

Meeting Speak

Larger conferences sometimes provide a conference **preprint,** a bound copy of all the handouts and papers for every session. This is most typical at medical and scientific conferences where the sessions are quite technical.

How you set up registration depends on what kind of materials you provide. For example, assume all the registration packets are generic (they all contain the same info) and the only unique item is the attendee's name badge. Here you can place the name badges in alphabetical order on tables. As the attendees pick up their name badge, you check off their name and hand them a packet. Done.

If your packets contain name-specific information, such as name badges, receipts, letters, or other forms, it's important to make sure they get the correct personalized packet. The packets can be placed in alphabetical order behind registration, and attendees can go to a specific table or booth where a staff member can assist them.

Although we haven't specifically addressed what goes into an attendee packet, by now you get the idea. In Chapter 16, "The Stuff Meetings Are Made Of," we talked about the "stuff" meetings are made of, and a lot of those items go into the packets. Here are some items to consider:

➤ An attendee list (alphabetical)

➤ Conference *preprints*

➤ A meeting evaluation form and individual session evaluation forms

➤ A facility map, if not included in program

➤ Giveaways (conference gifts)

➤ Invitations

➤ Last-minute information not in the program

➤ Local maps, brochures, or magazines

➤ A name badge

➤ A program booklet or handout

➤ Receipts

➤ Ribbons

➤ Special handouts

➤ Tickets

Food for Thought

If you have room, place several tables near the registration area so attendees have a place to review their packets and set their stuff down.

When laying out your registration area, pretend you're an attendee and walk through the process. You want to make it easy and quick. Consider the following points:

➤ Is the registration area in a logical, central place?

➤ Which direction will people come from?

➤ Can they see the signage?

➤ Is there enough room for lines of people? Can people with disabilities easily register?

➤ Is there a place attendees can go if they have questions or need time to fill out forms?

➤ Can attendees pick up their materials from any of the registration staff, or must they go to a specific table/booth?

➤ Do you need a special registration area for exhibitors, VIPs, speakers, or sponsors?

➤ Will you have onsite registration for those who didn't register early?

➤ Do you need to collect payment? Do you need a phone line for credit card verification?

➤ Do you need Internet access?

➤ Do you need tables for displays, pamphlets, or handouts?

➤ Do you need tables for vendors or CVB staff? Hotel staff?

You need to answer these questions early in the planning process because you need to plan for location, space, signage, equipment rental, booth rental, additional furniture rental, packet preparation, and on and on.

Registration is where most attendees, exhibitors, vendors, speakers, and even facility staff will go to ask questions and get help. Therefore, it's very important to have someone there at all times registration is listed as open who can make decisions and answer questions. Remember that your registration staff will be busy. Any questions your staff cannot answer should be referred quickly to someone who can help. If you cannot have the "answer person" stay in the registration area (maybe because it's you and you have to be everywhere), put your staff members on radios or cell phones so they can reach you instantly.

Staffing and Training

A big question is how much help you need onsite. It really depends on the number of attendees and the complexity of your meeting. A rule of thumb is one staff person per every 100 attendees—give or take. However, also factor in all the events in your meeting. If you have only general sessions and/or a few breakouts, you will need less staff than if you also have exhibits, offsite functions, tours, big-name VIPs or celebrities, numerous breakouts, and so on.

Before you leave your office, you should meet with your staff and develop a list of responsibilities. Make sure people understand what tasks they are responsible for, and what kinds of decisions they can and cannot make, and to whom to direct questions. Also make sure each staff member knows the roles of the other people on staff to avoid confusion. These responsibilities should be in writing.

If you hire staff just for your onsite needs, you need to train them upon arrival. Since you may not know them and they have not been a part of your planning process, it is difficult to put them into positions that generate a lot of questions. Therefore, it's especially important that they are used efficiently and know the chain of command. They are great for registration support. They also know the venue, so they can assist with questions about the city and surroundings.

During your meeting, you should have a wind-up (or is it a wind-down?) meeting with your staff at the end of each day. Make it a short meeting, 15 to 30 minutes tops. The purpose is to get feedback, determine any problems or issues, and make adjustments. These feedback sessions are very useful and help everyone get some closure on the day. Listen to the negative feedback and give some positive feedback. It makes a big difference. Take notes so you can factor in these comments and suggestions at your next meeting.

The Inside Scoop

Unless you have a very small program, it's best to have at least two people working a meeting. One should be glued to the registration desk so the other can run around to check rooms, make on-the-spot decisions, and solve last-minute problems.

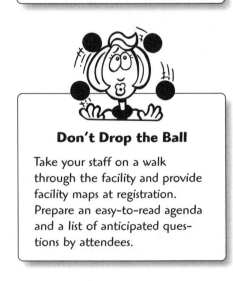

Don't Drop the Ball

Take your staff on a walk through the facility and provide facility maps at registration. Prepare an easy-to-read agenda and a list of anticipated questions by attendees.

Signage

Another thing you will need to do is place your signs. Wait! Did we talk about signage? Whoops. Well, let's discuss it here. Signs are always important to direct attendees and provide pertinent information.

In many cases, the information on the signs won't or can't be known until several weeks or even days prior to your meeting. However, well before then, you need to decide what kind of signs you need, their style, their size, and approximately how many. Here are some questions to consider:

➤ Do you want a logo or meeting theme on them?

➤ Do you have specific colors?

➤ Do you need directional signs with arrows?

➤ How will you display the signs? Easels? Stand-alone? Hanging? What are the facility's guidelines on signs: color, size, print, and placement?

➤ Will you need the ability to make signage onsite?

➤ Do you want to acknowledge sponsors? Vendors? In-kind contributors?

In addition, you may want a banner or large organization logo at registration or in a general session. Talk to your facility about your options for displaying these. Also, what kind of signage do you need at your registration area? If you have multiple registration booths, you will need to direct attendees to specific booths. In this case, the vendor that provides the booths can also create signage for them. Whatever signage you need, make sure they are large enough and are displayed high enough to be easily seen.

If you are able to go on a pre-meeting site visit, it's an excellent idea to walk through the facility and map out the placement of your signs, especially the directional ones. That way, you can determine the number, size, and style. If you can't, use a facility diagram and discuss your needs with your convention services manager or catering manager. Also bring along blank sign stock so you can make signs on the spot.

Don't Drop the Ball

Hanging banners usually require special equipment and labor. You also may have to get special permission from the facility and may be assessed a fee.

Food for Thought

For directional signs, use removable arrows that can be adhered using Velcro.

Behind the Scenes

You may think you have a lot of meetings with the facility staff. Well, they have meetings about your meeting (without you), too. Before you arrive, each department completely reviews the needs of your group. Staff schedules are created and pertinent information is posted and distributed.

The Inside Scoop

Make sure your sales and catering contacts understand the goals and objectives for your meeting. They should also have a good idea of the attendee profile and as much information as possible on arrival/departure patterns, eating habits, and so on. The more they know about you, the better they can serve you.

Don't Drop the Ball

Before you retire each evening, it is a good idea to review tomorrow's BEOs and function sheets with the banquet or convention services manager. Try to be one step ahead in terms of meeting execution.

In addition, most hotels have a weekly staff or operations meeting to review all groups arriving within the next few weeks. They review the number of arrivals and departures, the occupancy percentage, VIPs, meal functions, special requests, and other important information.

It is quite an operation behind the scenes in preparation for your group. The facility has to schedule staff, order food and beverages, prepare the paperwork, create the daily in-house meeting agenda for the entire hotel, make sure the necessary equipment is available, and communicate all the information amongst themselves in preparation for your arrival.

Welcome to My (Early!) Morning

The banquet and convention services department personnel get up very early and are at work before your attendees wake up. Typically, they are scheduled 24 hours a day to set your meeting rooms and to make sure things are ready to go at the agreed times.

The staff uses the BEOs or function sheets to set your meeting rooms, so make sure they are 100 percent accurate when you sign off on them. Keep your contact updated on changes and do it in writing.

Sometimes your meeting rooms are set the night before so they will be ready when you are in the morning. If you can, check your meeting rooms the night before to make sure all is ready for your meeting the next day. In any case, always check the rooms 30 to 60 minutes prior to the meeting start times. If there are any discrepancies, report them immediately to the convention services or banquet staff. Most A/V equipment is *not* set at night because of security reasons.

Mid-Morning Relay Race

About mid-morning and mid-afternoon, your group will take a break. Make sure the facility staff can access the meeting rooms during the break to "refresh" the meeting rooms. Don't assume this automatically happens. The facility has many meetings going at the same time and it literally becomes a race to get from room to room. Keep your contacts informed if you are running late or are still on schedule. If you are running late, lunch, afternoon breaks, or dinner may need to be pushed back a bit, but try to stay on time.

> **Food for Thought**
>
> When checking rooms, ask the setup crew, banquet staff, and A/V personnel if they have the latest changes just in case something didn't get passed on to them.

Come and Get It!

Meals are another busy time for the facility's staff. They need to be aware of the meeting's schedule (and any changes) so they can serve the meal at the designated time. They also need to make sure the banquet room is set and the staff is ready to go. You should check the room, too, just to make sure everything is ready according to your BEO.

If you have a program during your meal, you probably don't want the banquet staff clearing tables, making noise, and walking in front of your attendees. Consider scripting your program to accommodate the needs of the facility, speakers, and attendees.

Bumps in the Road

You will always have a few bumps in the road during your meetings. Here's a list of potential problems and what to do to reduce or eliminate them:

➤ **Changes not communicated to staff.** Constantly have a dialogue going with staff. Don't assume that everything is taken care of.

➤ **Power outages.** Make sure you have flashlights available and know the hotel's evacuation procedure and backup power source(s).

➤ **Broken A/V equipment.** Make sure the A/V company has extra of everything in inventory. For critical presentations, have a spare in the room. (You'll probably have to pay for it, but consider it insurance.) It's a good reason to use the in-house A/V company.

➤ **Missing items.** Did attendees leave items in the room yesterday? Check all rooms immediately following the last session, or you may have to go dumpster digging to retrieve lost items. Yuck!

➤ **It's tooooooo coooooooold.** Rooms should be cool in the morning. Once the bodies pile in, the room warms up. Don't be too quick to turn up the heat (unless icicles are growing on your attendees). Hot rooms make people sleepy, inattentive, and can make them nauseous.

➤ **Your mic is dead.** When doing your room checks, test the mics, by speaking into them, not tapping them. Insist that new batteries be placed in all wireless microphones prior to using them—especially general session mics!

➤ **Your meeting room has changed.** Make sure your contract states that you must agree in writing prior to changing your assigned meeting rooms. If rooms are changed anyway, make sure all the postings are correct. The facility staff should provide signs or people to direct participants to the new location.

➤ **An attendee was walked (to another hotel).** Try to negotiate a no-walk policy for your group. If you can, stay on top of the hotel's occupancy and work directly with the front office manager to bring the walked person back the next day.

Do some of these things sound like hotel staff responsibilities and not yours? Yes, it is true. However, meeting professionals must always look out for their meetings. Sometimes you will run into staff turnover, lack of staff, lack of motivation, or just plain sloppiness. Staying on top of the details prevents problems from occurring. Stay in tune with the facility and its staff.

Problem Solving

Even the best, most thorough planner will have some problem or issue to deal with onsite. What happens if a speaker changes his or her mind and needs a piece of equipment that A/V doesn't have? What if your keynote gets stuck in traffic or an attendee complains about his room and wants a refund? What if your shipping company loses the shipment with your registration materials or more people than you guaranteed show up for a meal function?

Once onsite, you have to make decisions—fast. And at this point, almost all problems have an effect on the facility and its staff, not to mention your staff, too. The key here is to discuss the problem with your onsite manager and others who are involved. They really do want your meeting to be a success and, with your help, will do whatever they can to make it work. Working with committed and creative people is one of the greatest things about this business.

The Home Stretch

Onsite can be fun if you are on top of things. A lot of the hard work is done in advance when preparing the paperwork and documents for the meeting. To end this chapter, we want to leave you with 10 tips for survival while onsite:

1. Preprogram your cell phone with the number of all your vendors. This includes the hotel you are staying at.

2. Always confirm your onsite deliveries with all of your vendors. Ask to see the package room where the boxes are kept. Check the incoming package log to see if any of the boxes belong to your group.

3. Don't leave anything of value in the meeting rooms unattended.

4. Have your office rekeyed if you plan to keep valuables in the room such as computer equipment. For keycard locks, place a lockout on it. Access to the room is limited to the people to whom you give keys.

5. For large meetings, get on the in-house radio system with the hotel staff. This gives you immediate access to help when you need it. Learn their radio lingo, and you will fit in just fine.

6. Carry a small, retractable blade (on a keychain or in your fanny pack). You'll be amazed at how many boxes you'll open.

7. Use the name badge holder (behind the tag) to store room keys, money, and business cards.

8. Wear comfortable shoes, wear comfortable shoes, wear comfortable shoes.

9. Have big bowls of chocolate in your office. Don't share.

10. Get a massage at the spa when the meeting is over.

Onsite should be the best part of the planning process. All your hard work is paying off, and there is light at the end of the tunnel! Once the meeting is over, stay an extra day, meet with the facility staff to review the meeting, and take a little time to relax. You deserve it.

The Least You Need to Know

➤ Develop your registration process and layout so that it makes sense in the facility's environment.

➤ A well-trained conference staff makes the meeting flow much more smoothly.

➤ A lot of work and planning go on behind the scenes, and you probably aren't the only group in-house. Plan ahead so you don't have to make major changes to your program onsite.

➤ Enlist the help of the facility when problems arise.

Chapter 24

Yikes! Help! Emergency!

In This Chapter

➤ Learn how to define a crisis

➤ See what kind of negative things can and do happen onsite

➤ Discover what professional security services do

➤ Learn three strategies for dealing with bad situations

Planners spend so much time getting every meeting detail right that it's easy to put planning for the unexpected on the back burner. Just because you don't expect bad things to happen doesn't mean you shouldn't be prepared.

As a planner, you need to understand the importance of protecting your attendees, organization, and property and reducing overall risk. You spend a lot of money planning a successful meeting, so don't watch your efforts go up in smoke by overlooking safety and security issues. This chapter sheds some light on preventing and dealing with bumps in the road.

What Is a Crisis?

In the meetings industry, you will hear the term *crisis management*. Before you can begin to manage a crisis, however, shouldn't you know what one is? A crisis in the meetings industry could be defined as when things don't go as planned. It happens all the time. But come on, really, how do you define a true crisis? We think that the definition is subjective and is relative to the impact on your attendees and your meeting.

For example, if you are allowing a choice of chicken or beef for a meal and run out of chicken (leaving only beef), that's not a crisis. It may be disappointing, annoying, or embarrassing, but it's not a crisis. If, however, your attendees come down with food poisoning, that's a crisis.

A specific definition of a crisis is difficult to pinpoint because people react and handle issues and stress differently. If your highly paid celebrity keynote speaker is flying over the city in a holding pattern and can't make the opening session, whether you have a crisis depends on how you and your decision-makers handle it. Here is a list of some of the things that can have a negative impact on your meeting:

How would you classify the following: a real crisis (C) or a paper cut (PC)?

Meeting Speak

Crisis management is a process to plan for and implement decisions to avoid or control undesirable events.

Food for Thought

When onsite, you should have a first-aid kit, have fast access to someone who is certified in CPR, know where (and how far) the nearest hospital is, and how to contact the facility emergency staff.

➤ Bomb threats (C)
➤ Chemical spills (C)
➤ Crime (C)
  ➤ Assault
  ➤ Theft
➤ Fire (C)
➤ Lost materials (generally a PC)
➤ Lunch buffet ran out of food (PC)
➤ Medical emergencies (C)
  ➤ Allergic reactions
  ➤ Choking
  ➤ Death
  ➤ Disease
  ➤ Injuries from falls
  ➤ Food poisoning
  ➤ Heart attack
  ➤ Illness
  ➤ Other serious conditions or injuries
➤ Natural disasters (C)
  ➤ Earthquakes
  ➤ Floods
  ➤ Hurricanes
  ➤ Storms
  ➤ Tornadoes

➤ Personal crises (C or PC ... it depends)

➤ Power outages (C or PC)

➤ Speaker no-shows (PC)

➤ Strikes (C or PC)

➤ Terrorism or threat thereof (C)

Your Motto—Be Prepared

You are running an important training seminar that requires numerous handouts. One hour before the session, you find that all the handouts have been mistakenly thrown out. The seminar is useless without them. What do you do?

Your organization spent $80,000 creating a multimedia video rolling out its new logo to be presented at the opening general session. The night before, you find out it's back at the home office. What do you do?

The Inside Scoop

If you have attendees from overseas, ask them to provide medical insurance documentation during registration. You don't want a situation in which they need medical treatment in the United States but have no means to pay for it.

A huge snowstorm up and down the East Coast is preventing 40 percent of your attendees from getting to your meeting. Many are calling to cancel altogether. What do you do?

When faced with a crisis or a paper-cut situation, follow these suggestions:

➤ First and foremost, don't panic. It serves no purpose. You must collect information, discuss options, and make fast decisions, and you can't do that very well if you are upset or let the situation get to you. Take a deep breath and know you'll get through it.

➤ You cannot anticipate every scenario, but it is very important that you plan for the ones with the largest impact. Before your meeting, take the time with your staff, the facility, and local emergency personnel to think through the "what-ifs" and come up with crisis management methods.

➤ Work with the facility, vendors, your staff, and all others who are involved. In any emergency, crisis, or bad situation, you must rely on the talents and experience of others. Get their feedback and let them help in areas in which they have expertise.

Don't Drop the Ball

Ask your staff not to guess or speculate on potential outcomes and to only state facts. Otherwise, rumors and misinformation spread, and it will make your task that much harder.

The bottom line is to plan and prepare for the unexpected. As the lead planner, you will be expected not only to make decisions but to provide leadership. It's important to temper your emotions and provide clear and honest communication. As long as attendees know that solutions are forthcoming, they will be calmer and happier.

Written Plans

You can't remember every meeting detail, can you? You have to write things down, especially information that must be communicated to others. Therefore, there's no way you can develop backup plans and not put them in writing. You, your staff, the facility's staff, and many others need direction, and the written backup plan is the place to start.

Food for Thought

For natural disasters, an emergency plan includes moving people to a secure, safe location and providing medical attention and good communication.

Don't Drop the Ball

Obtain the names, titles, and phone and pager numbers for all people responsible for a facility's emergency procedures. Meet with them at the start of your meeting.

When creating an emergency backup plan, one of the first things you should do is obtain a copy of the facility or hotel's emergency procedures. Review it and ask questions. It is important for you to understand how the facility implements its plan and who is responsible in various categories.

Ask yourself how your meeting fits in with their procedures. Understand the chain of command. You should take the important parts of the facility's procedures and create your own supplemental document for your meeting (and staff). This document should provide an outline of what to do under certain circumstances. Be as specific as possible. These procedures should also be easy to read. In an emergency, people don't have time (and won't) thumb through lengthy volumes of material.

Do you need a written backup plan for nonemergency procedures? Maybe. It's your call. Many circumstances develop fast, and you will have to work with a variety of people to solve them quickly. If a speaker does not show up, referring to a procedure won't do much. But consider the value of identifying some common problems, putting them in writing, and reviewing them with your staff. Written procedures provide a reference point on which people can base their decisions.

Professional Security Services

Depending on the needs of your meeting or event, you may choose to hire a security services company. These companies specialize in onsite event security

and management. The following are some of the
services they provide:

➤ Controlled access into and out of meeting/
event areas

➤ Establishment of emergency action plans

➤ Onsite security staff

➤ Protection of proprietary information

➤ Protection of equipment, valuable items

➤ VIP and celebrity security

Food for Thought

Have emergency information
printed separately from the program and on special colored
cards so that the information
stands out.

To decide whether you need a security firm, consider the following factors:

➤ Will your meeting have diplomats, celebrities,
or VIPs? They may come with their own security, but you might consider hiring
some additional people, especially to work with their security personnel.

➤ What is the location of your event? Will you be in an area where crime or political turmoil is a factor?

➤ Is there a scheduled event or deadline that might expose your meeting to risk?
A strike deadline or a nearby major sporting event?

➤ What is your meeting's topic? Is it controversial? Is there a concern for the
safety of speakers or attendees?

➤ Is there potential for theft of materials or intellectual property?

With meetings costing significant sums, it is worth considering the value that a professional security company offers. It only takes one incident or one unforeseen event
to turn your entire meeting into a negative, and the financial cost could be great.

Other Minor Frustrations

Frustrations may not fall into the category of emergency procedures or crisis management (although sometimes attendees make you feel like you are in a crisis), but they
do need to be addressed. You'll spend much more time dealing with little frustrations
than with big dilemmas.

Last-Minute Requests

There are last-minute requests and then there are last-minute requests. When you are
onsite, you need to be responsive to the needs of your meeting and your attendees.
You don't have the time or the resources to honor everyone's requests. What are we
talking about? Here are just a few examples of things you will be asked to do:

Food for Thought

Always get a reservation list (with room numbers) of attendees staying in the hotel. You never know when you need to contact an attendee or attendees quickly.

The Inside Scoop

When considering whether to honor someone's request, ask yourself what's the worst thing that will happen if you don't. You don't want to do or say the wrong thing and run the risk of turning a minor issue into World War III.

➤ Mail an attendee's registration materials home (at your expense).

➤ Modify a speaker's evaluation form right before he begins speaking. (You can do this during his talk, can't you?)

➤ Leave the staff office open after hours.

➤ Change the banquet lunch menu the day before because one of the organizers doesn't like it.

➤ Add an LCD projector but not pay for it. Instead, take it from an existing room and return it later.

➤ Change an attendee's return airline reservation.

➤ Deliver something to someone's room.

➤ Watch someone's briefcase or suitcase for the day.

This list could go on and on. You want to be helpful, but where do you draw the line? Sometimes you can't honor a request (like changing the menu). Other times, it's unethical (like not paying for the LCD projector). Still other times, it's just plain not your job (like mailing the materials—you've got enough to do). In some cases, however, there are good reasons to help (like making airline reservations for an attendee from overseas because his English is poor).

What you do is up to you. You should take each request on a case-by-case basis. Sometimes you'll have to bite the bullet and do things you think are silly or wasteful of your time; other times, you'll have to put your foot down. Use your judgment.

Oh Puleese!

People get up in arms about very minor issues. People like to complain. It's too hot; it's too cold. The food was terrible. I can't read the speaker's slides from the back. Sometimes the requests (or complaints) border on the ridiculous. A veteran planner gave us a great piece of advice years ago: She said to listen. Many times, people just want to be heard. They have a problem and want someone to do something. Many times you can't solve it, but tell the person you'll try. Sometimes the problem solves itself. Sometimes it doesn't matter. Take heart and take notes. You just might want to write about it someday.

The Least You Need to Know

➤ Plan ahead for emergencies with written procedures.

➤ Review all procedures with your staff.

➤ Professional security services can provide a full range of pre-event and onsite assistance.

➤ It's okay to say no to last-minute requests.

Chapter 25

It's Not Over Till It's Over

In This Chapter

➤ See why you must always double-check your master bill

➤ Learn some tips on tipping

➤ Learn what goes into your meeting's final report

➤ Understand some of the ethical dilemmas planners face

Just when you think the meeting is over and you're done, you realize there's still quite a bit of wrap-up to do.

In this chapter, we focus on tying up the loose ends, paying bills, tabulating evaluations, tipping, and generating reports. We also talk about ethics. Ethics defines behavior, and it influences many of the planning decisions we make.

Paying the Bills

We recommend that you sign off on your *banquet checks* and review all charges to your master account every day. You should also review, one more time, your master bill charges with accounting before you leave and keep a copy of all documentation. Now comes the easy part (or at least the fairly easy part).

Meeting Speak

A **banquet check** is the standard document used to break down the charges for a specific event, usually food and beverage.

The Inside Scoop

It's our experience that there are always errors on the master bill, mostly minor. Be prepared to spend some time reviewing the bill in detail. The sooner you call errors to the facility's attention, the sooner they can revise the bill and get paid.

In many cases, you will not receive the master bill for three to six weeks after your meeting, sometimes longer. Why? Well, it takes a few days for all the charges to get posted. Then someone from accounting needs to collect the charges, review your contract to make sure you've met your contractual obligations with respect to revenue, and start calculating. Plus, yours isn't the only meeting invoice accounting is working on. Consider stipulating in the contract that you will have a final bill in hand within three weeks of your meeting.

Eventually, you will receive your master bill with the associated backup. If you reviewed your charges daily and again before you left the facility, reviewing the bill should be easy. However, be on the lookout for last-minute additions such as shipping and additional food and beverage or A/V charges. Sometimes you'll find a charge for an attendee that gets put on your account by mistake. No matter how confident you are that you've approved everything, review each charge carefully.

In addition, make sure all concessions or conditions outlined in your contract are met. Make sure your final bill reflects the following:

➤ Correct calculation of complimentary rooms

➤ Any food and beverage discounts

➤ Any A/V discounts

➤ Removal of state or local sales tax, if applicable

➤ Deposits

➤ All charges billed correctly

Tipping ... Didn't We Do That?

Yes and no. When onsite, a number of people work on your behalf to get things done. Your convention services manager or catering manager is responsible for communicating your needs to the facility staff, which includes the following:

➤ Audio-visual staff

➤ Banquet staff

➤ Bell staff

➤ Concierge

➤ Front desk staff

➤ Housekeeping

➤ Recreation director(s)

➤ Setup crew

➤ Shipping/receiving staff

➤ Many others

They are the backbone of the facility and are the people who make it happen. Sadly, sometimes they go unnoticed and unthanked. Should you thank them by giving them a tip? Isn't that what the food-and-beverage service charge/gratuity was for? Let's shed some light on this.

The terms "service charge," "gratuity," and "tip" are frequently used interchangeably by meeting facilities, but they really mean different things. What you need to ask a facility is what service charges/gratuities you are paying for and to whom they are distributed. There are many people who contribute to the success of your meeting but are not included in the distribution of the service charges and/or mandatory gratuities. Bottom line is: Be sure to ask and understand who is covered and who is not in both the service charge and gratuity categories.

Tipping is always very appreciated but is not expected. We do it at each meeting because we want to recognize the people who have provided great service.

Food for Thought

If you want to thank a group, like the banquet staff, housekeepers, or telephone operators, and don't know their names, put some money in an envelope with a nice thank you note and ask the group's supervisor to distribute.

Food for Thought

If you forget to bring thank you notes, ask your sales contact for blank note cards. He or she usually will have some on hand and will gladly give you some, especially if you specify that they are for staff tips!

If tipping is important to you, at the start of your meeting, begin a "tip list." Throughout the meeting, write down the names and departments of people who help you. On the last day of your meeting, look at your list (it may get lengthy) and assign dollar amounts. It's a nice touch to put the tips in individual handwritten thank you notes.

One big question is how much to tip. You might decide to give a banquet staffer $10, your A/V technician $30, and your convention services manager $50. It really depends on the amount and level of service you received and your budget. If your A/V person ran around nonstop for four days and worked miracles, $30 may not be enough. A quick way to get cash onsite for tipping is to request a cash advance against your master bill. Ask your onsite contact if this is possible.

The Inside Scoop

Tips don't have to be in cash, especially if you have a large group and many people were involved. Chocolates, candy, and other edible treats for "the crew" are always welcome and go a long way. Others may appreciate T-shirts or conference tote bags with the meeting logo. Be sure to ask your contact what the facility's rules are before distributing any of these items or cash. In some cases, the employees will need permission to take these items out of the building or accept money.

When the time comes to distribute tips, it's best to do it in person with a verbal thank you. When you can't do that, ask your convention services manager or catering manager to do the honors. If you need a record for accounting purposes, ask that individual to sign your distribution list.

Tabulating the Evaluations

Evaluations are one of the last important meeting details to handle. Depending on the complexity of your evaluation form, it may take a few days or weeks to get them tabulated.

Don't Drop the Ball

Before you leave the facility, make sure you have collected all your evaluations, especially if they were left in various locations. Once you leave, poof—they're gone.

When you return to your office, it's a good idea to get started tabulating evaluations quickly. We know from experience that the longer it takes to get to them, the harder they are to finish. This is because your body and mind move on to the next project, and it's so hard to go back. If possible, assign the tabulation to one or more staff and get it finished.

Once they are completed, you should prepare a cohesive synopsis. The synopsis may include your interpretations and recommendations for the next meeting. Send them to all of the decision-makers as well as the people who were involved in planning the meeting. Also consider sending a copy to your sponsors and exhibitors so that the value of your meeting is reinforced.

You should also provide all of your speakers with a copy of their evaluations(s). Speakers probably are not interested in the full synopsis of the meeting, just their portion. However, if your overall evaluations contain pertinent speaker-related information, send that along, too.

Final Facility Reports

Make sure you receive a final report from the facility. The report should include a recap of everything you contracted for (rooms, food and beverage, A/V, and so on) and final comments, if possible, about how the meeting attendees used the facilities.

It is also helpful to know if the attendees used airport transportation, ate and drank in the restaurants and bars, used room service, and so on.

Your Final Report

After you have received all of the bills, tabulated your evaluations, and received your facility reports, it's time to put them all together in one final meeting report. Don't worry; it's not a huge project. You just need to consolidate the useful info into a report that outlines your meeting. The final report should have the info described in the meeting history report form as well as the following:

➤ Meeting name and dates

➤ Location

➤ Goal(s)

➤ Objectives

➤ Numbers of registrants (paid)

➤ Number of complimentary registrants, VIPs, sponsors, exhibitors, cancellations, no-shows, and so on

➤ Comments

➤ Evaluation summaries

➤ Conclusions

➤ Other information you deem relevant

Food for Thought

Send the facility a copy of the evaluations that pertain to the facility and service. They want to know, too!

Don't Drop the Ball

Make it a part of your contract that the facility agrees to provide detailed information about your meeting in a recap report.

The final report is valuable because it contains your meeting history. Chances are someone, probably you, will do this meeting again. The decision-makers, planning committee, and facility sales staff will ask a lot of questions. You won't remember the details, and in the early planning process, you will refer to this document often. The great thing is that all the important info you need is in one place!

Ethics

Ethics is an important topic in any industry and is always a hot topic in meetings industry circles. Meeting planners must make many decisions, some having large financial implications. It's quite common for vendors to "sweeten the pot" with personal incentives, gifts, and deals. The full range of temptations is enough for an entire chapter; unfortunately, we don't have room for this discourse. However, we want to highlight a few of the ethical discussions that meeting planners (and suppliers) are having. As you will see, there are two sides to every story.

To FAM or Not to FAM

Familiarization (FAM) trips are usually multiday, all-expense-paid trips to a location for the purpose of showcasing specific hotels, restaurants, other facilities, and attractions. Often a planner can bring a guest. Since the venues are marketing themselves, they fly you in, limo you around, wine you, dine you, lavish you with nice gifts, and house you in upgraded accommodations. Sounds like tremendous fun, huh? But you also get tours of many facilities, meet upper management, see a lot of the area, get tons of info, and get to ask a lot of questions. If you are asked to go on a FAM trip, what would you do?

➤ Go because you are seriously considering the location.

➤ Go because you've never been there and you want to check it out.

➤ Go because you can take your family and make a vacation out of it.

➤ Go some other time when you can pay for it yourself.

The Debate on the Rebate

Almost all hotels will pay a commission or a rebate on the sleeping room revenue if negotiated prior to contract signing. Asking for a commission or rebate on sleeping room revenue may or may not increase the cost of the sleeping rooms. It depends on whom you talk to. Commissions are paid primarily to third-party planners or to travel agents, and rebates are paid back to the meeting host.

There are two debates here, both about disclosure. The first debate centers on whether the third party should disclose to the client (the meeting host) that they are receiving a commission from the hotel. In many cases, the hotel will insist that it be disclosed and put into the contract. The second debate centers on whether any rebate or commission, no matter who gets it, should be disclosed to the attendees. If it does not affect the room rate, what difference does it make? Do attendees really care? If you do tell them, will it open up a can of worms? So, now you've booked a meeting and are getting a nice rebate for your organization (let's say $7 per room night). What would you do?

➤ Take the money and run.

➤ Take the money because it really helps your bottom line.

➤ Take the money but disclose it to your attendees.

➤ Only get net (noncommissionable) rates.

Other Ethical Issues

Other ethical dilemmas that planners face include receiving gifts from vendors, using someone else's creative theme or meeting design ideas from a proposal, receiving a free weekend vacation from a hotel as a thank you, and receiving tickets, dinners, or other perks from vendors.

Another interesting "reward" is awarding hotel points. Some major hotel chains offer hotel points, which are like frequent flyer miles, to planners who book meetings at their property. Planners can redeem these points for free stays and other things. You get the idea. Depending on the size of your meeting, these points can be substantial.

Many of the industry's associations have codes of ethics or guidelines for professional behavior. If you are not sure about a specific situation, you can always check these guidelines for help in making your decision.

It's not enough for planners to make decisions about meeting-related details; some decisions require a reflection on what is ethical. Ethics are always being debated in the meetings industry and that's good. It's not okay to look the other way or to do something just because the industry allows it. When faced with an ethical quandary, ask yourself, "Is it the right thing to do?"

The Least You Need to Know

➤ Your master bill needs to be reviewed carefully and compared to your contract. Resolve discrepancies immediately while the meeting is fresh in your mind.

➤ Tipping facility staff is not expected, but it's pretty common and is appreciated.

➤ Your final meeting report is one of your most important resources for next time.

➤ When making important decisions, consider the ethics behind them. You are your reputation.

Chapter 26

For Suppliers Only (Planners May Take a Peek)

In This Chapter

➤ Learn the top five ways to lose a customer

➤ Learn six steps to a great partnership

➤ Learn the number one mistake a hotel salesperson makes on a site inspection

➤ Understand how to educate your customers

➤ See what kinds of information a planner wants to see in a post-meeting report

This chapter will give meetings industry suppliers an inside look at what meeting planners are looking for when purchasing goods and services. It also will help suppliers foster positive, mutually beneficial business relationships with meeting planners.

For planners, this chapter provides a glimpse of what other planners look for when working with suppliers. It is always helpful to have a frame of reference to help you determine your best course of action. It is nice to know you are not alone!

Of course, the best relationships are honest and open, and you both learn from one another. In these changing times, we all need to work together to maximize the benefits of our business relationships.

Five Ways to Lose a Customer

We start with this topic not to be negative but to send a wake-up call to all suppliers that many times you will never know the real reason for the loss of business. It is true that the meetings industry is cyclical; it is either a suppliers' or buyers' market. The point is that things change, and treating your customers the same all the time is a tried and true way to keep them in good times and in bad.

Here are the top five ways to lose (or not win) a customer:

1. Send a contract with items that are different than what was discussed or send a contract without items a planner will be charged for onsite.

2. Don't return phone, fax, and e-mail inquiries promptly.

3. Don't show genuine interest in the client and his or her business (for example, by serving cookie-cutter proposals and contracts).

4. Leave messages like "Hi. I'm _____. I am calling to find out if you plan meetings. Please call me at _____."

5. Be inflexible. There is a difference between being inflexible and genuinely not being able to honor a request. It comes down to educating your clients. Inflexibility is often perceived when, in reality, there is a real business reason behind not taking a piece of business. Explain why.

Six Steps to a Great Partnership

On the flip side, there are ways to be a true partner to meeting planners. These may sound too simple, and you may already think you do them. The real question is "Do you?"

1. Ask questions and listen to what meeting planners say.

2. Return phone, fax, and e-mail inquiries promptly.

3. Understand client needs before responding. Read the RFPs and ask a lot of questions if needed. Provide solutions.

4. Know your product and/or services.

5. Know your competition and your competitive advantages.

6. Be sincere.

Know Your Property/Product/Service

One of the most frustrating experiences a planner has with a supplier is when a supplier does not know his or her product or service inside and out. For example, things like freight elevators, electrical outlets, loading docks, and how many people fit into meeting rooms are just some examples of things suppliers often do not know. If you are not sure, conduct site inspections when there are different groups in house to see how your facility works best.

Site Visits

When a planner conducts a site visit, he or she is there to determine whether the facility is a good match for a particular meeting. If you have done your homework prior to the site visit, you know the program and other ancillary needs of the group. You should first talk with the planner and sit down and map out a plan as to how you can accommodate the group. Come up with some ideas and present them to the planner. All too often, the planner is left to map out the program in a facility without expert advice. Explain how exhibitors will load in and out, where the stage should be placed in the ballroom, and how the breakouts fit into the allotted space. Tell the planner what works best in your facility. After all, you've seen many more programs in your facility than the planner has.

Show the planner what he or she wants and needs to see. Explain where you envision the meetings, meals, and other activities taking place. Paint a picture for the planner and help the person place his or her meeting in your facility.

The Inside Scoop

Learn your property inside and out. Take a tour with the chief engineer, A/V personnel, and the convention services manager. Be able to answer questions with confidence.

Don't Drop the Ball

The number one mistake made by salespeople on a hotel site inspection is not having done their homework. Understand the meeting's needs and how your facility can accommodate them.

Know These Things, Too

Planners want to know that their business is important. If you understand their business, they will see that you are a valuable resource, and the relationship will start out strong. Here are some other things meeting planners ask about that salespeople should know:

➤ The location of meeting room light switches and thermostats

➤ A/V equipment basics

➤ Food and beverage basics

➤ Outlet hours of operations

➤ Area attractions

➤ Off-site dinner/reception venues

➤ Directions to the airport

➤ Facility emergency procedures

In addition, know your competition and your competitive advantages. Also update the planner on changes such as personnel, property name changes, special promotions, policy changes, renovations, and construction dates. These could impact planner decisions.

Prepare to Solicit

Your goal is to build rapport, analyze needs, show how your facility can meet those needs, and build a trust-based relationship. Soliciting for customers isn't the same as it used to be. Planners, just like everyone else, have too much on their plate and really don't want to be bothered with calls, faxes, and e-mails from organizations they will never do business with.

Find out where you can go online to market your property and where to find clients looking for space. Here's a hint: Surf the main Web sites we have highlighted in the book. Take a look at all the marketing opportunities on these sites.

Participate in some of the meeting industry online discussions. Get your name out there! Networking still works in the new century. The days of pulling the trace files (those should be replaced by a computer) and cold calling are gone. If you are not good at using e-mail and getting on the Web, take a class or ask someone for help.

Exactly how do you reach planners who need your products and services? If we knew the exact answer, we'd be on a beach somewhere forever. You will have to figure out which ones work for you and create some of your own, too!

Food for Thought

Make sure your collateral material is relevant and easy to read. Your Web site should be user-friendly and should address the most frequently asked questions. Get rid of "canned" solicitation letters.

Here are some of the rules for finding customers:

➤ Plan your strategy.

➤ Determine your target market.

➤ Hang out at meetings and other places your target market frequents.

➤ Do your homework. If you call a prospective client, know why you are calling and make a connection.

➤ Work hard for referrals and follow up.

➤ Use technology efficiently. Find out where you can find potential customers on-line.

➤ Always carry business cards and never be timid about striking up conversations with strangers.

Random, cold solicitations are obsolete. By networking, garnering referrals, and personalizing solicitations based on needs, you'll see a bigger bang for your marketing buck.

You are better off spending $3,000 to attend a meeting and tradeshow and by meeting planners in sessions while you both learn, than by sending unsolicited marketing materials via mail, fax, or e-mail. Heck, you are better off attending conferences and spending time just networking in the hallways!

Educate the Customer

Educating the customer is an important and often overlooked role of every supplier. We all know that supply and demand drives availability and rates. We also know there are great pieces of business and not-so-great pieces of business. Educate your customers on the value of their business. If a customer is aware that there are ways to make his or her business better for a property, you both win.

Educating customers means being honest and telling them exactly why you can't book their business. On the flip side, it means telling them why you want their business. Maybe it fills a hole for you, but they think it is great because there are a lot of food functions. Level with them. Be open and honest to begin with, and long-term relationships can develop.

Inquiry Calls

The inquiry call, from a potential customer, is the first opportunity to educate him or her. To begin with, you do not know the experience level of the person making the inquiry. To respond properly, the first thing you should find out is the caller's

Food for Thought

Keep on top of the meetings industry. Subscribe to trade publications and read about the issues and challenges planners face on a daily basis.

The Inside Scoop

It comes down to providing a solution to the customer's problem. Find out very specific details about the piece of business. Nine times out of ten, we receive canned proposals. The sales manager didn't read the RFP and failed to qualify the business. Guess who has the best chance to book the meeting? The one who paid attention.

Don't Drop the Ball

Determine at the beginning of the inquiry whether you have a first-timer on your hands or a 25-year veteran. Then you will know how to approach the business.

Don't Drop the Ball

Be up front on items such as setup fees, labor charges, comp rooms, upgrades, and delivery charges. Explain what a "tentative hold" is and how long you will hold space, if at all, before a contract is signed.

level of understanding of the meetings industry. You do this by asking a few open-ended questions about the meeting, the organization, and where you might have met before. You'll know in a few minutes where the person stands in the experience department. If he or she has read this book, you are in trouble!

Once you have evaluated the person's business, explain in detail why you are submitting a proposal or declining it. Explain what would make it good business. Do you need more food and beverage revenue? Do you need a higher room rate? Exactly what are the criteria?

Preparing a Proposal

The next opportunity to educate the customer is in the proposal. The inquiry determines how you structure your proposal, but you now have the occasion to be very detailed as to how the business fits into your facility. Make sure to include all costs associated with doing business with your organization. All too often, planners get onsite and find unforeseen details turning into budget busters. For example, what is the cost of copies? Computer usage? Valet parking? Service charges and taxes? At what percentage do attrition charges kick in? Newer meeting planners may not anticipate these charges and may not realize it until too late simply because they have little or no experience.

Some suppliers will argue that if planners don't ask, you don't tell. If this is your philosophy, you may have a one-time customer. Forget repeat business.

Proposals should ...

➤ Be customized.
➤ Be concise and to the point.
➤ Be on time.
➤ Respond to customer's requests.
➤ Be creative and demonstrate your understanding of the business.

Contracts

Once the proposal goes to a contract stage, review and explain it to the planner. Especially pay attention to the cancellation, attrition, and insurance sections. You should also tell planners who will be their contact for planning the meeting, and you should review their deadlines as specified in the contract. Next, explain your accounting and billing process. An informed customer is a happy customer.

Anticipate Needs

This is where you can really help newer meeting planners use your facility to their benefit. Until a planner is actually onsite for the meeting, there are many things that can get overlooked. By asking the right questions, you can figure out all of his or her needs in advance and eliminate unnecessary frustrations onsite.

Here are some great questions to ask planners:

➤ **Where will your attendees eat when there are no food functions planned?** This will clue you in to when and if to staff the F&B outlets.

➤ **When and how do you expect your attendees to arrive?** This will clue you in to those motor coaches about to pull up to the front door.

➤ **Tell me about the most successful part of the meeting last year.** This will clue you in to specific things that you should make sure work well.

➤ **Tell me what you would change about last year's meeting site and service.** This will clue you in to how you can become the hero.

➤ **Explain how you envision the general session setup.** This will clue you in to space and setup issues like 24-hour holds.

➤ **Tell me about your attendees.** This will clue you in to the types of services you need to offer during the meeting. Will your health club be busy?

➤ **Tell me about your exhibitors. What kinds of products and services do they exhibit?** This will give you a heads up on the elephant they plan on bringing in the front doors of the lobby entrance.

You get the idea. This is where you ask pointed questions and let planners describe their meeting and their needs. We are sure you can come up with a hundred other questions.

Provide Their Meeting History

Suppliers will ask about a planner's past meeting history. Therefore, it is necessary for suppliers to provide this information in a timely manner so that planners can maintain an accurate history.

Meeting Speak

A **cover** is a meal served to one attendee. If you serve 200 people for dinner, you serve 200 covers.

Statistics

Statistics include guestrooms picked up per day compared to the room block, guestrooms picked up at certain intervals prior to arrival, food-and-beverage revenues, *covers* and guarantees by food function, revenue generated in the outlets, A/V revenue, rental fees, and general statistics about the meeting.

Observations

Observations, in addition to statistics, are very helpful to planners when planning future meetings. Provide comments from the various department heads on how the group was serviced. Break it down by department and create a report for all to complete. Include the following:

➤ **Reservations.** Room pickup, suite usage.

➤ **Bell stand.** Self-parking and valet usage, comments about bell staff usage.

➤ **Front desk.** Arrival and departure patterns, late check-outs, no-shows.

➤ **Housekeeping.** Rollaway and refrigerator usage.

➤ **Switchboard.** Number of additional lines, wake-up call usage, phone call traffic in general.

➤ **Food and beverage outlets.** Number of covers and revenue in each outlet for the group.

➤ **Security.** List calls from attendees and if there were any problems.

➤ **Accounting.** Deposit received, any special billing issues.

➤ **Banquets.** Number of covers served versus guarantees. Total revenue by function. Note any special meal requests.

➤ **Audio-visual.** List any last-minute requests, the total amount billed.

Indicate whether the final numbers are inclusive of service charges and taxes. Even go so far as to include the final calculations. Planners will appreciate detailed information when they refer to the report in the future.

Ask all departments to contribute to post-meeting reports. This is a program you can institute in the hotel by asking all departments to provide a report within a few days of every group's departure. Include statistics as well as general comments and even suggestions for improvement. This process also forces the staff to pay closer attention to the details—an added bonus!

This report should be sent to the client within a few weeks of departure. There are some major chains already doing this, but more could jump on the bandwagon.

The Least You Need to Know

➤ Know your property, product, or service. Know it inside and out. Enough said.

➤ Do your homework prior to writing a proposal and conducting a site inspection. Know exactly how the meeting fits in to your property and be prepared to discuss it.

➤ Be up front on all charges associated with doing business with your facility.

➤ Provide all groups with a post-meeting report.

Chapter 27

Alphabet Soup

In This Chapter

➤ Learn the certification designations available in the meetings industry

➤ Find out what colleges and universities offer degrees and/or certificates in meeting management

➤ Learn what kind of education you need to become a meeting planner

➤ Discover some resources for finding a job in the meetings industry

The meetings industry, like most industries, has its own educational process and certifications. If you are serious about the meetings industry as a career path, you may want to work toward a certification. Many of the associations listed in this book offer certification programs for their specific discipline. This chapter will help you sort out your options.

We'll tell you about resources for finding positions within the meetings industry. We'll also tell you about college degrees and how to find schools that offer meeting-planning programs. Finally, we address how associations are stepping up to the plate to provide cutting-edge education via distance learning and seminars and conferences.

Education is a lifelong process, and keeping up with the industry takes time and effort to maintain the knowledge base necessary for future success.

Certification—Is It for You?

Okay, so you think your name would look good with a few initials behind it? Many people do. We know many talented certified planners. We also know many meeting planners who do not have any certifications, and they too are excellent planners. Whether or not you decide to obtain a certification depends on your particular situation and what type of education you need to do your job. Within the meetings industry, certification is quite visible and can lead to higher salaries.

The Inside Scoop

A certification designation is a stepping stone for professional excellence. It demonstrates your dedication to your profession. It is not a reason to stop learning once you have achieved it. It is not a piece of paper that says you are better than people who do not have a certification.

Currently, there are two main certification designations for meeting planners:

1. **Certified Meeting Professional (CMP).** Founded and organized through the Convention Industry Council (CIC). You can find more information at www.conventionindustry.org.

2. **Certificate in Meeting Management (CMM).** The first university-endorsed meeting professional designation, it is awarded by Meeting Professionals International (MPI). You can find more information at www.mpiweb.org.

In addition, there are many other certification designations within the meetings industry that apply to either planners and suppliers or both. Here's a partial list including the association that confers the designations:

American Hotel and Motel Association (www.ahma.com)

Certified Hospitality Sales Professional (CHSP)

Certified Hotel Administrator (CHA)

Certified Lodging Manager (CLM)

Certified Hospitality Educator (CHE)

Certified Food & Beverage Executive (CFBE)

Certified Rooms Division Executive (CRDE)

Certified Hospitality Housekeeping Executive (CHHE)

Certified Human Resources Executive (CHRE)

Certified Engineering Operations Executive (CEOE)

Certified Hospitality Supervisor (CHS)

American Society of Association Executives (www.asaenet.org)

Certified Association Executive (CAE)

Hospitality Sales and Marketing Association International (www.hsmai.org)

Certified Hospitality Marketing Executive (CHME)

International Association of Assembly Managers (www.iaam.org)

Certified Facilities Executive (CFE)

International Association of Exhibition Management (www.iaem.org)

Certified in Exhibition Management (CEM)

International Special Events Society (www.ises.com)

Certified Special Events Professional (CSEP)

National Association of Catering Executives (www.nace.net)

Certified Professional Catering Executive (CPCE)

National Speakers Association (www.nsaspeaker.org)

Certified Speaking Professional (CSP)

Society of Incentive and Travel Executives (www.SITE-intl.org)

Certified Incentive and Travel Executive (CITE)

For a lot of people, years of experience are worth their weight in gold. A planner who plans multiple meetings and is active in the industry gets more education on the job than a planner who plans one or two meetings a year. Only you can determine in what areas you need more education and training.

Higher Education

You may want to consider a degree or certificate program from a college or university. There are many programs available in meeting management. Even degrees in tourism and hotel and restaurant management can lead to some pretty exciting careers!

Food for Thought

When you investigate a certification designation, find out for how long the designation is valid and what the requirements are for renewing it.

Degrees/Certificates

Many colleges and universities offer certificates or degrees in meeting, event, convention, exhibition, tourism, hotel, and restaurant management. The exact courses vary by institution. Here is a sampling:

California State University
Fullerton, CA
www.takethelead.fullerton.edu/catalog/catalog/meetplan.htm

Cornell University
Ithica, NY
www.hotelschool.cornell.edu

George Washington University
Washington, DC
www.gwu.edu/emp

Indiana University Purdue University Indianapolis
Indianapolis, IN
www.iupui.edu/~indyhper/tcem_courses.htm

Michigan State University
East Lansing, MI
www.bus.msu.edu/shb

New York University
New York, NY
www.scps.nyu.edu/chtta

Northeastern University
Tahlequah, OK
www.nsuok.edu

Roosevelt University
Chicago, IL
www.roosevelt.edu/tourismstudies

University of Nevada
Las Vegas, NV
www.unlv.edu/Tourism

University of Wisconsin—Stout
Menomonie, WI
www.uwstout.edu/programs/bshrtm

You also should check with local community colleges in your area. Many are getting on the bandwagon and offering certificates in meeting planning. If you are not sure where to call, check with your state chapter of the industry associations. They will send you in the right direction.

Distance Learning

Distance learning no longer lets your hectic schedule preclude you from pursuing a degree. Taking classes online allows you to learn from the comfort of your own computer in your pajamas if need be. Most colleges and universities are beginning to offer courses online, so be sure to check. Some of the ones in the preceding list offer online courses, too.

Associations

It will be no big surprise to you that associations are a great place to further your professional educational needs. Most of them offer seminars, conferences, and conventions featuring the newest trends, the latest technology, and cutting-edge speakers. This is another great reason to be a member of at least one association. Associations also offer distance learning programs. Check out their Web sites for opportunities in this area. If you can't attend their meetings, at least you may be able to take advantage of their educational offerings.

Continuing Education Units (CEUs)

When you join an association that offers a certificate program, you will more than likely have to earn continuing education credits (CEUs) for the certification and recertification process. Each certification designation will have its own rules and stipulations for the program. In some instances, you will have to qualify to sit for the exam. For example, you may be required to have five years of employment experience in the field to become certified.

Conferences and Seminars

Attending conferences and seminars is one of the best ways to learn a lot in a small amount of time. The networking allows time to problem-solve and is worth the registration fee. The opportunity to meet colleagues face-to-face provides the motivation and energy to do a better job back at the office. Connecting and sharing with your peers is powerful. Sharing what works and how to do things better will never replace a computer screen or a textbook.

Get a Job! Get a Life!

People who want to become meeting planners often ask us what degree or education they need to get a job. This is a very good question and is one that has many different answers and perspectives.

First of all, if you ask planners today how they became meeting planners you will hear the following top five reasons:

1. By accident.
2. It fit into their current duties.
3. Their boss volunteered them to plan a meeting.
4. They were good at organizing parties and events.
5. They love people and the challenge of getting things done under pressure.

These days, it is not as easy to "fall into" a meeting-planning job as it used to be. With employers realizing that they need strategic thinkers and leaders, the planner positions are taken more seriously and are categorized at higher levels. In some companies, being a CMP or CMM is a requirement.

So, in answer to the question of what you need in the way of education, we offer the following advice:

➤ Obtain a certification, degree, or certificate in the meetings industry.

➤ Be willing to start out in a support role in a meeting-planning department.

➤ Don't limit your job possibilities to a "meeting planner" or "assistant" title. Look at hotels, CVBs, DMCs, and event-planning companies for other opportunities. Even being a sales assistant in a hotel can give you valuable experience. You also get to meet all the clients who need planners!

➤ Get an internship at a hotel or CVB.

➤ Be persistent.

Networking is still a great way to find a job in the meetings industry. Attend industry functions, talk to both planners and suppliers, and in general, be active in the industry!

There are also some very good Web sites you can visit to peruse the job opportunities and submit your resume. For starters, take a look at these:

➤ www.meetingjobs.com

➤ www.mim.com/jobboard

➤ www.hotel-jobs.com

➤ www.hcareers.com

➤ www.searchwide.com

Most of the industry associations listed in this book also have job boards on their Web sites. Just by surfing the Web sites mentioned in this book, you will find many places to look for a job.

The Least You Need to Know

➤ A certification designation is a stepping stone to professional excellence.

➤ It is never too late to earn a certificate or degree in meeting management.

➤ Investigate colleges, universities, and local community colleges for certificate and degree programs in meeting management.

➤ There are many online job boards on which you can post a resumé or search through job listings.

Chapter 28

Oh, the Insanity of It All

In This Chapter

➤ Learn a four-step process for standing firm on meeting planning decisions

➤ Discover ways to look out for number one

➤ See how being too busy takes you away from the really important things in your life

➤ Learn some simple tricks to keep control of the information flow in and out of your office

---

Today's lifestyles demand our full attention. We are constantly exposed to new technology, higher stress levels, increased job responsibility, a nonstop business climate, the need for more education, family commitments, and that nagging feeling of always being "behind" in whatever we are supposed to do.

Meeting planning can really stress you out. You are responsible for tons of details including budgets, goals, objectives, negotiating contracts, marketing, brochure development, travel plans, speakers, VIPs, registration, meeting supplies, and making it all happen onsite. The real kicker is that meeting planning is all based on deadlines, and there are real consequences for missing those deadlines. Meeting planning is a huge responsibility.

This chapter is for you, the meeting planner. Who really knows what you do besides you? We do. We can help by sharing with you some thoughts and ideas we have come up with during our tenure in the meetings business.

How Much More Can I Take?

Planning revolves around details, and it's always amazing how much time the little things take up. Your best bet is to get and stay organized. Here are a few good, quick tips that we use:

➤ Assign each task a priority: low, medium, high, or urgent.

➤ Every day, do at least three items more than you add to your list. Start with the highest priority.

➤ Respond to low- or mid-level e-mails and voicemails after hours if possible.

➤ Create a "waiting on" response list so you can see at a glance who you are waiting on.

➤ Don't let things pile up. File at the end of every day.

➤ Review and modify your next day's list before you leave the office.

➤ When you need information, make phone calls early in the day.

➤ Use caller ID and/or e-mail filters to screen calls or e-mails.

➤ Throw out redundant information.

➤ Take some time each day to relax.

Taking some time out also helps keep things in perspective. There will be times when a problem develops and you have to answer to people who don't understand the situation or what you do. They get upset, your staff gets upset, and you get upset. Situations can escalate to the point that even the littlest deals turn into big deals. Slow down, take a deep breath, and most of all, don't take it personally.

Don't Drop the Ball

When things get tense, rally the troops. If you have support staff, take care of them. Buy lunch, tell jokes, provide snacks and toys in the office—make it fun.

Food for Thought

Continue your professional education. Go to meeting planning educational seminars and conferences; read trade, business, and training magazines; consider certification.

Who's Clueless?

Meeting planning is just now becoming recognized as a profession. Planners should be involved in the strategic part of meetings, not just logistics. All too often, the planner role is just administrative in nature, and that can be a mistake. Don't get stuck in the dirt. Think big picture.

One word of caution: You will run into nonplanners who think they know more than you when it comes to planning meetings. Sometimes that leads to stupid mistakes. If you run into a situation in which your organization or managers want to do something you know will not work, stand up for what you know. Act professionally and state your viewpoint based on experience. What is your recourse, however, if you are asked to so something that you know will not work and that could possibly have a negative impact on your meeting? Consider using this four-step process:

1. Go to the person/group making the request and explain why you think the idea won't work. Back up your explanation with facts and provide an alternative solution.

2. Garner support from within your organization or from seasoned veterans in the meetings industry. Make sure you clearly state your case and your alternative solution.

3. If you are still asked to implement the request, make sure you document your recommendation in writing and give a copy to all decision-makers prior to the event or meeting. Then, if your predictions come true, you cannot be held responsible.

4. Follow up after the event or meeting and evaluate the outcome. Learn from your experience.

As an example, consider the company executive who does not consider the meeting planner an integral part of the company's strategic-planning process. The planner has no strategic role and is told to just plan the meeting logistics. In this scenario, if the planner has no idea about goals, objectives, and the reasons for the meetings, how can this person communicate needs to a potential vendor? How can he or she determine the right site for the meetings? How can he or she negotiate a contract that meets the needs of each meeting? The answer is he or she can't. The planner can only plod along and check off one detail after another.

Consider another company in which the meeting planner is part of the organization's strategic-planning advisory group and is well versed in why meetings are held within the organization. This person is in a much better position to select the right site, set the meeting rooms, internally market the meeting to the attendees, and negotiate contracts. The meeting planning process is more strategic in nature, and as a result, contracts are negotiated to meet those needs. The right sites are selected to support the meetings' goals and objectives, and attendees understand why they are attending the meetings.

Food for Thought

When you get recognition for a job well done, take it and don't be afraid to toot your own horn.

To reach a strategic position in your organization, you need to constantly educate your superiors as to how you bring value to the organization. Document how and when you saved the company money, and how much, because of your negotiation skills or how you leveraged your buying power by signing a multiyear meeting contract. It is very easy to spend a lot of money on meetings. It takes a talented meeting planner to keep tabs on the purse strings and be recognized for it.

What's So Hard About That?

Then there are the people who think your job is nothing but fun, fun, fun and can't believe you get paid for it. We have not come across any other industry in which so much responsibility is placed on individuals who have little or no experience and have to learn the hard way—by doing. Think about the awesome responsibility you have and how it can really affect your organization. For example, if your contracts are not negotiated effectively because you have no idea about your history and the company ends up paying huge attrition fees, that affects the company. The flip side is that a well-negotiated contract can avoid attrition fees altogether.

We know of one meeting planner who got sick and tired of not making what her peers made in other departments so she researched the skill sets, documented that she has huge responsibilities that can make or break budgets in her company, and won a well-deserved pay raise.

Look Out for #1

Ever notice how busy everyone is? Doesn't it seem that everyone's response to "How are you?" is "I'm busy"? How did this happen? We remember a time when work was more manageable and you went home each night feeling good about the workload in your office. You rarely even brought work home. The "B" word (balance) is affecting us all. These days you are lucky if you are caught up.

The Inside Scoop

The good news is we can have better control of our time if we take the time (no pun intended) to sort through and determine the really important stuff.

Planners are constantly under deadline pressures and have a lot of last-minute tasks to accomplish. These things tend to get in the way of accomplishing your goals and objectives.

Would you like to take back your life and maintain some sense of balance? If so, make a list of things you do that are not really important and stop doing them. Your list might look like this:

➤ Making too many volunteer commitments, both professional and personal

➤ Making too many business commitments

➤ Watching too much television

➤ Attending business-related social gatherings

➤ Stacking unread mail or magazines, hoping to get to them later

Make a list of the really important things you need to do and do them! This list could include the following:

➤ Be home to tuck the kids into bed every night, or scratch the dog's ears.

➤ Make more home-cooked dinners and eat at least one meal a day with family or friends.

➤ Upgrade your technology and your knowledge of it to make your life easier.

➤ Go for a walk or a bike ride; smell the roses.

➤ Have lunch with your favorite person.

➤ Take a vacation every year and leave your pager and cell phone at home.

Here are some additional tips to take control:

➤ **Delegate at home and at work.** Delegate when you can. If you are a volunteer, make sure you are not doing the majority of the work.

➤ **Look at your to-do list and do the "worst" thing first.** Once the hard part is over, the rest of your day is much easier.

➤ **Listen to your body.** If you are a morning person, try to accomplish the most important things when you are at your best. If you are a night person, work at night. Do not fight your body's internal clock.

➤ **Hire outside help.** Hire help to clean your house, mow your grass, or even run errands. You can find professional services or perhaps even neighborhood teenagers. Your time is important and has value.

➤ **Simplify your life.** Get rid of things you don't use and throw out excess stuff.

➤ **Accept that it is okay to do less.** Sometimes it is okay to do nothing. Silence can be golden.

Many people find validation in crossing items off a to-do list. This is not living; it is just accomplishing tasks. Think about it. Is this how you measure your success? What do you really want to do? How do you really want to spend your time?

Meeting planners tend to carry over their *big* checklists into their personal lives. Before you know it, you are running your life like you run a meeting. Sometimes our kids have to say, "Mom, you are not at a meeting." Understand this and your life will be less stressful.

Meeting Speak

A **coach** is an individual with experience and leadership to guide and help you achieve your goals.

Get a Coach

Ever heard of having a *coach?* A life coach? A career coach? A family coach? Yes, they exist and can be a valuable part of helping you make changes. Not only have you committed to make changes, you now have to report progress to someone. Talk about motivation!

A coach brings a different perspective to your life. Sometimes just knowing that other people are going through the same thing is comforting. Plus, a coach is less expensive than a psychiatrist. Check out www.coachfederation.com for more information and to find a coach.

Friends and Family

Make time for friends and family. Do you eat dinner with them? Do you celebrate events such as birthdays and holidays? Make sure family is a top priority and carries more weight than work does. Try not to miss important events because you are too busy. Establish family traditions. This is especially important if you have young children or elderly parents. The worst thing that can happen is you go through life on a huge racetrack, and one day you wake up and realize you didn't spend enough time with your family and friends. Don't let it happen.

When the Goin' Gets Tough

When the goin' really gets tough, write your obituary. Sit down and write who you are or what you want to be remembered for. It really puts things into perspective. You will find out very quickly that being busy all the time and accumulating a million frequent flyer miles is not something people will remember you for. You will also find that whatever is creating havoc in your life really doesn't matter much in the whole scheme of things.

The Office Never Closes

With technology racing faster than the speed of sound, you never catch up. In fact, when you are onsite at one meeting, you may have several others piling up at the office! Or, at the very least, your other work is piling up, too. Not to mention the voice and e-mail messages waiting for your attention.

E-mail is one big game of gotcha! You are helpless and are tagged "it" with the click of a mouse—unless, of course, you program one of those handy little e-mail messages that says you are out of the country for the next several months. You can also program your voicemail not to accept messages. We really like that one.

However, the reality of it is you need to be reachable and need to control the flow of information in and out of your office. Here are some ideas for helping you manage this flow:

➤ Delegate time-consuming tasks, such as mailings, to other staff members or outsource this work if possible.

➤ Network with other meeting-industry professionals to find out how they do things. If you belong to any industry associations, these are perfect places to find other people with similar job responsibilities. If you do not belong to any associations, join one now! Didn't we say that already?

➤ Say no to time wasters such as extended lunches or seminars whose content hold little or no value to you.

➤ Understand your job and ask the question, "Is this task really important to the bottom line?" If the answer is no, don't do it. Try it. You may be surprised.

> **Don't Drop the Ball**
>
> In these high tech days, many people are using hand held PDAs (personal digital assistants). They allow you to keep a large number of contacts handy, record calendar information, and send and receive e-mail. They can really increase your productivity.

Juggling Multiple Meetings

It would be great if you could plan one meeting at a time, but more than likely, you will be responsible for several at any given time. Here are some ideas to make it easier to manage them and to save time in the booking process:

➤ Book multiple meetings at the same hotel or with the same hotel chain.

➤ Schedule site visits together. Piggyback meetings in the same city.

➤ Create a standard RFP for all your meetings.

➤ Hire an industry attorney to create a meetings contract or at least an addendum that addresses your needs.

➤ Keep good meeting-history records.

Staying Ahead

In our work, the key to staying ahead in this fast-paced world is to stay focused on a defined set of issues. For example, a meeting planner has a defined role—simply put, to plan meetings. A supplier's role is to meet the planner's needs within the scope of the meeting. To succeed, we need to organize ourselves in a way that progress can be monitored and improved upon. Good luck!

The Least You Need to Know

➤ Solid organization is necessary to stay in control of the details.

➤ In any dispute over meeting decisions, state your viewpoint and stand up for what you know.

➤ Each day, tackle the "yuckiest" thing first. The rest of the day will seem much easier.

➤ Keep balance in your work and life.

Sample Forms
and Checklists

Here are some handy forms for you to copy and use. You can customize them for your needs or use them the way they are. Make your own forms along the way, too. Meeting planners just love forms and checklists!

Breakout Evaluation

1. Name of breakout session: _____

   Date: _____

2. Presenter name: _____

3. The information presented is useful to my work: Yes ❏   No ❏

4. The delivery method was appropriate: Yes ❏   No ❏

5. The handouts were relevant and covered the subject: Yes ❏   No ❏

6. Please rate each of the following:

	Excellent	**Good**	**Fair**	**Poor**
Speaker knowledge of topic	❏	❏	❏	❏
Delivery style	❏	❏	❏	❏

Suggestions for improvement:

_____

_____

_____

_____

Return form to: <add your contact information here>

Conference Evaluation

	Excellent	Good	Fair	Poor

1. Please rate each of the following:

   Educational value of overall conference: ❑ ❑ ❑ ❑

2. How would you rate the conference logistics?

   Schedule ❑ ❑ ❑ ❑

   Registration process ❑ ❑ ❑ ❑

3. Please rate the hotel:

   Service ❑ ❑ ❑ ❑

   Food and beverage ❑ ❑ ❑ ❑

   Meeting rooms ❑ ❑ ❑ ❑

   Audio-visual ❑ ❑ ❑ ❑

4. Do you have suggestions for next year's conference?

   Keynote speakers: _____

   Breakout topics: _____

   Activities: _____

   Schedule: _____

5. Were your professional goals and objectives met during the conference?
   Yes ❑   No ❑

6. What did you learn that you will put into use once you return to the office?

   _____

   _____

7. What didn't you learn that you thought you would?

   _____

   _____

8. Did the promotional material adequately describe the educational value of the conference?   Yes ❑   No ❑

   If not, do you have any suggestions for improvement?

   _____

   _____

9. How do you rate the conference fee?   High ❑   Just right ❑   Low ❑

10. Do you plan on attending the conference next year? Yes ❑   No ❑   Maybe ❑

11. Are you a member?   Yes ❑   No ❑

12. What is your title? _____

13. Name/phone number (optional) _____

Return form to: <add your contact information here>

Exhibitor Evaluation

Please share your comments on the value of being an exhibitor. Your feedback will be extremely helpful in planning future conferences.

	Excellent	Good	Fair	Poor
1. Please rate each of the following:				
Overall exhibit experience	❏	❏	❏	❏
Overall schedule	❏	❏	❏	❏
Networking with attendees	❏	❏	❏	❏
Booth registration process	❏	❏	❏	❏
Pre-conference info	❏	❏	❏	❏
Cost of booth	❏	❏	❏	❏
Meeting facility overall	❏	❏	❏	❏
2. Please rate exhibitor services company:				
Service	❏	❏	❏	❏
Pre-conference information	❏	❏	❏	❏
Pricing	❏	❏	❏	❏
Package handling	❏	❏	❏	❏

3. List suggestion(s) for improvement:

_____

_____

4. How did you first learn about this conference?
   - ❏ Word of mouth
   - ❏ Info mailed to you
   - ❏ Web site
   - Other: _____

5. We will return again next year as an exhibitor.
   - ❏ Yes—please send information
   - ❏ No
   - If not, why: _____

6. Include your name and affiliation (optional).
   - Name: _____
   - Affiliation: _____

Return form to: <add your contact information here>

Room Pick-Up Report

Meeting name: _____

Meeting dates: _____

	Hotel Information	Meeting Sponsor
Name	_____	_____
Address	_____	_____
City	_____	_____
State/ZIP	_____	_____
Contact name	_____	_____
Phone	_____	_____
Fax	_____	_____
E-mail	_____	_____
Web site	_____	_____

Total

Days to Arrival	Date	Date	Date	Total Pick-Up	Revenue
Contracted block	_____	_____	_____	_____	$_____
Pick-up 6 weeks out	_____	_____	_____	_____	$_____
Pick-up 5 weeks out	_____	_____	_____	_____	$_____
Pick-up 4 weeks out	_____	_____	_____	_____	$_____
Pick-up 3 weeks out	_____	_____	_____	_____	$_____
Pick-up 2 weeks out	_____	_____	_____	_____	$_____
Pick-up 1 week out	_____	_____	_____	_____	$_____
Pick-up 1 day out	_____	_____	_____	_____	$_____
Pick-up day of	_____	_____	_____	_____	$_____
Actual pick-up	_____	_____	_____	_____	$_____

Room rate(s):	$_____	Total room revenue:	$_____
Suite rate(s):	$_____	Number of suites used:	_____
Complimentary policy:	_____	Number of comps:	_____
Number of no-shows:	_____	No-show percentage:	_____
Number of cancellations:	_____	Cancellation percentage:	_____
Room tax percentage:	_____		

Additional information: _____

Food and Beverage Pick-Up Report

Meeting name: _____

Meeting dates: _____

Contact name: _____

Phone/fax/e-mail: _____

Meal Function	Guarantee	Actual Served	Cost/Person	Total Cost
Date: _____				
Continental breakfast	_____	_____	_____	_____
A.M. break	_____	_____	_____	_____
Lunch	_____	_____	_____	_____
P.M. break	_____	_____	_____	_____
Reception	_____	_____	_____	_____
Dinner	_____	_____	_____	_____
Date: _____				
Continental breakfast	_____	_____	_____	_____
A.M. break	_____	_____	_____	_____
Lunch	_____	_____	_____	_____
P.M. break	_____	_____	_____	_____
Reception	_____	_____	_____	_____
Dinner	_____	_____	_____	_____

Total Food and Beverage Cost* $_____

*not including taxes and gratuity

Gratuity Percentage: _____   Gratuity taxed? yes/no   ×_____% Gratuity

F & B Tax Percentage: _____ $_____

Entertainment
Group(s) and Cost(s): _____   ×_____% Tax

Decorations and Costs: _____

TOTAL $_____

Observations about food functions: _____

Site Visit Checklist

Property name: _____

Contact person: _____ **Phone:** _____

Distance from airport:
     Miles: _____
     Minutes: _____
Transportation available: _____
Nearby restaurants: _____
Nearby shopping: _____

Arrival Experience
(list comments)
Check-in: _____
Check-out: _____
Lobby area: _____
Bell stand service: _____
Front desk service: _____

Guest Rooms
No. of guest rooms:
     Kings: _____
     Dbl/Dbl: _____
     Suites: _____
Amenities in rooms: _____
Condition: _____
No. of phone lines: _____   Data port?   Yes   No

Food and Beverage Outlets
No. of outlets: _____
Names: _____
Hours of operation: _____

Meeting Space
Condition: _____
Square footage: _____
No. of breakout rooms/size: _____

_____
_____

Airwalls soundproof?   Yes   No
Temperature controls in rooms?   Yes   No
Lighting quality: _____
Sound system(s): _____
List any obstructions: _____
Room signage clear?   Yes   No
AV company onsite?   Yes   No
    Name: _____
Restrooms nearby?   Yes   No

Questions

Is the hotel unionized?   Yes   No
    Which departments? _____
Are there any renovation or construction plans?   Yes   No
What other groups are in-house over these dates? _____
Is the hotel ADA compliant?   Yes   No
    Issues: _____
Are there any big events in town over these dates?   Yes   No
Will the hotel likely be sold out during meeting dates? Yes   No
Call reservations. Rate quoted during meeting dates: _____
What is the guest emergency procedure?
    Medical: _____
    Fire: _____
    Other: _____

Breakout Session Speaker Agreement

<Date>
<Name>   <Title>
<Organization>   <Address>
<City, State, ZIP>

Title of Session: _____   Start Time: _____

Date: _____   End Time: _____

Thank you for agreeing to be a presenter at our conference. In exchange for your time, you will receive a complimentary registration to the conference. Although we are unable to cover your expenses related to the conference, we will copy your hand-outs if you provide an original at least fourteen days in advance of your presentation.

Please send us the following information as soon as possible:

1. A brief resumé of your education and experience for your introduction.
2. Audio-visual requirements for your breakout session. Please note that all rooms will be set crescent style with a podium and table for the speaker's use.

   ___ Overhead projector and screen   ___ Flipchart

   ___ VCR and Monitor   ___ LCD projector

   ___ Slide projector   ___ Wireless microphone

Please note you are responsible for making your own housing reservation. Please call 000-000-0000. Enclosed is a tentative conference agenda for your planning purposes.

I hereby agree to present at the <name of conference>. I affirm that, to my knowledge, none of the material presented, either verbally or in written materials, infringes upon any copyright or any person's right of privacy. I will not libel or slander any other person, facility, company, product, or service during my presentation. If such affirmation is breached, I indemnify and hold harmless <insert your organization here> and all contracted service providers.

I also understand I cannot make a "sales pitch" for any specific firm, publication, or service during my presentation. I can provide participants with an opportunity to purchase publications or materials at the conclusion of my session.

____ I agree to have my session audiotaped and the tapes reproduced for sale with the proceeds going to <insert designee of proceeds>.

Accepted: _____

Date: _____

Print Name: _____

Please fax or mail this agreement along with your brief resumé to: <add your information here>

Meeting-Related Web Sites

This appendix lists all the Web sites referenced in this book. It represents just a very small sampling of the wide variety of meeting-related Web sites. To find the latest, most comprehensive, hyperlinked list of hundreds of Web sites, go to www. corbinball.com.

Associations and Organizations

www.ahiattorneys.org	Academy of Hospitality Industry Attorneys
www.ahma.com	American Hotel and Motel Association
www.ammc.org	Association of Meeting Management Consultants
www.asaenet.org	American Society of Association Executives
www.ascap.com	American Society of Composers, Authors, and Publishers
www.bmi.com	Broadcast Music, Inc.
www.conventionindustry.org	Convention Industry Council
www.iacconline.org	International Association of Conference Centers
www.iacvb.org	International Association of Convention and Visitors Bureaus
www.iaem.org	International Association for Exhibition Management
www.iasbweb.org	International Association of Speakers Bureaus
www.ifea.com	International Festivals and Events Association
www.ises.com	International Special Events Society
www.mpiweb.org	Meeting Professionals International
www.nsaspeaker.org	National Speakers Association
www.nsfre.org	National Society of Fund Raising Executives
www.officialtravelinfo.com	OfficialTravelInfo.com
www.pcma.org	Professional Convention Management Association
www.sesac.com	Society of European Stage Authors and Composers

Certifications

www.asaenet.org	Certified Association Executive (CAE)
www.conventionindustry.org	Certified Meeting Professional (CMP)
www.hsmai.org	Certified Hospitality Marketing Executive (CHME)
www.iaam.org	Certified Facilities Executive (CFE)
www.ises.com	Certified Special Events Professional (CSEP)
www.mpiweb.org	Certification in Meeting Management (CMM)
www.nace.net	Certified Professional Catering Executive (CPCE)
www.nsaspeaker.org	Certified Speaking Professional (CSP)
	CPAE—Council of Peers Award for Excellence
www.site-intl.org	Certified Incentive and Travel Executive (CITE)

Gifts, Giveaways, and Meeting Supplies

www.4imprint.com	4imprint
www.awards.com	Awards.com
www.branders.com	Branders
www.bravanta.com	Bravanta.com
www.landsend.com	Lands' End
www.marcomeetings.com	Marco
www.nambe.com	Nambe
www.pcnametag.com	pc/nametag
www.seton.com/events	Seton
www.tiffanys.com	Tiffany's

Industry Jobs

www.coachfederation.com	International Coach Federation
www.hcareers.com	Hospitality Careers Online
www.hotel-jobs.com	Hospitality Jobs Online
www.meetingjobs.com	Meeting Candidate Network
www.mim.com/jobboard	Meetings Industry Mall Job Board

Meeting Management Resources

www.all-hotels.com	all-hotels.com
www.conferencedirect.com	ConferenceDirect
www.conferon.com	Conferon

Meeting Management Resources

www.corbinball.com	Corbin Ball Associates
www.eventweb.com	EventWeb
www.helmsbriscoe.com	HelmsBriscoe
www.hotrateshotdates.com	HotRatesHotDates
www.meetingscoach.com	MeetingsCoach
www.meetingsnet.com/mpsg	Meeting Planners Survival Guide
www.mim.com	Meetings Industry Mall
www.mpoint.com	mpoint.com by Plansoft
www.theguide.com	Guide to Unique Meeting and Event Facilities
www.tradeshowresearch.com	Successful Exhibiting

Meeting Technology Software

www.allmeetings.com	AllMeetings.com
www.badgepro.com	BadgePro
www.bluedot.com	bluedot.com
www.b-there.com	b-there.com
www.cardscan.com	CardScan
www.ceosoft.com	Scheduler Plus
www.cvent.com	cvent.com
www.dea.com	Event Management Systems
www.certain.com	Event Planner Plus and Meeting Planner Plus
www.ekeba.com	Complete Event Manager
www.eventsource.com	EventSource.com
www.event411.com	Event411.com
www.expocad.com	Expocad
www.meetingmatrix.com	MeetingMatrix
www.mpoint.com	mpoint.com by Plansoft
www.netsimplicity.com	Meeting Room Manager
www.optimumsettings.com	Optimum Settings
www.passkey.com	Passkey.com
www.pcnametag.com	pc/nametag
www.peopleware.com	PeoplewarePro
www.psitrak.com	MeetingTrak
www.regweb.com	RegWeb
www.seeuthere.com	seeUthere.com

continues

continued

Meeting Technology Software

www.senada.com	Senada.com
www.starcite.com	Starcite
www.timesaversoftware.com	Room Viewer and Event Sketch
www.viewcentral.com	ViewCentral

Trade Publications

www.btnonline.com	*Business Travel News*
www.corbinball.com	*Corbin Ball Associates*
www.meetingsnet.com	*Adams Business Media*
www.meetings-conventions.com	*Meetings and Conventions*
www.meetingnews.com	*MeetingNews*
www.midwestmeetings.com	*Midwest Meetings*
www.meetings411.com	*Meetings West, Meetings South, Meetings East*
www.smallmarketmeetings.com	*Small Market Meetings*
www.successmtgs.com	*Successful Meetings*
www.wheremagazine.com	*Where Magazine*

Trade Shows and Expositions

www.expochange.com	ExpoExchange
www.freemanco.com	Freeman Decorating
www.gesexpo.com	GES Exposition Services

Glossary

à la carte   Each item is priced and sold individually on the menu.

adult learning techniques   Methods used to teach and retrain individuals who are returning to an educational setting.

agenda   An outline of the meeting schedule.

amenity   An item placed in a guestroom such as food and beverages or some other gift. In-room amenities are also shampoos, bathrobes, and stuff!

American Society of Association Executives (ASAE)   An association for managers and executives of associations.

appliqué   A small, self-stick, embroidered design used for name badges, lapels, and clothes. Used for themes and identifiers.

association planner   An individual who plans meetings for associations.

attrition   A reduction in numbers from what you promised the meeting facility. The numbers are the guestrooms and food and beverage meal covers from which the facility forecasts its potential revenue and profit. Attrition is also called slippage or drop-off.

back of the house   The area in a meeting facility that the staff uses and that is not open to the public.

banquet check   The standard document used to break down the charges for a specific event, usually food and beverage charges.

banquet event order (or banquet prospectus)   A hotel information sheet for staff members that lists the details of a meal function including times, the number of people, the menu, special instructions, audio-visual equipment, and billing information.

booking pattern   Arrival and departure days of the week for a group or individual.

break-even point   The point at which your meeting neither makes nor loses money.

breakout session   Presentations focused on specific topics.

buyers market   A business climate in which the customer can negotiate better deals and has more flexibility in the negotiating process.

call for presentations   An application to apply for the opportunity to be a presenter at a meeting or conference. Conference organizers are usually looking for specific topics, and carefully following the application guidelines gives you a better chance of being selected.

catering manager   A person who plans and manages meal functions at a hotel.

city-wide   Large meetings that cannot be held in just one location. Attendees stay in hotels throughout the city and usually meet at a large convention center or venue.

coach   An individual with experience and leadership who guides people and helps them achieve specific goals.

commissionable rate   A guestroom rate in which the hotel agrees to pay a specific percentage back to a designated organization. An industry standard for third-party meeting planners and travel agents is 10 percent. A net rate is void of any commissions.

comp   A meeting industry term that means complimentary.

company meeting   A meeting for people from the same company or organization. These include board, staff, and sales meetings and focus on information exchange, problem solving, and decision making.

concession   Something you receive over and above the standard offering.

conference   A meeting for people who have a shared discipline or industry, usually for educational reasons.

contingency plans   Written documents, prepared in advance, that address every conceivable emergency or other urgent issue.

continuing education units (CEUs)   A requirement of many professional associations that individuals earn a specific number of CEUs to maintain their original certification status.

convention   An assembly of delegates who formulate a platform and select candidates and/or take legal action. They also focus on a common topic or issue.

convention and visitors bureau (CVB)   A not-for-profit organization representing destinations. A CVB is typically funded by a combination of membership dues, taxes, and government funding. CVB members are organizations that provide products and services to planners, such as hotels, restaurants, and attractions.

Convention Industry Council (CIC)   Consists of 26 organizations representing the convention, meetings, and exhibition industries as well as travel and tourism.

convention services manager   A person who plans and manages the meeting details at a hotel.

corporate planner   An individual who plans meetings for corporations.

cover   A meal served to one attendee. If you serve 200 people for dinner, you serve 200 covers.

cutoff date   The date on which the hotel releases your room block back to general inventory.

data record   The unique collection of information about a specific object.

destination management company (DMC)   A company that helps planners in a destination or city. These companies can arrange tours, plan and manage your meeting, plan a themed event, and conduct a spouse/guest program, among other things.

evaluation   Written feedback about a meeting or event from attendees, sponsors, exhibitors, and organizers.

exhibitor   A person or group that displays products or services at a tradeshow or exhibition.

exposition   A booth-type format to display services and products to consumers and the public.

exposition services contractor (or decorator)   The company that provides the booth, signs, setup, and other services needed for a tradeshow or exposition.

familiarization (FAM) trip   A trip hosted by a destination or a CVB and its members for the sole purpose of showcasing the city as a meeting location.

food and beverage minimum   An amount you must spend for food and beverage, not including taxes, gratuities, or service charges. If you spend below the amount, you pay the difference between the minimum and the actual amount spent.

function books   Schedule books for reserving meeting space in a hotel.

general session   A meeting format that addresses all attendees.

giveaway   Any gift-like item given to attendees at a meeting, usually for promotional purposes. Sometimes referred to as an amenity.

goal   The foundation of a meeting. It explains why the meeting is being held and provides a road map for the planning process.

gratuity   A voluntary amount of money given in exchange for a service performed. Also referred to as a tip.

guarantee   The number of people you expect to attend a meal function. This number usually is due to the property 36 to 72 hours prior to the function. You pay either the guaranteed number or the number of people served, whichever is greater.

hold all space   All meeting space in the hotel is being held by a group. If you have a hold all space, it should be stated in the contract along with a date when your agenda is due.

indemnification   An agreement in which one party agrees to protect the other party from liability, damages, or out-of-pocket expenses that may occur in connection with a particular transaction.

independent planner   An individual who plans meetings for various organizations on a contract basis.

in-kind donations   Products or services donated to a cause in lieu of money.

inquiry call   An initial contact with a supplier or vendor for the purpose of asking about its product or service.

keynote speaker   A presenter who talks about the primary issue(s).

lanyard   A necklace or neck cord that attaches to the name badge so it can be hung around a person's neck.

lavaliere microphone   A small microphone that can be attached to clothing, allowing hands to be free.

learner outcomes   A term that is synonymous with "course objectives."

lumen   A unit of luminous flux equal to the light emitted in a unit of solid angle by a uniform point source of one candle intensity.

marshalling yard   An area away from the facility where exhibitors wait to be called to the dock for unloading.

meet-and-greet   Commonly used at airports to meet special passengers and either direct them to ground transportation or take them to their final destination.

meeting   A congregation of two or more people to further a common cause.

meeting history   A statistical record of a past meeting or event including guestrooms used, food and beverage functions, and other meeting data.

meeting management company   A company that provides meeting management services to organizations.

meeting manager   A person who organizes, plans, and executes activities for individuals who meet for a common cause.

meeting or convention resumé   An information sheet for hotel staff members regarding the entire meeting. It outlines the VIPs, agenda, contact information, rooming list, and group profile.

meeting professional   An individual who plans and provides services for meetings and events.

Meeting Professionals International (MPI)   The largest association for meeting professionals.

meetings industry   The collective resources that design, implement, and support meetings and events.

milestone   A significant point in a process or development. Missing a milestone usually has significant consequences.

MIM list   An online discussion group moderated by a well-known leading educator and expert in the meetings industry.

monitor   Someone who introduces the speaker, keeps the meeting on track, gets help with audio-visual equipment if needed, and distributes and collects the evaluations (if applicable). The monitor is often a volunteer.

mutual indemnification   A term that means both parties will be responsible for their own negligent acts or omissions if they cause a loss to the other party or cause the other party to defend itself against an asserted claim in connection with a particular transaction.

national sales office (NSO)   A sales office for hotel companies that represents all of their properties and facilities.

net square foot   The method by which some facilities charge for exhibit space. Net square footage is the space the exhibitors actually use—not including aisles, pillars, food stations, and seating.

no-show   A person who has a reservation for a guestroom and does not show up. There are two kinds of no-shows. One is someone who has a reservation guaranteed until a specific time. The second has a guaranteed reservation. This means the person has guaranteed to the hotel that he or she will pay for the room. If the person is a no-show, the hotel charges his or her credit card or keeps the deposit.

objective   A measurable, attainable target that, when completed, contributes to the accomplishment of the goal.

on-consumption   To charge only for the items consumed. This mostly applies to food and beverage items.

one-stop shop   A process in which you plan the meeting and meal functions with one person at the hotel versus two or three.

onsite   A term used by planners to mean that you are at the meeting facility, having your meeting. You are *onsite*.

outcome objective   Relates to the needs of a meeting's attendees.

outsource   To solicit and hire services from outside a company, group, or organization.

post-convention meeting   A meeting with the host facility's staff just after the conclusion of the conference or meeting to review the meeting.

pre-convention meeting   A meeting with the host facility's staff just prior to the start of the conference.

preprints   A bound copy of all the handouts and papers for every session. This is most typical at medical and scientific conferences where the sessions are quite technical.

process objective   Describes the how-to approach for accomplishing something.

Professional Convention Management Association (PCMA)   An association for meeting professionals focusing on meetings, conventions, and exhibitions.

relational database   A structured set of data made up of records so that data can be searched and accessed across different databases.

request for proposal (RFP)   An outline of all pertinent meeting specifications.

reservation list   The list of reservations under a specific group's room block.

return on investment (ROI)   The process of evaluating a meeting in terms of value to the stakeholders involved in it.

rooming list   A list of people for whom you are making room reservations. This includes check-in and check-out dates, room type, special comments, and billing information.

sellers market   A business climate in which the meeting facility has such strong demand that it can charge higher rates and be selective about the business it books.

service charge   A mandatory charge added to a service. For example, hotels often charge a flat service charge for food and beverage and audio-visual services.

silent auction   Raises funds by displaying items up for bid. The participants provide their bids in writing. At the end of the specified time period, the person with the highest bid keeps the item.

speakers bureau   An organization that represents professional speakers. You can use its services for free. The speaker pays the representation fee directly to the bureau.

special event   A high-profile gathering. This term covers a wide variety of activities such as sporting events, fundraisers, tributes, community programs, festivals, parades, road shows, and more.

specification sheet (spec sheet)   A list of meeting rooms and the number of people they can hold in various setups.

sponsor   An organization or individual who contributes money, product, or service.

stakeholder   Someone who has a vested interest in the success of the meeting such as the vice-president of the company paying the bill.

suppliers   Vendors and organizations that supply products and services for meetings and events.

target rate   The lowest group rate available on a given day.

tradeshow   A booth-type format to communicate and sell services and products to members of a specific group.

transient demand   Demand for guestrooms by individual travelers.

venue   A location of a specific function.

walk   A term used for a person who has a guaranteed reservation but is moved to another hotel because the hotel is overbooked. If you are walked, the facility will compensate you by taking you to another hotel and paying for the room and a phone call home. This is also known as a dishonored reservation.

Index

I

T

317

IDIOTSGUIDES.COM
Introducing a new and different Web site

Millions of people love to learn through *The Complete Idiot's Guide*® books. Discover the same pleasure online in **idiotsguides.com**–part of The Learning Network.

Idiotsguides.com is a new and different Web site, where you can:

❋ Explore and download more than 150 fascinating and useful mini-guides–FREE! Print out or send to a friend.

⊕ Share your own knowledge and experience as a mini-guide contributor.

🗨 Join discussions with authors and exchange ideas with other lifelong learners.

🏛 Read sample chapters from a vast library of *Complete Idiot's Guide*® books.

✗ Find out how to become an author.

✂ Check out upcoming book promotions and author signings.

🏠 Purchase books through your favorite online retailer.

Learning for Fun. Learning for Life.

IDIOTSGUIDES.COM • LEARNINGNETWORK.COM

Copyright © 2000 Pearson Education